1007950478

Teaching Mathematics in the Visible Learning Classroom

High School

Teaching Mathematics in the Visible Learning Classroom

High School

John Almarode, Douglas Fisher,
Joseph Assof, John Hattie,
and Nancy Frey

FOR INFORMATION:

Corwin

A SAGE Company

2455 Teller Road

Thousand Oaks, California 91320

(800) 233-9936

www.corwin.com

SAGE Publications Ltd.

1 Oliver's Yard

55 City Road

London, EC1Y 1SP

United Kingdom

SAGE Publications India Pvt. Ltd.

B 1/I 1 Mohan Cooperative Industrial Area

Mathura Road, New Delhi 110 044

India

SAGE Publications Asia-Pacific Pte. Ltd.

3 Church Street

#10-04 Samsung Hub

Singapore 049483

Program Manager, Mathematics: Erin Null
Editorial Development Manager: Julie Nemer
Editorial Assistant: Jessica Vidal
Production Editor: Tori Mirsadjadi
Copy Editor: Amy Hanquist Harris
Typesetter: C&M Digitals (P) Ltd.
Proofreader: Liann Lech
Indexer: Nancy Fulton
Cover Designer: Rose Storey
Marketing Manager: Margaret O'Connor

Copyright © 2019 by Corwin.

All rights reserved. When forms and sample documents are included, their use is authorized only by educators, local school sites, and/or noncommercial or nonprofit entities that have purchased the book. Except for that usage, no part of this book may be reproduced or utilized in any form or by any means, electronic or mechanical, including photocopying, recording, or by any information storage and retrieval system, without permission in writing from the publisher.

All trademarks depicted within this book, including trademarks appearing as part of a screenshot, figure, or other image, are included solely for the purpose of illustration and are the property of their respective holders. The use of the trademarks in no way indicates any relationship with, or endorsement by, the holders of said trademarks.

Printed in the United States of America.

Library of Congress Cataloging-in-Publication Data

Names: Almarode, John, author.

Title: Teaching mathematics in the visible learning classroom, high school / John Almarode [and four others].

Description: Thousand Oaks, California : Corwin, A Sage Company, [2019] | Includes bibliographical references and index.

Identifiers: LCCN 2018021319 | ISBN 9781544333144 (pbk. : alk. paper)

Subjects: LCSH: Mathematics teachers—In-service training. | Mathematics—Study and teaching (Secondary)

Classification: LCC QA10.5 .T43 2018 | DDC 510.71/2—dc23
LC record available at https://lccn.loc.gov/2018021319

This book is printed on acid-free paper.

18 19 20 21 22 10 9 8 7 6 5 4 3 2 1

DISCLAIMER: This book may direct you to access third-party content via Web links, QR codes, or other scannable technologies, which are provided for your reference by the author(s). Corwin makes no guarantee that such third-party content will be available for your use and encourages you to review the terms and conditions of such third-party content. Corwin takes no responsibility and assumes no liability for your use of any third-party content, nor does Corwin approve, sponsor, endorse, verify, or certify such third-party content.

Contents

List of Videos	ix
Acknowledgments	xi
About the Authors	xiii

Introduction — 1

What Works Best	2
What Works Best When	6
The Path to Assessment-Capable Visible Learners in Mathematics	10
How This Book Works	13

Chapter 1. Teaching With Clarity in Mathematics — 17

Components of Effective Mathematics Learning	20
Surface, Deep, and Transfer Learning	21
Moving Learners Through the Phases of Learning	26
Surface Learning in the Secondary Mathematics Classroom	27
Deep Learning in the Secondary Mathematics Classroom	29
Transfer Learning in the Secondary Mathematics Classroom	29
Differentiating Tasks for Complexity and Difficulty	31
Approaches to Mathematics Instruction	33

Checks for Understanding	35
Profile of Three Teachers	37
Maria Rios	37
Benjamin Wittrock	38
Li Shuzhen	38
Reflection	40

Chapter 2. Teaching for the Application of Concepts and Thinking Skills — 43

Ms. Rios and Systems of Linear Equations	44
What Ms. Rios Wants Her Students to Learn	47
Learning Intentions and Success Criteria	48
Guiding and Scaffolding Student Thinking	50
Teaching for Clarity at the Close	54
Mr. Wittrock and Three-Dimensional Shapes	63
What Mr. Wittrock Wants His Students to Learn	66
Learning Intentions and Success Criteria	68
Guiding and Scaffolding Student Thinking	70
Modeling Strategies and Skills	71
Teaching for Clarity at the Close	73
Ms. Shuzhen and Statistical Reasoning	80
What Ms. Shuzhen Wants Her Students to Learn	80
Learning Intentions and Success Criteria	82
Modeling Strategies and Skills	83
Teaching for Clarity at the Close	87
Reflection	92

Chapter 3. Teaching for Conceptual Understanding — 93

Ms. Rios and Systems of Linear Equations	94
What Ms. Rios Wants Her Students to Learn	95
Learning Intentions and Success Criteria	95
Instructional Approaches That Promote Conceptual Understanding	98

Modeling Strategies and Skills	101
Teaching for Clarity at the Close	104

Mr. Wittrock and the Volume of Three-Dimensional Shapes   111
- *What Mr. Wittrock Wants His Students to Learn* — 112
- *Learning Intentions and Success Criteria* — 114
- *Instructional Approaches That Promote Conceptual Understanding* — 116
- *Teaching for Clarity at the Close* — 119

Ms. Shuzhen and Independent Versus Conditional Probability   128
- *What Ms. Shuzhen Wants Her Students to Learn* — 128
- *Learning Intentions and Success Criteria* — 129
- *Modeling Strategies and Skills* — 130
- *Instructional Approaches That Promote Conceptual Understanding* — 131
- *Teaching for Clarity at the Close* — 133

Reflection   139

Chapter 4. Teaching for Procedural Knowledge and Fluency   141

Ms. Rios and Systems of Linear Equations   142
- *What Ms. Rios Wants Her Students to Learn* — 143
- *Learning Intentions and Success Criteria* — 143
- *Modeling Strategies and Skills* — 146
- *Guiding and Scaffolding Student Thinking* — 149
- *Instructional Approaches That Promote Procedural Knowledge* — 150
- *Teaching for Clarity at the Close* — 155

Mr. Wittrock and Trigonometric Relationships   160
- *What Mr. Wittrock Wants His Students to Learn* — 164
- *Learning Intentions and Success Criteria* — 165
- *Instructional Approaches That Promote Procedural Knowledge* — 166
- *Teaching for Clarity at the Close* — 169

Ms. Shuzhen and Probabilities of Compound Events	175
What Ms. Shuzhen Wants Her Students to Learn	175
Learning Intentions and Success Criteria	176
Modeling Strategies and Skills	177
Instructional Approaches That Promote Procedural Knowledge	178
Teaching for Clarity at the Close	180
Reflection	185

Chapter 5. Knowing Your Impact: Evaluating for Mastery — 187

What Is Mastery Learning?	188
Using Learning Intentions to Define Mastery Learning	189
Establishing the Expected Level of Mastery	190
Collecting Evidence of Progress Toward Mastery	192
Ensuring Tasks Evaluate Mastery	201
Ensuring Tests Evaluate Mastery	204
Feedback for Mastery	207
Task Feedback	209
Process Feedback	210
Self-Regulation Feedback	214
Conclusion	215
Final Reflection	218

Appendices

A. Effect Sizes	219
B. Teaching for Clarity Planning Guide	224
C. Learning Intentions and Success Criteria Template	229
D. A Selection of International Mathematical Practice or Process Standards	230
References	**233**
Index	**235**

List of Videos

Introduction

Video 1: What Is Visible Learning for Mathematics?

Video 2: Creating Assessment-Capable Visible Learners

Chapter 1. Teaching With Clarity in Mathematics

Video 3: What Does Teacher Clarity Mean in High School Mathematics?

Chapter 2. Teaching for the Application of Concepts and Thinking Skills

Video 4: Learning Intentions and Success Criteria in an Application Lesson

Video 5: Modeling a Close Read

Video 6: Collaborative Learning in an Application Task

Chapter 3. Teaching for Conceptual Understanding

Video 7: Setting the Stage for Conceptual Learning

Video 8: Managing Student-Led Dialogic Learning

Video 9: Making Learning Visible Through Learner Notebooks

Video 10: Feedback Through Peer-Assisted Reflection

Video 11: Consolidating Knowledge Through Direct/Deliberate Instruction

Chapter 4. Teaching for Procedural Knowledge and Fluency

Video 12: Differentiating Instruction to Support Surface, Deep, and Transfer Learning

Video 13: Supporting Surface Learning Needs With a Peer Tutor

Video 14: Checking for Understanding as Procedural Knowledge Deepens

Video 15: Supporting Learners' Extension Into Transfer

Chapter 5. Knowing Your Impact: Evaluating for Mastery

Video 16: Evaluating for Mastery

Note From the Publisher: The authors have provided video and web content throughout the book that is available to you through QR (quick response) codes. To read a QR code, you must have a smartphone or tablet with a camera. We recommend that you download a QR code reader app that is made specifically for your phone or tablet brand.

 Videos may also be accessed at resources.corwin.com/vlmathematics-9-12

Acknowledgments

We are forever grateful for the teachers and instructional leaders who strive each day to make an impact in the lives of learners. Their dedication to teaching and learning is evident in the video clips linked to the QR codes in this book. The teachers at Health Sciences High & Middle College have graciously opened their classrooms and conversations to us, allowing us to make mathematics in the Visible Learning classroom evident to readers. Louisa County Public Schools did the same. The learners they work with in the Louisa County Public Schools are better simply because they spent time with the following people:

   Mr. Peter Coen, Louisa County High School

   Mr. Daniel Barrett, Louisa County High School

   Mr. Jesse Cleaver, Louisa County High School

   Mr. William Patrick, Louisa County High School

   Mr. Chad Bunovich, Louisa County High School

   Dr. Lisa Chen, Assistant Superintendent for Instruction

We are extremely grateful to Superintendent Doug Straley for allowing us into the schools and classrooms of Louisa County, helping to make our work come alive.

Ms. Ashley Norris is an excellent teacher in Columbia County Public Schools in Georgia. She is actively engaged in implementing Visible Learning into her mathematics classroom. Her contributions to Chapter 5 provide a clear example of how she has taken the Visible Learning research and translated the findings into her teaching and learning. We are forever grateful to her for sharing her journey with us so that we could share these examples with you.

About the Authors

John Almarode, PhD, has worked with schools, classrooms, and teachers all over the world. John began his career in Augusta County, Virginia, teaching mathematics and science to a wide range of students. In addition to spending his time in preK–12 schools and classrooms, he is an associate professor in the Department of Early, Elementary, and Reading Education and the codirector of James Madison University's Center for STEM Education and Outreach. In 2015, John was named the Sarah Miller Luck Endowed Professor of Education. However, what really sustains John—and what marks his greatest accomplishment—is his family. John lives in Waynesboro, Virginia, with his wife, Danielle, a fellow educator; their two children, Tessa and Jackson; and their Labrador retrievers, Angel and Forest. John can be reached at www.johnalmarode.com.

Douglas Fisher, PhD, is Professor of Educational Leadership at San Diego State University and a teacher leader at Health Sciences High & Middle College. He is the recipient of a William S. Grey Citation of Merit and NCTE's Farmer Award for Excellence in Writing, as well as a Christa McAuliffe Award for Excellence in Teacher Education. Doug can be reached at dfisher@mail.sdsu.edu.

Joseph Assof is an 11th- and 12th-grade mathematics teacher and the math department chair at Health Sciences High & Middle College in San Diego, CA. He leads his department's reform efforts to align to the Common Core Standards—with a focus on high-quality instruction. He is a member of the San Diego County Math Leaders Task Force, whose mission is to support every student in meeting the rigorous expectations of the Common Core. Joseph's classroom is featured in a number of *Visible Learning for Mathematics, Grades K–12* videos.

ABOUT THE AUTHORS

John Hattie, PhD, has been Laureate Professor of Education and Director of the Melbourne Education Research Institute at the University of Melbourne, Australia, since March 2011. He was previously Professor of Education at the University of Auckland, as well as in North Carolina, Western Australia, and New England. His research interests are based on applying measurement models to education problems. He has been president of the International Test Commission, has served as adviser to various ministers, chairs the Australian Institute for Teachers and School Leaders, and in the 2011 Queen's Birthday Honours was made "Order of Merit for New Zealand" for his services to education. He is a cricket umpire and coach, enjoys being a dad to his young men, is besotted with his dogs, and moved with his wife as she attained a promotion to Melbourne. Learn more about his research at www.corwin.com/visiblelearning.

Nancy Frey, PhD, is Professor of Literacy in the Department of Educational Leadership at San Diego State University. She is the recipient of the 2008 Early Career Achievement Award from the National Reading Conference and is a teacher leader at Health Sciences High & Middle College. She is also a credentialed special educator, reading specialist, and administrator in California.

Introduction

Please allow us to introduce you to Ashley Norris, Maria Rios, Benjamin Wittrock, and Li Shuzhen. These four mathematics teachers set out each day to deliberately, intentionally, and purposefully impact the learning of their students. They recognize these important elements:

- They have the capacity to select and implement various teaching and learning strategies that enhance their students' learning in mathematics.

- The decisions they make about their teaching have an impact on student learning.

- Every student can learn mathematics, and they need to take responsibility to teach *all* learners.

- They must continuously question and monitor the impact of their teaching on student learning (adapted from Hattie & Zierer, 2018).

Through the videos accompanying this book, you will meet additional secondary mathematics teachers and the instructional leaders who support them in their teaching. Collectively, the **mindframes** of these teachers—or their ways of thinking about teaching and learning—lead to action in their mathematics classrooms, and their actions lead to outcomes in student learning. This is where we begin our journey through *Teaching Mathematics in the Visible Learning Classroom*.

Visible Learning occurs when teachers *see* learning through the eyes of their students and students *see* themselves as their own teachers. How do teachers of mathematics see relations, functions, equations, geometric proofs, trigonometric identities, and logarithmic functions through the eyes of their students? In turn, how do teachers develop

> **Mindframes** are ways of thinking about teaching and learning. Teachers who possess certain ways of thinking have major impacts on student learning.

assessment-capable visible learners—students who see themselves as their own teachers—in the study of numbers, operations, and relationships? Conceptualizing, implementing, and sustaining Visible Learning in the secondary mathematics classroom by identifying *what works best* and *what works best when* is exactly what we set out to do in this book.

Mathematics learning involves the balance of conceptual understanding, procedural knowledge, and the application of concepts and thinking skills to a variety of mathematical contexts. By *balance*, we mean that no one dimension of mathematics learning is more important than the other two. Conceptual understanding, procedural knowledge, and the application of concepts and thinking skills are each essential aspects of learning mathematics. Mathematics classrooms where *teachers see learning through the eyes of their learners and learners see themselves as their own teachers* result from specific, intentional, and purposeful decisions about each dimension of mathematics instruction critical for student growth and achievement. This book explores each of these components in secondary mathematics teaching and learning through the lens of *what works best* in student learning at the surface, deep, and transfer phases. We are not suggesting that teachers implement procedural knowledge, conceptual understanding, and application in isolation, but through a series of linked learning experiences and challenging mathematical tasks that result in students engaging in both mathematical content and practices or processes.

Our Learning Intention: To understand what works best in the secondary mathematics classroom.

What Works Best

Identifying what works best draws from the key findings from *Visible Learning* (Hattie, 2009) and also guides the classrooms described in this book. One of those key findings is that *there is no one way to teach mathematics or one best instructional strategy that works in all situations for all students*, but there is compelling evidence for certain strategies and approaches to have a greater likelihood of helping students reach their learning goals. In this book, we use the effect size information that John Hattie has collected and analyzed over many years to inform how we transform the findings from the Visible Learning research into learning experiences and challenging mathematical tasks that are most likely to have the strongest influence on student learning.

For readers less familiar with Visible Learning, we would like to take a moment to review what we mean by *what works best*. The Visible Learning database is composed of over 1,800 meta-analyses of studies that include over 80,000 studies and 300 million students. Some have argued that it is the largest educational research database amassed to date. To make sense of so much data, John Hattie focused his work on meta-analyses. A **meta-analysis** is a statistical tool for combining findings from different studies with the goal of identifying patterns that can inform practice. In other words, a meta-analysis is a study of studies. The mathematical tool that aggregates the information is an effect size and can be represented by Cohen's *d*. An **effect size** is the magnitude, or relative size, of a given effect. Effect size information helps readers understand not only that something does or does not have an influence on learning, but the relative impact of that influence.

For example, imagine a hypothetical study in which learning mathematics while walking on a treadmill results in relatively higher mathematics scores. Schools and classrooms around the country might devote large monetary resources to buying treadmills for mathematics classrooms. However, let's say the results of this hypothetical study indicate that the "treadmill effect" had an effect size of 0.03 in mathematics achievement when compared to those students that did not walk on a treadmill, an effect size pretty close to zero. Furthermore, the large number of students participating in the study made it almost certain there would be a difference in the two groups of students (those using a treadmill vs. those not using a treadmill). As an administrator or teacher, would you still advocate for spending a large amount of your district or school budget on treadmills? How confident would you be in the impact or influence of your decision on mathematics achievement in your district or school?

This is where an effect size of 0.03 for the "treadmill effect" is helpful. Understanding the effect size helps us know how powerful a given influence is in changing achievement—in other words, the impact for the effort or return on the investment. The effect size does not just help us understand what works, but what works *best*. With the increased frequency and intensity of mathematics initiatives, programs, and packaged curricula, deciphering where to best invest resources and time to achieve the greatest learning outcomes for all students is challenging and frustrating. For example, some programs or packaged curricula are

> A **meta-analysis** is a statistical tool for combining findings from different studies with the goal of identifying patterns that can inform practice.

> **Effect size** represents the magnitude of the impact that a given approach has on learning.

Video 1
What Is Visible Learning for Mathematics?

To read a QR code, you must have a smartphone or tablet with a camera. We recommend that you download a QR code reader app that is made specifically for your phone or tablet brand. Videos can also be accessed at *https://resources.corwin.com/vlmathematics-9-12*

hard to implement and have very little impact on student learning. Some programs and packaged curricula are easy to implement and still have limited influence on student growth and achievement in mathematics. Teaching mathematics in the Visible Learning classroom involves searching for those things that have the greatest impact and produce the greatest gains in learning, some of which will be harder to implement and some of which will be easier to implement.

As we begin planning for our first-period algebra class or our afternoon geometry class, knowing the effect size of different influences, strategies, actions, and approaches to teaching and learning proves helpful in deciding where to devote our planning time and resources. Is a particular approach (e.g., classroom discussion, exit tickets, the use of calculators, jigsaw, computer-assisted instruction, creating simulations, cooperative learning, instructional technology, presenting clear success criteria, developing a rubric, etc.) worth the effort for the desired learning outcomes of that day, week, or unit? John Hattie was able to demonstrate that influences, strategies, actions, and approaches with an effect size greater than 0.40 allow students to learn at an appropriate rate, meaning *at least* a year of growth for a year in school. Effect sizes greater than 0.40 mean more than a year of growth for a year in school. Figure I.1 provides a visual representation of the range of effect sizes calculated in the Visible Learning research.

Before this level was established, teachers and researchers did not have a way to determine an acceptable threshold; thus, we continued to use weak practices, often supported by studies with statistically significant findings.

Consider the following examples. First, let us consider classroom discussion. Should teachers devote resources and time to planning for the facilitation of classroom discussion? Will this approach to mathematics provide a return on investment rather than "chalk talk," where we work out lots of problems on the board for them to include in their notes? With classroom discussion, teachers intentionally design and purposefully plan for learners to talk with their peers about specific problems or approaches to problems (e.g., comparing approaches to solving a quadratic, completing the square or using the quadratic formula) in collaborative groups. Peer groups might engage in working to solve complex problems or tasks (e.g., data analysis, geometric proofs, maximization problems, or solving systems of equations in an authentic context). The students would not

> EFFECT SIZE
> FOR CLASSROOM
> DISCUSSION = **0.82**

THE BAROMETER OF INFLUENCE

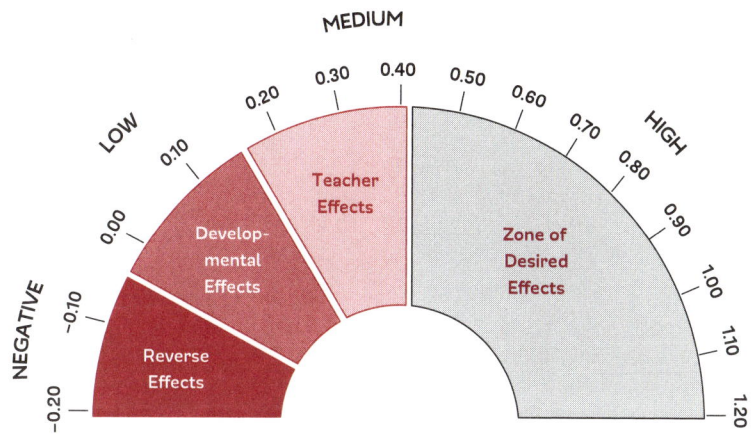

Source: Adapted from Hattie, J. (2009). *Visible Learning: A Synthesis of Over 800 Meta-Analyses Relating to Achievement.* Figure 2.4, page 19. New York, NY: Routledge.

Figure I.1

be **ability grouped** (tracking or streaming), but rather grouped by the teacher to ensure academic diversity in each group as well as language support and varying degrees of interest and motivation. As can be seen in the barometer in Figure I.2, the effect size of classroom discussion is 0.82, well above our threshold of accelerated learning gains.

Therefore, someone teaching mathematics in the Visible Learning classroom would use classroom discussion to understand mathematics learning through the eyes of their students and for students to see themselves as their own mathematics teachers. Talking about mathematics content and practices or processes helps us see learning through the eyes of our students and allows them to see themselves as their own teachers.

Second, let us look at the use of calculators. Within academic circles, teacher workrooms, school hallways, and classrooms, there have been many conversations about the use of the calculator in mathematics. There have been many efforts to reduce the reliance on calculators and the development of technology-enhanced items on assessments in mathematics. Using a barometer as a visual representation of effect sizes, we see that the use of calculators has an effect size of 0.27. The barometer for the use of calculators is in Figure I.3.

> **EFFECT SIZE FOR ABILITY GROUPING = 0.12**
>
> **EFFECT SIZE FOR RESPONSE TO INTERVENTION = 1.29**

Ability grouping is the long-term grouping or tracking of learners based on their ability. This is different from grouping students to work on a specific concept, skill, or application or to address a misconception.

THE BAROMETER FOR THE INFLUENCE OF CLASSROOM DISCUSSION

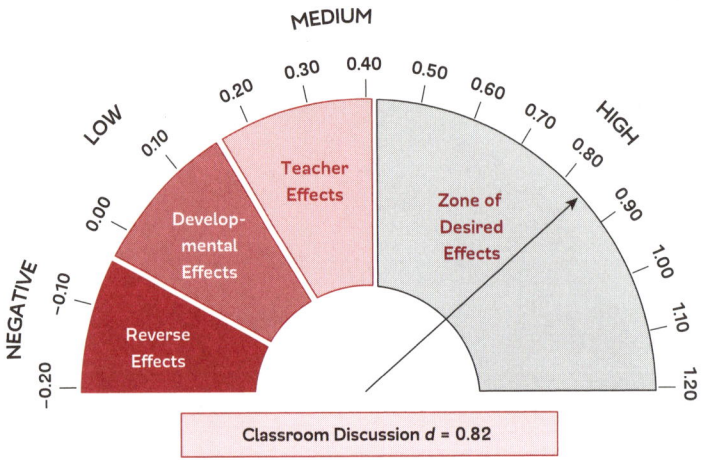

Classroom Discussion d = 0.82

Source: Adapted from Hattie, J. (2009). *Visible Learning: A Synthesis of Over 800 Meta-Analyses Relating to Achievement.* Figure 2.4, page 19. New York, NY: Routledge.

Figure I.2

EFFECT SIZE OF USE OF CALCULATORS = 0.27

As you can see, the effect size of 0.27 is below the zone of desired effects of 0.40. The evidence suggests that the impact of the use of calculators on mathematics achievement is low. However, closer examination of the five meta-analyses and the 222 studies that produced an overall effect size of 0.27 reveals a deeper story to the use of calculators. Calculators are most effective in the following circumstances: (a) when they are used for computation, deliberate practice, and learners checking their work; (b) when they are used to reduce the amount of cognitive load on learners as they engage in problem solving; and (c) when there is an intention behind using them (e.g., solving by graphing or approximation problems). This leads us into a second key finding from John Hattie's Visible Learning research: *We should not hold any influence, instructional strategy, action, or approach to teaching and learning in higher esteem than students' learning.*

What Works Best When

Visible Learning in the mathematics classroom is a continual evaluation of our impact on student learning. Regarding the calculator example, their use is not really the issue and should not be our focus. Instead, our focus should be on the intended learning outcomes for that day and how calculators support that learning. Visible Learning is

THE BAROMETER FOR THE INFLUENCE OF USING CALCULATORS

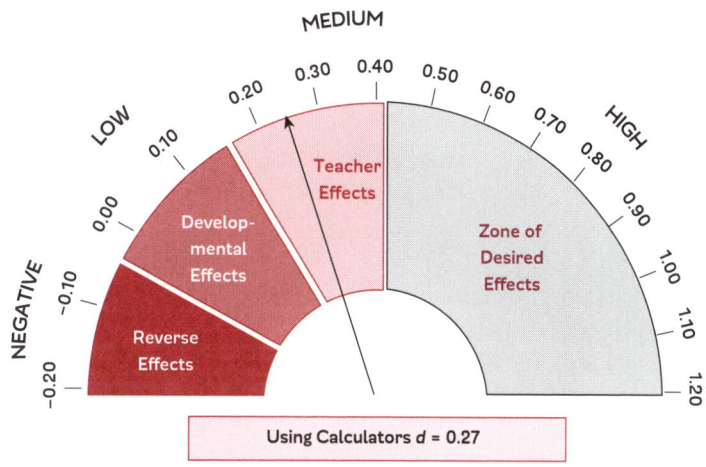

Source: Adapted from Hattie, J. (2009). *Visible Learning: A Synthesis of Over 800 Meta-Analyses Relating to Achievement.* Figure 2.4, page 19. New York, NY: Routledge.

Figure I.3

more than a checklist of dos and don'ts. Rather than checking influences with high effect sizes off the list and scratching out influences with low effect sizes, we should match the *best* strategy, action, or approach with the learning needs of our students. In other words, is the use of calculators the right strategy or approach for the learners at the right time for this specific content? Clarity about the learning intention brings into focus what the learning should be for the day, why students are learning about this particular piece of content and process, and how we *and* our learners will know they have learned the content. Teaching mathematics in the Visible Learning classroom is not about a specific strategy, but a location in the learning process.

Over the next several chapters, we will show how to support mathematics learners in their pursuit of conceptual understanding, procedural knowledge, and application of concepts and thinking skills through the lens of *what works best when*. This requires us, as mathematics teachers, to be clear in our planning and preparation for each learning experience and challenging mathematics tasks. Using guiding questions, we will model how to blend what works best with what works best *when*. You can use Figure I.4 in your own planning. This is also found in Appendix B and online at **resources.corwin.com/vlmathematics-9-12**.

Teaching Takeaway

Using the right approach at the right time increases our impact on student learning in the mathematics classroom.

HOW TO USE APPENDIX B WHEN PLANNING FOR CLARITY

I have to be clear about what content and practice or process standards I am using to plan for clarity. Am I using only mathematics standards or am I integrating other content standards (e.g., writing, reading, or science)?

Rather than what I want my students to be doing, this question focuses on the learning. What do the standards say my students should learn? The answer to this question generates the **learning intentions** for this particular content.

Once I have clear learning intentions, I must decide when and how to communicate them with my learners. Where does it best fit in the instructional block to introduce the day's learning intentions? Am I going to use guiding questions?

As I gather evidence about my students' learning progress, I need to establish what they should know, understand, and be able to do that would demonstrate to me that they have learned the content. This list of evidence generates the **success criteria** for the learning.

ESTABLISHING PURPOSE

1 **What are the key content standards I will focus on in this lesson?**
Content Standards:

2 **What are the learning intentions (the goal and *why* of learning, stated in student-friendly language) I will focus on in this lesson?**
Content:
Language:
Social:

3 **When will I introduce and reinforce the learning intention(s) so that students understand it, see the relevance, connect it to previous learning, and can clearly communicate it themselves?**

SUCCESS CRITERIA

4 **What evidence shows that students have mastered the learning intention(s)? What criteria will I use?**

I can statements:

online resources This planning guide is available for download at resources.corwin.com/vlmathematics-9-12.

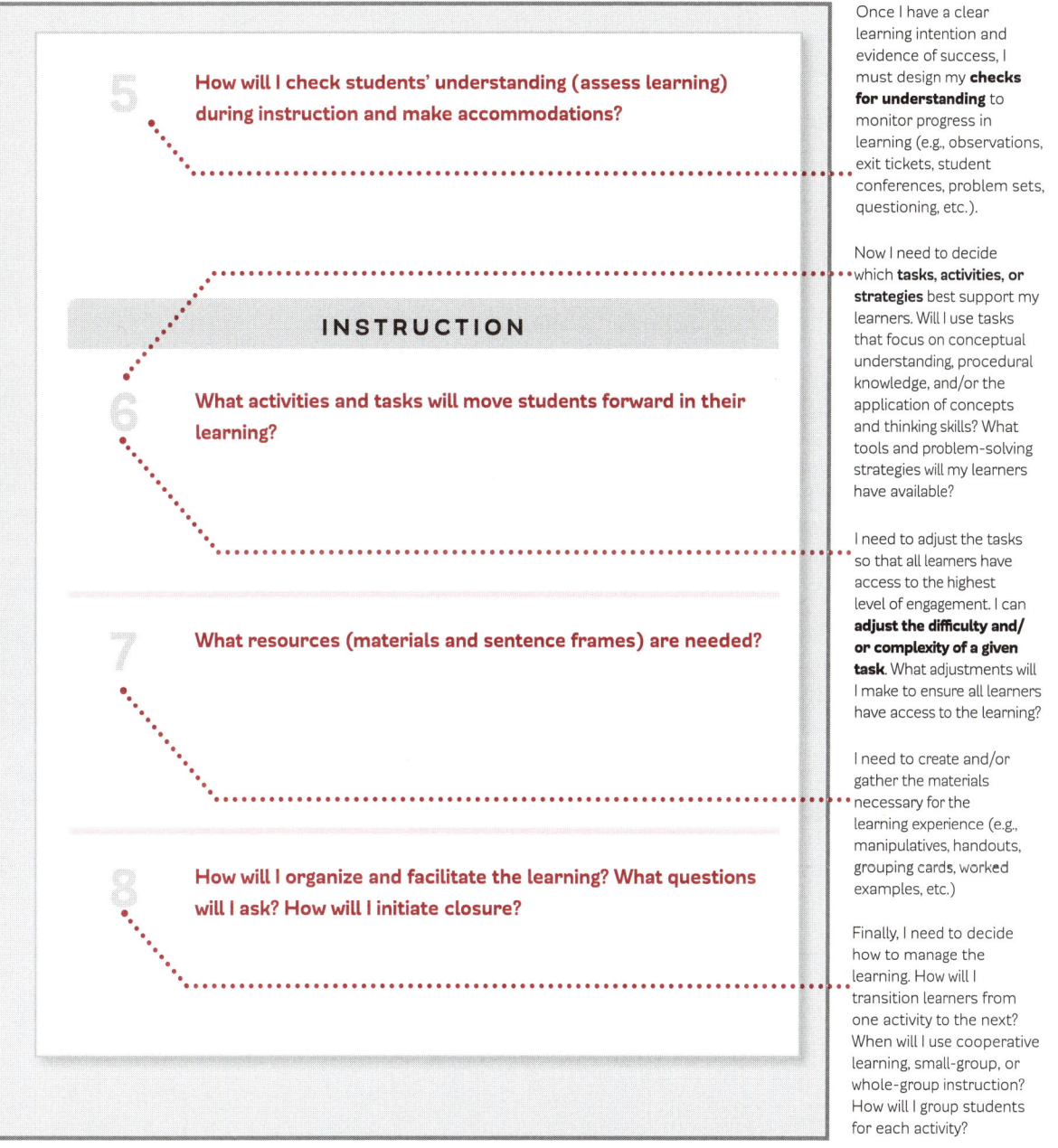

5 How will I check students' understanding (assess learning) during instruction and make accommodations?

Once I have a clear learning intention and evidence of success, I must design my **checks for understanding** to monitor progress in learning (e.g., observations, exit tickets, student conferences, problem sets, questioning, etc.).

INSTRUCTION

Now I need to decide which **tasks, activities, or strategies** best support my learners. Will I use tasks that focus on conceptual understanding, procedural knowledge, and/or the application of concepts and thinking skills? What tools and problem-solving strategies will my learners have available?

6 What activities and tasks will move students forward in their learning?

I need to adjust the tasks so that all learners have access to the highest level of engagement. I can **adjust the difficulty and/or complexity of a given task**. What adjustments will I make to ensure all learners have access to the learning?

7 What resources (materials and sentence frames) are needed?

I need to create and/or gather the materials necessary for the learning experience (e.g., manipulatives, handouts, grouping cards, worked examples, etc.)

8 How will I organize and facilitate the learning? What questions will I ask? How will I initiate closure?

Finally, I need to decide how to manage the learning. How will I transition learners from one activity to the next? When will I use cooperative learning, small-group, or whole-group instruction? How will I group students for each activity?

Figure I.4

Through these specific, intentional, and purposeful decisions in our mathematics instruction, we pave the way for helping learners see themselves as their own teachers, thus making them assessment-capable visible learners in mathematics.

The Path to Assessment-Capable Visible Learners in Mathematics

Teaching mathematics in the Visible Learning classroom builds and supports assessment-capable visible learners (Frey, Hattie, & Fisher, 2018). With an effect size of 1.44, providing a mathematics learning environment that allows learners to see themselves as their own teacher is essential in today's classrooms. The QR code in the margin provides a glimpse of two collaborative mathematics classrooms. In both classrooms, the teachers work together to deliberately, intentionally, and purposefully provide learning experiences that build and support assessment-capable visible learners. Through effective co-teaching, these teachers provide *all* learners access to rich mathematics learning.

The following characteristics apply to assessment-capable visible mathematics learners:

> **EFFECT SIZE FOR ASSESSMENT-CAPABLE VISIBLE LEARNERS = 1.33**

1. They are active in their mathematics learning. Learners deliberately and intentionally engage in learning mathematics content and practices or processes by asking themselves questions, monitoring their own learning, and taking the reins of their learning. They know their current level of learning.

   An assessment-capable visible learner says, "I am comfortable finding the simultaneous solution for a system of equations using graphing but need more learning on the elimination and substitution approach. I know there are examples in my interactive notebook that I can use to prepare for tomorrow's challenge problem."

2. They are able to plan the next steps in their progression toward mastery in learning mathematics content. Because of the active role taken by an assessment-capable visible mathematics learner, these students can plan their next steps and select the right tools (e.g., manipulatives, problem-solving approaches, and/or metacognitive strategies) to support working toward given learning

intentions and success criteria in mathematics. For example, a student might respond to feedback, saying, "There is a more efficient way to solve this quadratic equation. I am going to use completing the square this time to see if I can find a more precise answer." They know what additional tools they need to successfully move forward in a task or topic.

Video 2
Creating Assessment-Capable Visible Learners

https://resources.corwin.com/vlmathematics-9-12

> An assessment-capable visible learner says, "To find the solution to the system of equations, I am going to use substitution. Looking at the graph of this system of equations, the solution does not appear to be a pair of integers. Substitution will allow me to find a more accurate and precise solution."

3. They are aware of the purpose of the assessment and feedback provided by peers and the teacher. Whether the assessment is informal, formal, formative, or summative, assessment-capable visible mathematics learners have a firm understanding of the information behind each assessment and the feedback exchanged in the classroom. Put differently, these learners not only seek feedback, but they recognize that errors are opportunities for learning, monitor their progress, and adjust their learning (adapted from Frey et al., 2018) (see Figure I.5).

> An assessment-capable visible learner says, "Yesterday's exit ticket surprised me. Ms. Norris wrote on my paper that I needed to revisit the process for isolating x and then substituting the expression into the second equation. So today I am going to work out the entire process in my notebook and try not to skip steps or do parts of the process in my head."

Over the next several chapters, we will explore how to create a classroom environment that focuses on learning and provides the best environment for developing assessment-capable visible mathematics learners who can engage in the mathematical habits of mind represented in one form or another in every standards document. Such learners can achieve the following:

1. Make sense of problems and persevere in solving them.

2. Reason abstractly and quantitatively.

3. Construct viable arguments and critique the reasoning of others.

4. Model with mathematics.

ASSESSMENT-CAPABLE VISIBLE LEARNERS

ASSESSMENT-CAPABLE LEARNERS:

 **KNOW** THEIR CURRENT LEVEL OF UNDERSTANDING

 **KNOW** WHERE THEY'RE GOING AND ARE CONFIDENT TO TAKE ON THE CHALLENGE

 **SELECT** TOOLS TO GUIDE THEIR LEARNING

 **SEEK** FEEDBACK AND RECOGNIZE THAT ERRORS ARE OPPORTUNITIES TO LEARN

 **MONITOR** THEIR PROGRESS AND ADJUST THEIR LEARNING

 **RECOGNIZE** THEIR LEARNING AND TEACH OTHERS

Source: Adapted from Frey, Hattie, & Fisher (2018).

Figure I.5

5. Use appropriate tools strategically.

6. Attend to precision.

7. Look for and make use of structure.

8. Look for and express regularity in repeated reasoning (© Copyright 2010. National Governors Association Center for Best Practices and Council of Chief State School Officers. All rights reserved.).

How This Book Works

As authors, we assume you have read *Visible Learning for Mathematics* (Hattie et al., 2017), so we are not going to recount all of the information contained in that book. Rather, we are going to dive deeper into aspects of high school mathematics instruction that are critical for students' success, helping you to envision what a Visible Learning mathematics classroom like yours looks like. In each chapter, we profile three high school teachers who have worked to make mathematics learning visible for their students and have influenced learning in significant ways. Each chapter will do the following:

1. Provide effect sizes for specific influences, strategies, actions, and approaches to teaching and learning.

2. Provide support, through research, for specific strategies and approaches to teaching mathematics.

3. Incorporate content-specific examples from secondary mathematics curricula.

4. Highlight aspects of assessment-capable visible learners.

Through the eyes of algebra, geometry, and statistics teachers, as well as the additional secondary mathematics teachers in the accompanying videos, we aim to show you the mix and match of strategies you can use to orchestrate your lessons in order to help your students build their conceptual understanding, procedural fluency, and application of concepts and thinking skills in the most visible ways possible—visible to you and to them. As you may have noticed, you will see instances of classrooms that use a collaborative teaching situation. While some of the co-teachers have a special education background, it is important to note that the teachers work as equal collaborative partners who are there to support all learners. They plan together, they teach together, and they evaluate their impact on student learning together. Teaching mathematics in a Visible Learning classroom *can be done* with all students and in any classroom. If you're a mathematics specialist, mathematics coordinator, or methods instructor, you may be interested in exploring the vertical progression of these content areas preK–12 within Visible Learning classrooms and see how visible learners grow and progress across time and content areas. While you may identify with one of the teachers from a content perspective, we encourage you to read all the vignettes to get a full sense of the variety of choices you can make in your instruction, based on your instructional goals.

In the first chapter, we focus on the aspects of mathematics instruction that must be included in each lesson. We explore the components of effective mathematics instruction (conceptual, procedural, and application) and note that there is a need to recognize that student learning has to occur at the surface, deep, and transfer levels within each of these components. Surface, deep, and transfer learning served as the organizing features of *Visible Learning for Mathematics*, and we will briefly review them and their value in learning. Finally, Chapter 1 contains information about the use of checks for understanding to monitor student learning. Generating evidence of learning is important for both teachers and students in determining the impact of the learning experiences and challenging mathematical tasks on learning. If learning is not happening, then we must make adjustments.

Following this introductory chapter, we turn our attention, separately, to each component of mathematics teaching and learning. However, we will walk through the process, starting with the application of concepts and thinking skills, then direct our attention to conceptual understanding, and finally, procedural knowledge. This seemingly unconventional approach will allow us to start by making the goal or endgame visible: learners applying mathematics concepts and thinking skills to other situations or contexts.

Chapter 2 focuses on *application* of concepts and thinking skills. Returning to our three profiled classrooms, we will look at how we plan, develop, and implement challenging mathematical tasks that scaffold student thinking as students apply their learning to new contexts or situations. Teaching mathematics in the Visible Learning classroom means supporting learners as they use mathematics in a variety of situations. Returning to Figure I.4, we will walk through the process for establishing clear learning intentions, defining evidence of learning, and developing challenging tasks that, as you already have come to expect, encourage learners to see themselves as their own teachers. The final section of this chapter will focus on how to differentiate mathematical tasks by adjusting their difficulty and/or complexity, working to meet the needs of all learners in the mathematics classroom.

Chapter 3 and Chapter 4 take a similar approach with conceptual understanding and procedural knowledge, respectively. Using Chapter 2 as a reference point, we will return to the three profiled classrooms and explore the conceptual understanding and procedural knowledge that provided the foundation for their learners applying ideas to different mathematical situations. For example, what influences, strategies, actions, and approaches support a learner's conceptual understanding of systems of equations, the unit circle, or inferential statistics? As in Chapter 2, we will talk about differentiating tasks by adjusting the difficulty and complexity of these tasks.

In this book, we do not want to discourage the value of procedural knowledge. Although mathematics is more than procedural knowledge, developing skills in basic procedures is needed for later work in each area of mathematics, from complex numbers to conditional probability. As in the previous two chapters, Chapter 4 will look at what works best when in supporting students' fluency in procedural knowledge. Adjusting the difficulty and complexity of tasks will once again help us meet the needs of all learners.

In the final chapter of this book, we focus on how to make mathematics learning visible through evaluation. Teachers must have clear knowledge of their impact so that they can adjust the learning environment. Learners must have clear knowledge about their own learning so that they can be active in the learning process, plan the next steps, and understand what is behind the assessment. What does evaluation look like so that teachers can use it to plan instruction and to determine the impact they have on learning? As part of this chapter, we highlight the value of feedback and explore the ways in which teachers can provide effective feedback to students that is growth producing. Furthermore, we will highlight how learners can engage in self-regulation feedback and provide feedback to their peers.

This book contains information on critical aspects of secondary mathematics instruction that have evidence for their ability to influence student learning. In the appendices, we provide additional resources for implementing these critical aspects of secondary mathematics instruction. We're not suggesting that these be implemented in isolation, but rather that they be combined into a series of linked learning experiences that result in students engaging in mathematics learning more fully and deliberately than they did before. Whether calculating slope or the area under the curve, we strive to create a mathematics classroom where we *see* learning through the eyes of our students and students *see* themselves as their own mathematics teachers. As learners progress from simplifying rational expressions to solving related rates, teaching mathematics in the Visible Learning classroom should develop and support assessment-capable visible mathematics learners.

TEACHING WITH CLARITY IN MATHEMATICS

1

CHAPTER 1 SUCCESS CRITERIA:

(1) I can describe teacher clarity and the process for providing clarity in my classroom.

(2) I can describe the components of effective mathematics instruction.

(3) I can relate the learning process to my own teaching and learning.

(4) I can give examples of how to differentiate mathematics tasks.

(5) I can describe the four different approaches to teaching mathematics we use in this book.

> A **learning intention** describes what it is that we want our students to learn.

> **Success criteria** specify the necessary evidence students will produce to show their progress toward the learning intention.

> EFFECT SIZE FOR LEARNING INTENTION = **0.68** AND SUCCESS CRITERIA = **1.13**

> EFFECT SIZE FOR COOPERATIVE LEARNING = **0.40**

> EFFECT SIZE FOR COOPERATIVE LEARNING COMPARED TO COMPETITIVE LEARNING = **0.53**

In Ms. Norris's algebra class, students are learning to create equations in one variable and then use those equations to solve problems. On the board, she has clearly provided her learners with a learning intention and success criteria for the lesson:

Learning Intention: I am learning that authentic situations can be modeled or represented with equations.

Success Criteria

1. I can create an equation that models an authentic situation.
2. I can determine which type of function best models the situation (linear, exponential, or quadratic).
3. I can justify my decisions in creating my equation.

There are many different approaches for engaging learners in creating equations and inequalities. Today, Ms. Norris provides her learners with a contextual situation and then, after assigning them to cooperative learning teams, asks learners to come up with an equation that models the specific situation.

> *Four people can sit comfortably at a rectangular table. If two tables are placed together, this arrangement will comfortably seat six people. If three tables are placed together, the arrangement will comfortable seat eight people. How many people can comfortably sit at 10 tables if they are placed together? How many tables are needed for a group of 100 people?*

Ms. Norris provides each cooperative learning team with different manipulatives (e.g., tiles, index cards, grid paper, and counters) that they can choose to use in accomplishing this task and deriving an equation. She tells students that they can choose to use some, all, or none of the manipulatives. Furthermore, she encourages them to use any strategy that they believe would be appropriate for completing this task. One cooperative learning team decided to use scissors and paper to construct models of tables. Another cooperative learning team used the manipulatives to model different table configurations and explore if different types of configurations provided more or fewer seating options. One specific student asked, "Does this have to be an equation, or can we develop an inequality?" A third team of learners did not find the manipulatives helpful and began to discuss the information they needed to create an equation. Ms. Norris is pleased that her learners are actively monitoring which strategy works best for them on this particular task.

Ms. Norris is implementing the principles of Visible Learning in her algebra classroom. Our intention is to help implement these principles in your own classroom. By providing learners with a challenging task, a clear learning intention, and success criteria, cooperative learning teams are engaging in conceptual understanding, procedural knowledge, and the application of concepts and thinking skills. Ms. Norris holds high expectations for her students in terms of both the difficulty and complexity of the task, as well as her learners' ability to deepen their mathematics learning by making learning visible to herself and each individual learner. As she monitors the learning progress in each team, holding every student accountable for his or her own learning, she takes opportunities to provide additional instruction when needed. Although her learners are engaged in cooperative learning with their peers, she regularly assesses her students for formative purposes. Ms. Norris is mobilizing principles of Visible Learning through her conscious awareness of her impact on student learning, and her students are consciously aware of their learning through this challenging task. Ms. Norris works to accomplish this through these specific, intentional, and purposeful decisions in her mathematics instruction. She has clarity in her teaching of mathematics, allowing her learners to have clarity and see themselves as their own teachers (i.e., assessment-capable visible mathematics learners). **Clarity** in learning means that both the teacher and the student know what the learning is for the day, why they are learning it, and what success looks like. This came about from using guiding questions in her planning and preparation for learning:

1. What do I want my students to learn?
2. What evidence shows that the learners have mastered the learning or are moving toward mastery?
3. How will I check learners' understanding and progress?
4. What tasks will get my students to mastery?
5. How will I differentiate tasks to meet the needs of all learners?
6. What resources do I need?
7. How will I manage the learning?

> **Teaching Takeaway**
>
> As part of learning content, students should have access to and learn to apply a variety of strategies for solving problems.

> EFFECT SIZE FOR STRATEGY MONITORING = 0.58

> **Clarity** in learning means that both the teacher and the student know what the learning is for the day, why they are learning it, and what success looks like.

> EFFECT SIZE FOR TEACHER CLARITY = 0.75

HOW VISIBLE TEACHING AND VISIBLE LEARNING COMPARE

Visible Teaching	Visible Learning
Clearly communicates the learning intention	Understands the intention of the learning experience
Identifies challenging success criteria	Knows what success looks like
Uses a range of learning strategies	Develops a range of learning strategies
Continually monitors student learning	Knows when there is no progress and makes adjustments
Provides feedback to learners	Seeks feedback about learning

Figure 1.1

 This figure is available for download at resources.corwin.com/vlmathematics-9-12

Video 3
What Does Teacher Clarity Mean in High School Mathematics?

https://resources.corwin.com/vlmathematics-9-12

Ms. Norris exemplifies the relationship between Visible Teaching and Visible Learning (see Figure 1.1).

Now, let's look at how to achieve clarity in teaching mathematics by first understanding how components of mathematics learning interface with the learning progressions of the students in our classrooms. Then, we will use this understanding to establish learning intentions and success criteria, create challenging mathematical tasks, and monitor or check for understanding.

Components of Effective Mathematics Learning

Mathematics is more than just memorizing formulas and then working problems with those formulas. Rather than a compilation of procedures—isolating the variable, subtracting exponents, plugging numbers into the quadratic formula, FOIL, PEMDAS—mathematics learning involves an interplay of conceptual understanding, procedural knowledge, and the application of mathematical concepts and thinking skills. Together, these compose mathematics learning, which is furthered by the following practice standards:

1. Making sense of problems and persevering in solving them
2. Reasoning abstractly and quantitatively

3. Constructing viable arguments and critiquing the reasoning of others

4. Modeling with mathematics

5. Using appropriate tools strategically

6. Attending to precision

7. Looking for and making use of structure

8. Looking for and expressing regularity in repeated reasoning (© Copyright 2010. National Governors Association Center for Best Practices and Council of Chief State School Officers. All rights reserved.)

Teaching mathematics in the Visible Learning classroom fosters student growth through attending to these mathematical practices. As highlighted by Ms. Norris in the opening of this chapter, this comes from linked learning experiences and challenging mathematics tasks that make learning visible to both students and teachers.

Surface, Deep, and Transfer Learning

In their high school years, students grow in mathematics learning through a progression that moves from understanding the surface contours of a concept into how to work with that concept efficiently by leveraging procedural skills, as well as applying concepts and thinking skills to an ever-deepening exploration of what lies beneath mathematical ideas. But understanding these progressions requires that teachers consider the levels of learning they can expect from students. We think of three levels, or phases, of learning: surface, deep, and transfer (see Figure 1.2).

Learning is a process, not an event. With some conceptual understanding, procedural knowledge, and application, students may still only understand at the surface level. We do not define *surface-level learning* as superficial learning. Rather, we define the **surface phase** of the learning as the initial development of conceptual understanding and procedural skill, with some application. In other words, this is the students' initial learning around finding the roots of a quadratic, understanding conceptually what the roots of the quadratic represent, and how to apply this learning to specific problems in algebra. Surface learning is

> **Surface learning** is the phase in which students build initial conceptual understanding of a mathematical idea and learn related vocabulary and procedural skills.

THE RELATIONSHIP BETWEEN SURFACE, DEEP, AND TRANSFER LEARNING IN MATHEMATICS

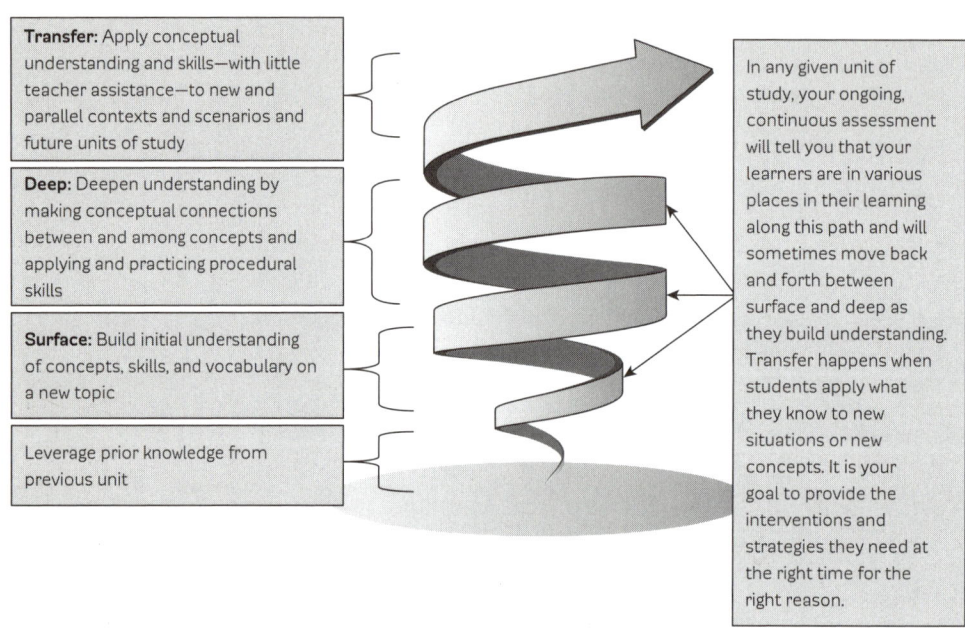

Source: Hattie et al. (2017). Spiral Image copyright EssentialsCollection/iStock.com

Figure 1.2

> **EFFECT SIZE FOR PRIOR ABILITY = 0.94 AND PRIOR ACHIEVEMENT = 0.55**

Deep learning is a period when students consolidate their understanding and apply and extend some surface learning knowledge to support deeper conceptual understanding.

often misrepresented as rote rehearsal or memorization and is therefore not valued, but it is an essential part of the mathematics learning process. You have to know something about the concept of the roots of an equation and process for solving the quadratic formula to be able to do something with that idea in an authentic situation.

With the purposeful and intentional use of learning strategies that focus on how to relate and extend ideas, surface mathematics learning becomes deeper learning. **Deep learning** occurs when students begin to make *connections* among conceptual ideas and procedural knowledge and then apply their thinking with greater fluency. As learners begin to monitor their progress, adjust their learning, and select strategies to guide their learning, they more efficiently and effectively plan, investigate, elaborate on their knowledge, and make generalizations based on their experiences with mathematics content and practices or processes.

If learners are to deepen their knowledge, they must regularly encounter situations that foster the transfer and generalization of their learning. **Transfer learning** is the point at which students take their consolidated knowledge and skills and apply what they know to new scenarios and different contexts. It is also a time when students are able to think more metacognitively, reflecting on their own learning and understanding. The American Psychological Association (2015) notes that "student transfer or generalization of their knowledge and skills is not spontaneous or automatic" (p. 10) and requires intentionally created events on the part of the teacher.

Figure 1.3 contains a representative list of strategies or influences organized by phase of learning. This is an updated list from *Visible Learning for Mathematics* (Hattie et al., 2017). Notice how many of these strategies and influences—clarity of learning goals, questioning, discourse, problem solving—align with the Effective Teaching Practices outlined by the National Council for Teachers of Mathematics and their book *Principles to Actions: Ensuring Mathematical Success for All* (2015; see Figure 1.4).

For the influences from the Visible Learning research, we placed them in a specific phase, based on the evidence of their impact and the outcomes that researchers use to document the impact each has on students' learning. For example, we have included concept maps and graphic organizers under deep learning. Learners will find it hard to organize mathematics information or ideas if they do not yet understand that information, whether it is a procedure, concept, or application. Without a conceptual understanding of the unit circle, mathematics students may classify trigonometric expressions or equations based on surface-level features (i.e., problems that involve sine while the others involve cosine) instead of deep-level features (i.e., problems that involve specific identities or inverses). When students have sufficient surface learning about specific content and practices or processes, they are able to see the connections between multiple ideas and create contextual representations of trigonometric equations, which allow for the generalization of mathematics principles. As a reminder, here are two key findings from the *Visible Learning* research:

1. There is no one way to teach mathematics or one best instructional strategy that works in all situations for all students.

2. We should not hold any influence, instructional strategy, action, or approach in higher esteem than students' learning.

> EFFECT SIZE FOR ELABORATION AND ORGANIZATION = 0.75

> **Transfer learning** is the point at which students take their consolidated knowledge and skills and apply what they know to new scenarios and different contexts. It is also a time when students are able to think more metacognitively, reflecting on their own learning and understanding.

> EFFECT SIZE FOR METACOGNITION = 0.60 AND EVALUATION AND REFLECTION = 0.75

HIGH-IMPACT APPROACHES AT EACH PHASE OF LEARNING

Surface Learning		Deep Learning		Transfer Learning	
Strategy	ES	Strategy	ES	Strategy	ES
Imagery	0.45	Inquiry-based teaching	0.40	Extended writing	0.44
Note taking	0.50	Questioning	0.48	Peer tutoring	0.53
Process skill: record keeping	0.52	Self-questioning	0.55	Synthesizing information across texts	0.63
Direct/deliberate instruction	0.60	Metacognitive strategy instruction	0.60	Problem-solving teaching	0.68
Organizing	0.60	Concept mapping	0.64	Formal discussions (e.g., debates)	0.82
Vocabulary programs	0.62	Reciprocal teaching	0.74	Organizing conceptual knowledge	0.85
Leveraging prior knowledge	0.65	Class discussion: discourse	0.82	Transforming conceptual knowledge	0.85
Mnemonics	0.76	Outlining and transforming notes	0.85	Identifying similarities and differences	1.32
Summarization	0.79	Small-group learning 0.47			
Integrating prior knowledge	0.93	Cooperative learning 0.40			
Teacher expectations 0.43					
Feedback 0.70					
Teacher clarity 0.75					
Integrated curricula programs 0.47					
Assessment-capable visible learner 1.33					

Source: Adapted from Almarode, Fisher, Frey, & Hattie (2018).

Figure 1.3

As teachers, our conversations should focus more on identifying where students are in their learning journey and moving them forward in their learning. This is best accomplished by talking about learning and measuring the impact that various approaches have on students' learning. If a given approach is not working, change it. If you experienced success with a particular strategy or approach in the past, give it a try, but make sure that the strategy or approach is working in this context. Just because

EFFECTIVE MATHEMATICS TEACHING PRACTICES

Establish mathematics goals to focus learning. Effective teaching of mathematics establishes clear goals for the mathematics that students are learning, situates goals within learning progressions, and uses the goals to guide instructional decisions.

Implement tasks that promote reasoning and problem solving. Effective teaching of mathematics engages students in solving and discussing tasks that promote mathematical reasoning and problem solving and allow multiple entry points and varied solution strategies.

Use and connect mathematical representations. Effective teaching of mathematics engages students in making connections among mathematical representations to deepen understanding of mathematics concepts and procedures and as tools for problem solving.

Facilitate meaningful mathematical discourse. Effective teaching of mathematics facilitates discourse among students to build shared understanding of mathematical ideas by analyzing and comparing student approaches and arguments.

Pose purposeful questions. Effective teaching of mathematics uses purposeful questions to assess and advance students' reasoning and sense making about important mathematical ideas and relationships.

Build procedural fluency from conceptual understanding. Effective teaching of mathematics builds fluency with procedures on a foundation of conceptual understanding so that students, over time, become skillful in using procedures flexibly as they solve contextual and mathematical problems.

Support productive struggle in learning mathematics. Effective teaching of mathematics consistently provides students, individually and collectively, with opportunities and supports to engage in productive struggle as they grapple with mathematical ideas and relationships.

Elicit and use evidence of student thinking. Effective teaching of mathematics uses evidence of student thinking to assess progress toward mathematical understanding and to adjust instruction continually in ways that support and extend learning.

Source: NCTM. (2014). *Principles to Actions: Ensuring Mathematical Success for All.* Reston, VA: NCTM, National Council of Teachers of Mathematics. Reprinted with permission.

Figure 1.4

both we and our students love the FOIL and PEMDAS mnemonics, for example, does not mean they will work for all students in your mathematics classroom—particularly if students lack understanding of the conceptual underpinnings of those procedures. Teachers have to monitor the impact that learning strategies have on students' mathematics learning and how they are progressing from surface to deep to transfer.

> The **SOLO Taxonomy** is a framework that describes learners' thinking and understanding of mathematics. The taxonomy helps conceptualize the learning process from surface, to deep, and then to transfer.

> **Teaching Takeaway**
>
> We must preassess our learners to identify their prior knowledge or background knowledge in the mathematics content they are learning.

Moving Learners Through the Phases of Learning

The **SOLO** (structure of the observed learning outcome) **Taxonomy** (Biggs & Collis, 1982) helps conceptualize the movement from surface to deep to transfer learning as a process of first branching out and then strengthening connections among ideas (see Figure 1.5). It is a framework that describes learners' thinking and understanding of mathematics. The taxonomy helps conceptualize the learning process from surface, to deep, and then to transfer.

As you reflect on your own students, you can likely think of learners who have limited to no prior experiences with the certain mathematics content. Take for example, logarithmic functions. Although learners have likely encountered real-world uses of logarithmic functions (e.g., the pH scale, Richter Scale, and decibels), many have had no experience with the mathematics behind those real-world applications. Thus, they have no relevant structure to their thinking. This means they are likely to struggle to articulate a single idea about the specific content.

Another example of this occurs with equations or formulas. They recognize that letters represent specific variables in an equation—say $A = \frac{1}{2}(b \times h)$—but are not going to be able to tell you what each variable is or represents in a triangle or make inferences about the effect on area if the base of a triangle is held constant and the height increased by a factor of 2. This part of the SOLO Taxonomy is referred to as the prestructural level or prestructural thinking. At the prestructural level, learners may focus on irrelevant ideas or avoid engaging in the content. This requires the teacher to support the learner in acquiring and building background knowledge. When teachers clearly recognize that a learner or learners are at the prestructural level, the learning experience should aim to build surface learning around concepts, procedures, and applications.

THE SOLO TAXONOMY

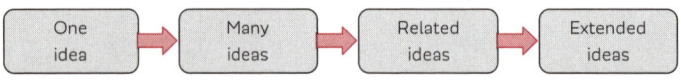

Source: Adapted from Biggs & Collis, 1982.

Figure 1.5

Surface Learning in the Secondary Mathematics Classroom

As learners progress in their thinking, they may develop single ideas or a single aspect related to a concept. Learners at this level can identify, name, follow simple procedures, highlight single aspects of a concept, and solve one type of problem (Hook & Mills, 2011). A student may identify what a logarithmic function looks like and how to represent "logs" in an equation or expression. They know that $A = \frac{1}{2}(b \times h)$ calculates the area of a triangle, that b represents the base, and h represents the height. They can only solve problems involving the exact type of triangle provided in an in-class example, such as in Figure 1.6.

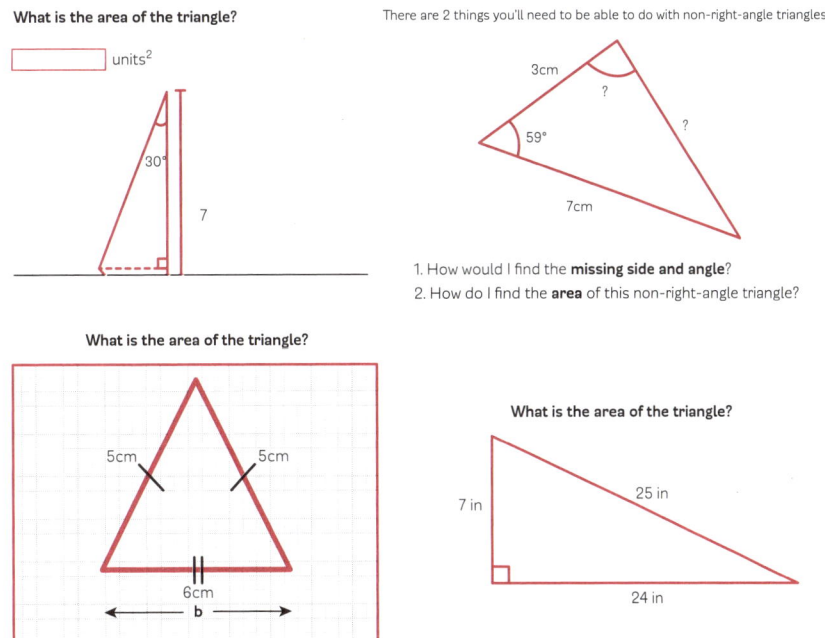

Figure 1.6

> **Teaching Takeaway**
>
> In the surface phase of learning, a student may be able to identify things, follow simple procedures, highlight single aspects of a concept, or solve one type of problem.

For example, learners can calculate the area of a right triangle only. Any variation to the problem will pose a significant challenge to this learner, requiring additional instruction (e.g., finding the area of a right triangle versus an isosceles or scalene triangle). With the right strategy at the right time, learners will continue to build surface learning by acquiring multiple ideas about concepts, procedures, and applications. Learners can then solve problems involving different variations of triangles (e.g., right triangles, isosceles triangles, and equilateral triangles) and describe coherently how to calculate the area of any triangle instead of simply executing the algorithm. However, each variation of a triangle is seen as a distinct scenario, not connected to the other variations of triangles.

As Ms. Norris does, we must establish learning intentions and success criteria based on where students are in their learning progression. Moving away from triangles and back to Ms. Norris's classroom, let us look at how we can develop learning intentions and success criteria for conceptual understanding, procedural knowledge, and application for learners at these two levels (one idea and many ideas) (see Figures 1.7 and 1.8).

SURFACE-PHASE LEARNING INTENTIONS FOR EACH COMPONENT OF MATHEMATICS LEARNING

Learning Intentions	Conceptual Understanding	Procedural Knowledge	Application of Concepts and Thinking Skills
Unistructural (one idea)	I am learning that relationships between numbers in a numeric pattern help me determine if the pattern is linear.	I am learning that I can use equations to model numeric patterns.	I am learning that equations generated from numeric patterns help me solve problems.
Multistructural (many ideas)	I am learning that the relationships between numbers in a numeric pattern can be linear or nonlinear.	I am learning that the equation I use to model numeric patterns depends on the relationships in the pattern.	I am learning that equations generated from numeric patterns help me solve problems with similar patterns.

Figure 1.7

SURFACE-PHASE SUCCESS CRITERIA FOR EACH COMPONENT OF MATHEMATICS LEARNING

Success Criteria	Conceptual Understanding	Procedural Knowledge	Application of Concepts and Thinking Skills
Unistructural (one idea)	I can explain why a given numeric pattern is linear.	I can create a linear equation in one variable from a numeric pattern.	I can use a linear equation to solve problems related to a given numeric pattern.
Multistructural (many ideas)	I can explain why a given numeric pattern is linear or nonlinear.	I can create an equation in one variable from a numeric pattern.	I can use an equation to determine if a given numeric pattern is linear or nonlinear.

Figure 1.8

Deep Learning in the Secondary Mathematics Classroom

Biggs and Collis (1982) conceptualize deep learning as identifying relationships between concepts or ideas. Learners at the deep level of the learning process focus on relationships and relational thinking about concepts, procedures, and applications. Returning to the area of a triangle, learners are able to compare and contrast the procedure for finding the area of right, isosceles, and equilateral triangles. Conceptually, learners deepen their understanding of base, height, and the relationship of these two values to any given angle in the triangle. They can analyze a specific situation and determine the best approach to finding the area of the triangle without specific guidance on which approach is most efficient and effective. The development of relational thinking paves the way for transferring these concepts and thinking, or as Biggs and Collis (1982) call it, *extending thinking*. The learning intentions and success criteria should reflect this level of thinking or readiness for our learners (see Figures 1.9 and 1.10 on the next page).

> **Teaching Takeaway**
>
> Learners in the deep phase can identify relationships between concepts and draw connections between concepts, procedures, and applications.

Transfer Learning in the Secondary Mathematics Classroom

The next step in the SOLO progression is for the learner to transfer learning to different contexts. At the extended level of thinking, learners formulate big ideas and generalize their learning to a new domain.

DEEP-PHASE LEARNING INTENTIONS FOR EACH COMPONENT OF MATHEMATICS LEARNING

Learning Intentions	Conceptual Understanding	Procedural Knowledge	Application of Concepts and Thinking Skills
Relational (related ideas)	I am learning that the specific context of the situation determines how to best represent the relationship (e.g., equation vs. inequality; linear vs. nonlinear).	I am learning that the equation or inequality I use depends on the specific context of the situation.	I am learning about the constraints by equations or inequalities.

Figure 1.9

DEEP-PHASE SUCCESS CRITERIA FOR EACH COMPONENT OF MATHEMATICS LEARNING

Success Criteria	Conceptual Understanding	Procedural Knowledge	Application of Concepts and Thinking Skills
Relational (related ideas)	I can compare and contrast numeric patterns that are linear, exponential, quadratic, or a rational function.	I can create equations and inequalities with one variable from a numeric pattern.	I can use my equation or inequality to solve problems.

Figure 1.10

Teaching Takeaway

Learners at the transfer phase begin to transfer their conceptual and procedural knowledge to different contexts and situations.

For example, an extended abstract thinker might predict how the area of a triangle varies as the height is increased or decreased, leaving the base constant. Learners at this level may begin to generalize this to other two-dimensional geometric shapes, recognizing that there are dimensions that maximize the area of a specific shape. Learners will begin to extend their thinking by using procedures in very different situations. For example, they might connect the height of a triangle to the height of a parallelogram, realizing that the term plays a similar role in the area calculations for each shape. Being clear about the learning intentions and success criteria is just as important in extending student ideas as with the previous levels of thinking (see Figures 1.11 and 1.12 on the opposite page).

TRANSFER-PHASE LEARNING INTENTIONS FOR EACH COMPONENT OF MATHEMATICS LEARNING

Learning Intentions	Procedural Knowledge	Conceptual Understanding	Application of Concepts and Thinking Skills
Extended abstract (extending ideas)	I am learning that equations and inequalities can be rearranged to highlight quantities of interest.	I am learning that equations and inequalities represent numeric relationships in authentic situations.	I am learning that I can use equations and inequalities to make inferences.

Figure 1.11

TRANSFER-PHASE SUCCESS CRITERIA FOR EACH COMPONENT OF MATHEMATICS LEARNING

Success Criteria	Procedural Knowledge	Conceptual Understanding	Application of Concepts and Thinking Skills
Extended abstract (extending ideas)	I can rearrange equations and inequalities to focus on a quantity of interest.	I can interpret solutions to equations and inequalities as viable or nonviable solutions in the specific context.	I can justify a decision using an equation and inequality.

Figure 1.12

With clear learning intentions and success criteria in place, we must design learning experiences and challenging mathematics tasks that result in students engaging in both mathematical content and practices or processes at the right level of thinking. This brings us to the question of rigor.

> EFFECT SIZE FOR "RIGHT" LEVEL OF CHALLENGE = 0.74

Differentiating Tasks for Complexity and Difficulty

As we have noted, there are three phases to students' learning: surface, deep, and transfer. Teachers have to plan tasks that provide students opportunities to learn and progress through these stages, as well as the flexibility to return to different phases of the learning when necessary. When students experience a "Goldilocks" challenge, the effect size is 0.74. A Goldilocks challenge is not too hard and not too boring. For example, if learners need additional surface learning around some aspect of procedural knowledge or conceptual understanding, we have the flexibility to go back, provide that instructional support, and then continue in the learning. The type of task matters as students move along in their thinking from surface to deep to transfer.

In *Visible Learning for Mathematics,* we shared the Common Core State Standards for Mathematics' definition of *rigor* as the balance of conceptual learning, procedural skills and fluency, and application. This is a good definition when applied to mathematics instruction, curricula, and learning as a whole. But we also want to go deeper to address the appropriate challenge of any mathematical *task*. In this book, we are using the term **rigor** to mean the balance of complexity and difficulty in a mathematics task, as well as to ensure it aligns with our learning intentions and success criteria.

> **Rigor:** The balance of difficulty and complexity in a given mathematical task.

As soon as someone mentions "rigorous tasks," we mentally formulate what that is in our own classrooms. Is rigor completing 50 problems for homework? Is rigor engaging in a mathematics brainteaser? To effectively design rigorous mathematics tasks that align with our learning intentions and success criteria, we have to better understand what is meant by difficulty and complexity. *Difficulty* is the amount of effort or work expected of the student, whereas *complexity* is the level of thinking, the number of steps, or the abstractness of the task. We can differentiate the level of difficulty and complexity for any task regardless of whether the task focuses on conceptual understanding, procedural knowledge, or the application. For example, in an advanced algebra class, learners are expected to understand the radian measure of an angle is the length of the arc on the unit circle subtended by the angle. These are the Success Criteria for that lesson:

1. I can explain the definition of a radian.

2. I can determine the length of the arc on the circle.

For these criteria, the teacher could lower the difficulty of tasks while maintaining the level of complexity by allowing learners to explain the definition of a radian using drawings, electronic devices, or communicating in her or his native language. In another example of adjusting the difficulty, learners could determine the length of the arc on a circle but with common central angles (30 degrees, 45 degrees, 60 degrees, or 90 degrees). As learners develop greater understanding of the concept and fluency in the procedure, the level of difficulty could be increased by requiring the learner to use the unit circle as a model for explaining the definition of a radian and determining the arc length for central angles such as 22 degrees or 37 degrees.

We do not believe that teachers can radically impact student learning by making them do a lot more work. Solving hundreds of equations (one form of increased difficulty) will not necessarily extend their thinking. Similarly, asking students to engage in a task that is too complex or not complex enough for their current level of thinking can also reduce the impact on student learning. Instead, we should balance difficulty and complexity in the design of learning tasks. Throughout this book, we will return to the concepts of difficulty and complexity as we discuss the various strategies and tasks our three profiled teachers use and share how they can adjust the difficulty and complexity of those tasks to meet the needs of all learners.

Approaches to Mathematics Instruction

Just as task design is an important consideration in the Visible Learning classroom, learners need to experience a *wide range* of tasks if they are going to become assessment-capable visible learners. They need opportunities to work with their teacher, with their peers, and independently so that they develop the social and academic skills necessary to continue to learn on their own. Although Ms. Norris decided to use a peer-led dialogic approach (cooperative learning groups), this is just one of four approaches to mathematics instruction we will use in this book. Three additional approaches are deliberate instruction, teacher-led dialogic, and independent learning.

Deliberate Instruction. Deliberate instruction, commonly referred to as *direct instruction*, has a negative reputation in education. This approach

> With clear learning intentions and success criteria in place, we must design learning experiences and challenging mathematics tasks that result in students engaging in both mathematical content and practices or processes at the right level of thinking.

EFFECT SIZE FOR SPACED VERSUS MASSED PRACTICE = **0.60**

> **Teaching Takeaway**
>
> Throughout a unit, learning tasks should balance conceptual understanding, procedural knowledge, and application in our mathematics classrooms. We should differentiate those tasks by adjusting the difficulty and complexity.

is mistakenly assumed to be synonymous with lecture. That is not the case. Deliberate instruction involves the following:

- Activation of prior knowledge
- Introduction of the new concept or skill
- Guided practice of the concept or skill
- Feedback on the guided practice
- Independent practice

To limit one's understanding of direct instruction to highly scripted programs is to overlook the practices that make it highly effective for developing surface-level knowledge. With an effect size of 0.60, direct instruction offers a pedagogical pathway that provides students with the modeling, scaffolding, and practice they require when learning new concepts and skills, as explained further by Hattie (2009):

> When we learn something new . . . we need more skill development and content; as we progress, we need more connections, relationships, and schemas to organize these skills and content; we then need more regulation or self-control over how we continue to learn the content and ideas. (p. 84)

Teacher-Led Dialogic. As learners develop the skills to engage in deepening dialogue, teacher-led dialogue allows the teacher to be present in student discussions about mathematics, facilitating the process to scaffold student conversation. In the end, the teacher will fade his or her support as students develop the necessary skills to take over and lead the conversations on their own. For example, a geometry teacher may use a teacher-led dialogic approach as she introduces the type of questioning essential in completing a geometric proof. Over time, after modeling the type of questioning and reasoning, the geometry teacher's role in this dialogue will lessen, gradually releasing the students to more independent work (i.e., less dependent on the teacher).

Student-Led Dialogic. Adolescents have a way of making themselves understood by their peers. There is a lack of clarity between the mathematical

> **EFFECT SIZE FOR DIRECT/DELIBERATE INSTRUCTION = 0.60**
>
> **EFFECT SIZE FOR SCAFFOLDING = 0.82**
>
> **EFFECT SIZE FOR DELIBERATE PRACTICE = 0.79**
>
> **EFFECT SIZE FOR FEEDBACK = 0.70**

ideas referred to by teachers and the concepts that students refer to in their understanding of content and practices or processes. In other words, students' thoughts and explanations can propel the learning of their peers. Whether solving problems, providing feedback, or engaging in reciprocal teaching, the collaborative act of peer-assisted learning in mathematics benefits all students in the exchange. In student-led dialogic learning, the role of the teacher is to organize and facilitate, but it is the students who are the ones that lead the discussion.

Independent. The learning continues, and in fact deepens, when students are able to employ what they have been learning. This can occur in three possible ways (Fisher & Frey, 2008):

- Fluency building
- Spiral review
- Extension

Fluency building is especially effective when students are in the surface learning phase and need spaced practice opportunities to strengthen automaticity. For instance, students who play online mathematics games or engage in mathematics problem solving independently are engaged in fluency-building independent learning.

Spiral review is one in which students revisit previously mastered content in order to prevent learning recidivism due to infrequent use. For instance, an entrance ticket, exit ticket, or homework assignment draws from content that was introduced in a previous week, unit, or quarter.

Extension occurs when learners are asked to use what they have learned in a new way. Independent learning through extension includes writing about mathematics, teaching information to peers, and engaging in mathematics investigations. There is no one way to teach mathematics. We should not hold any influence, instructional strategy, action, or approach to teaching and learning in higher esteem than students' learning.

Checks for Understanding

Checks for understanding offer both teachers and learners the opportunity to monitor the learning process as students engage in challenging

---

Teaching Takeaway

These approaches are in no particular order. Using the right approach at the right time increases our impact on student learning in the mathematics classroom.

EFFECT SIZE FOR QUESTIONING = 0.48

EFFECT SIZE FOR SELF-VERBALIZATION AND SELF-QUESTIONING = 0.55

EFFECT SIZE FOR HELP SEEKING = 0.72

EFFECT SIZE FOR SELF-REGULATION STRATEGIES = 0.52

> There is no one way to teach mathematics. We should not hold any influence, instructional strategy, action, or approach to teaching and learning in higher esteem than students' learning.

tasks and progress toward the learning intention. To ensure the learning is visible in our mathematics classroom, we must have the necessary information about student progress so that we provide effective feedback. In addition, learners must also have the necessary information about their progress so that they can effectively monitor progress and adjust their learning. Using the success criteria as a guide, checks for understanding include any strategies, activities, or tasks that make student thinking visible and allow both the teacher and learner to observe learning progress. When planning, developing, and implementing checks for understanding, the following two essential questions should guide our thinking as we create opportunities for students to respond:

1. What checks for understanding will tell my learners and me how they are progressing in their learning related to the learning intention(s) and success criteria?

2. What are we going to do with this information that will help with their next steps in learning?

Checks for understanding give us feedback about the impact of our teaching and should be driven by the learning intention and success criteria for that particular lesson or learning experience. For example, if the success criteria say to *describe*, the check for understanding should focus on or provide deliberate practice in *describing*. Someone teaching mathematics in the Visible Learning classroom should focus on assessment for the purpose of informing instructional decisions and providing feedback to learners. The following assumptions inform our collective understanding about teaching and learning:

1. Assessment occurs throughout the academic year, and the results are used to inform the teacher and the learner. Each period, time is set aside to understand students' mathematics learning progress and provide feedback to learners.

2. A meaningful amount of time is dedicated to developing mathematics content and practices or processes. Across every unit, students engage in sustained, organized, and comprehensive experiences

> EFFECT SIZE FOR PROVIDING FORMATIVE EVALUATION = 0.48

with all of the components: conceptual understanding, procedural knowledge, and application of concepts and thinking skills.

3. Solving problems and discussing tasks occurs every class period. These events occur with the teacher, with peers, and independently.

Profiles of Three Teachers

In addition to the videos accompanying each chapter of this book, we will follow the practices of three teachers throughout the remaining chapters. Just as we have provided specific examples throughout this chapter and in the videos, we will devote more time to take an in-depth look into the classrooms of three secondary mathematics teachers. We will give you a front-row seat as they make specific, intentional, and purposeful decisions in teaching mathematics in the Visible Learning classroom.

Maria Rios

Maria Rios teaches algebra in California. At her school, students do not need to pass any type of preassessment or screening test to enroll in algebra. In California, there are requirements that schools and districts articulate their math course pathway and the requirements for entrance into each class. For Ms. Rios, algebra is the default curriculum, and she believes that all students can master algebraic thinking. She works very hard to emphasize algebraic thinking each day, pushing back against a focus only on procedures (e.g., the concept of a solution to an equation vs. the steps to solving an equation). Ms. Rios teaches five periods of algebra per day, and her classes are very short (48 minutes each). Her learners are mainly Latino (75%) and speak Spanish as their heritage language. All of the students in the school qualify for free lunch, and 12% of the students receive special-education services. As Ms. Rios says,

> Algebra is another language, and my students are skilled at learning language, so I'm never surprised by their performance. They love the rich tasks we engage with, and they see math as an important part of what they need to learn to have a good life.

Teaching Takeaway

Unless we, as teachers, have clear success criteria, we are hardly likely to develop good checks for understanding for our learners.

Benjamin Wittrock

Benjamin Wittrock teaches geometry in Texas. He works at a career-focused high school that aims to prepare students for a range of law enforcement positions. The school educates about 1,200 students, and most of them are from the suburbs but choose to attend the school because of the internships and dual-enrollment college classes. Of the 1,200 students, 11% qualify for special-education services, and 15% are English learners. About 20% of the students qualify for free lunch each year, depending on the lottery results and who is admitted to the school. Mr. Wittrock's class sizes are smaller than many of his colleagues in other states, averaging 20 students per class. He is also the department chair for mathematics and serves on the district professional learning team. He is really interested in his students understanding trigonometric ratios and the relationships between geometry and trigonometry. He sees this as a vital connection between algebraic and geometric structures, and he views his course as sowing the seeds for analytic geometry. As he says,

> This is the make-or-break grade for advanced math. My students have a strong sense of algebra, and they have been working on algebraic thinking for years and years. But if they can master the concepts in geometry and relate them to algebra, their confidence grows, and I watch them go on to trig and calculus.

Li Shuzhen

Li Shuzhen teaches statistics to 11th- and 12th-grade students in Massachusetts. The class is one of the options her large, comprehensive high school offers as part of the mathematics curriculum. The class is so popular that there are now two full-time teachers who only teach statistics. The students at this school select their courses from a list of courses approved by the state for graduation credits. Parents and counselors approve the learners' selections. The stats class has a reputation for preparing students for their first college-level statistics course. As Ms. Shuzhen says, "Over 95% of college majors require a stats class, so I think high schoolers should have a stronger background in this subject." At this school, students are expected to take four years of mathematics, even though only three years are required to enter a four-year university. Her learners arrive with a wide range of reasons for enrolling in her statistics course, from avoiding math classes they believe are harder to wanting to learn about data. In addition, many of her learners have limited experience with statistics beyond the superficial exposure through the media and popular press (e.g., polls and weather forecasts). Ms. Shuzhen's classes average 33 students, and she teaches five periods per day. The school is typical of the area, with 30% African American, 35% Latino, 25% Caucasian, and 10% Asian Pacific Islander. Nearly 10% of the students qualify for special-education services, and 50% qualify for free lunch.

These three teachers, although located in different regions and contexts, operate under three important assumptions:

1. There is no one way to teach mathematics or one best instructional strategy that works in all situations for all students, but there is compelling evidence for tools that can help students reach their learning goals.

2. We should not hold any influence, instructional strategy, action, or approach to teaching and learning in higher esteem than students' learning.

3. Effective teaching and learning requires establishing clear learning intentions and success criteria, designing learning experiences and challenging mathematics tasks, monitoring student progress, providing feedback, and adjusting lessons based on the learning of students.

In the chapters that follow, you will encounter these three teachers and view the lesson plans they have developed for themselves. In order to establish a predictable pattern for displaying this information, we will use the Planning for Clarity questions (see Figure I.4). Lessons based on these guiding questions are not meant to be delivered in a strictly linear fashion, but rather are intended to serve as a way to guide your thinking about the elements of the lesson. In addition, through the videos accompanying this book, you will more briefly meet a number of teachers from other grade levels whose practices illustrate the approaches under discussion. While no book on lesson planning could ever entirely capture every context or circumstance you encounter, we hope that the net effect is that we provide a process for representing methods for incorporating Visible Learning for mathematics consistently in your secondary classroom.

Reflection

Mathematics instruction that capitalizes on Visible Learning is established upon principles of learning. Recognizing that learners develop procedural knowledge and conceptual understanding, and apply concepts and thinking, by engaging in surface, deep, and transfer learning allows us to intentionally and purposefully foster increasingly deeper and more sophisticated types of thinking in mathematics. This focus on the individual learner makes this approach inclusive of all learners, including those with language or additional learning needs.

Teaching mathematics in the Visible Learning classroom means leveraging high-impact instruction to accelerate student learning through surface, deep, and transfer phases of learning by engaging them in strategies, actions, and approaches to learning at the right time and for the right content. These challenging learning tasks have clear learning intentions and success criteria that allow students to engage in those tasks in a variety of ways and with a variety of materials. Learning becomes visible for the teacher and the students. In other words, an assessment-capable visible mathematics learner notices when he or she is learning and is proactive in making sure that learning is obvious. As we engage in discussions about mathematics learning in this book, we will return to these indicators that students are visible mathematics learners to explore how they might look in the classroom.

1. Take a moment and develop your own explanation of teacher clarity. What does teacher clarity look like in your mathematics classroom?

2. Using an upcoming lesson plan as an example, what components of mathematics instruction are you focusing on in the lesson? Think about how your lesson incorporates all or some of the following:

   a. Making sense of problems and persevering in solving them
   b. Reasoning abstractly and quantitatively
   c. Constructing viable arguments and critiquing the reasoning of others
   d. Modeling with mathematics
   e. Using appropriate tools strategically
   f. Attending to precision
   g. Looking for and making use of structure
   h. Looking for and expressing regularity in repeated reasoning

3. Using that same lesson plan, how will you or could you adjust the difficulty and/or complexity of the mathematics tasks to meet the needs of all learners?

4. Give some examples of learners engaged in surface learning, deep learning, and transfer learning. What are the observed learning outcomes of these students? What learning experiences best support learners at each level?

TEACHING FOR THE APPLICATION OF CONCEPTS AND THINKING SKILLS

2

CHAPTER 2 SUCCESS CRITERIA:

(1) I can describe what teaching for the application of concepts and thinking skills in the mathematics classroom looks like.

(2) I can apply the Teaching for Clarity Planning Guide to Teaching for Application.

(3) I can compare and contrast different approaches to teaching for application.

(4) I can give examples of how to differentiate the complexity and difficulty of mathematics tasks designed for application.

Assessment-capable visible learners in the mathematics classroom use mathematics in situations that require the application of mathematics concepts and thinking skills. How efficiently and effectively this occurs depends on the learners' conceptual understanding and procedural knowledge. When planning for clarity (see Figure I.4), we begin with the end in mind: What do I want my students to learn? In this chapter, we take the same approach. For Ms. Rios, Mr. Wittrock, and Ms. Shuzhen, what is the end goal for each of their learners? All three teachers expect their learners to apply mathematics concepts and thinking skills to authentic situations. Thus, our journey visiting classrooms in which Visible Learning is occurring begins with sharing how these three teachers, by design, teach for this purpose. The QR codes in the margin provide video examples of application in action from other mathematics classrooms. In Chapter 3 and Chapter 4, we will go back in time and look at how these classrooms got here.

The nature of the application of concepts and thinking skills differs *across* the three classrooms and *within* the three classrooms. How each teacher approaches these purposes depends on the learning needs of the students in his or her classroom. Therefore, you will see that Ms. Rios, Mr. Wittrock, and Ms. Shuzhen adjust the rigor—or complexity and difficulty—of the application task depending on where their learners currently are in the learning process (e.g., surface, deep, and transfer). For example, Ms. Rios adjusts the rigor of her application task for learners who need additional surface learning around the specific application task. Likewise, Mr. Wittrock and Ms. Shuzhen adjust the rigor of their application task to support learners who have gaps in their conceptual understanding. In all three classrooms, learners apply concepts and thinking skills to authentic scenarios. As we journey through these three classrooms, pay special attention to how each teacher differentiates the complexity and difficulty of the mathematics tasks so that all learners have access and the opportunity to apply concepts and thinking skills.

Ms. Rios and Systems of Linear Equations

Ms. Rios is excited—her algebra students have a conceptual understanding and procedural knowledge of systems of linear equations and are ready to transfer their learning to new and novel situations. Over the past few weeks, her students have been solving systems of linear equations algebraically, graphing systems of equations, and using linear functions to model authentic situations. She has designed an application task that she hopes will resonate with her students as a relevant and authentic coalescing of these concepts and procedures. Today, her students are going car shopping.

APPLICATION TASK: *ARE HYBRID CARS REALLY WORTH THE PRICE?*

Many car models are being offered in hybrid and non-hybrid varieties these days. In most cases, the hybrid version is more expensive to buy. However, hybrids typically use less gasoline than non-hybrids because their engines can also run on electricity. In this task, you will be advising car shoppers and helping them decide whether to buy a hybrid or non-hybrid vehicle. Your group will be assigned *one* car make and model from the following table. Assume the average cost of gasoline is projected to be $3.80 per gallon for the foreseeable future.

Car Make and Model	Non-Hybrid Model $	Hybrid Model $	Non-Hybrid Average MPG	Hybrid Average MPG	Average Yearly Miles Driven
Toyota Rav 4	$28,695	$30,025	25	42	12,500
Ford Fusion S	$22,120	$25,295	25	32	21,300
Lexus ES	$38,900	$41,820	24	40	8,500
Kia Optima EX	$31,795	$31,885	28	42	15,000

Source: www.fueleconomy.gov.

You will present your group's work on a collaborative poster. The poster must have four sections—one for each of today's success criteria. In each section, you will present your work, demonstrating mastery on that *I can* statement. For example, the first *I can* statement is this: *I can mathematically model a situation with a system of linear functions.* Under that section in your poster, you

(Continued)

(Continued)

will need to show two linear functions—one for the cost of the non-hybrid model of your assigned car and one for the cost of the hybrid model. Each function should be labeled to identify what each variable represents. The following is a sample layout of this poster:

[Your Assigned Car Type]	
• I can mathematically model a situation with a system of linear functions. Cost of non-hybrid model over time: y = mx + b Cost of hybrid model over time: y = mx + b	• I can solve a system of linear equations using my preferred method (algebraically or graphically). [Solve algebraically here. OR Solve graphically here.]
• I can use evidence to construct a claim about a real-world situation. The solution to the system of linear equations above means _____. Based on our evidence above, the _____ model is a better deal.	• I can logically communicate how my mathematical evidence supports my claim. Our claim is supported by _____. Additionally, _____.

online resources: This task is available for download at resources.corwin.com/vlmathematics-9-12.

Ms. Rios believes that all of her learners can engage in the application of concepts and thinking skills. As a seasoned practitioner of rich and rigorous mathematics tasks, Ms. Rios recognizes that in the absence of access, no rigor exists. For this reason, she has delineated the various skills required for successful completion by success criteria and designed a series of scaffolds that she can use to support her learners on an "as needed" basis. Thus, she intends to maximize the rigor for each individual by differentiating the level of supports for each of her learners. These supports include, but are not limited to, manipulatives, worked examples, and access to technology. Additionally, she recognizes that mathematically modeling and deriving functions from a context has proven challenging for her students almost universally. This is why she will be starting her lesson with a teacher-facilitated close reading of the

CHAPTER 2. TEACHING FOR THE APPLICATION OF CONCEPTS AND THINKING

task. She wants to make sure that *every* student has the opportunity to understand the context of the task, the given information, and the goal of the task before releasing them to work collaboratively in groups. After all, if teacher clarity is essential for her students' learning, then her students should have a general sense of what they are learning, why they are learning it, and what success looks like for this particular task.

> EFFECT SIZE FOR COGNITIVE TASK ANALYSIS = **1.29**

What Ms. Rios Wants Her Students to Learn

One metaphor used to describe tasks for transfer is the active connecting from one branch of a concept map to another. This becomes abundantly clear in applied mathematics where very rarely is a single branch of conceptual understanding or an individual offshoot of procedural knowledge useful in isolation. Application of mathematics is where the melding of ideas and skills allows us to make sense of the world around us.

This is evident in the litany of content standards typically addressed when teaching students application of mathematics, as seen in the following box:

> Application of mathematics is where the melding of ideas and skills allows us to make sense of the world around us.

MATHEMATICS CONTENT AND PRACTICE STANDARDS

A.REI.6.

Solve systems of linear equations exactly and approximately (e.g., with graphs), focusing on pairs of linear equations in two variables.

A.REI.11.

Explain why the x-coordinates of the points where the graphs of the equations $y = f(x)$ and $y = g(x)$ intersect are the solutions of the equation $f(x) = g(x)$; find the solutions approximately (e.g., using technology to graph the functions, make tables of values, or find successive approximations).

F.BF.1.

Write a function that describes a relationship between two quantities.

a. Determine an explicit expression, a recursive process, or steps for calculation from a context.

(Continued)

> (Continued)
>
> **Ms. Rios is helping her learners develop the following Standards for Mathematical Practice:**
>
> - Make sense of problems and persevere in solving them.
> - Use appropriate tools strategically.
> - Model with mathematics.

And while she acknowledges that other standards are absolutely addressed by this task, these are the ones that Ms. Rios has been explicitly teaching throughout this unit of study and intends to assess and capstone through today's mathematics task.

Learning Intentions and Success Criteria

With her focus on the three standards listed, Ms. Rios turns her attention to making the learning visible to her students. To do this, she develops the learning intentions and success criteria for this specific application task. Her approach is to develop learning intentions for content, language, and social intentions. Dividing learning intentions into *content*, *language*, and *social* varieties can provide teachers and students alike a clearer sense of the day's expectations. **Content learning intentions** answer the question "What is the math I am supposed to use and learn today?"

Language learning intentions give teachers a space to lay out the language demands of the day: Are students developing new academic or content vocabulary, are they practicing recently developed vocabulary within proper linguistic structures, or are they using those structures toward their actual communicative functions? **Language learning intentions** answer the question "How should I communicate my mathematical thinking today?" This is not limited to verbal communication and can include written or verbal representations of mathematical thinking.

Content learning intentions: What is the math I am supposed to use and learn today?

Language learning intentions: How should I communicate my mathematical thinking today?

EFFECT SIZE FOR TEACHING COMMUNICATION SKILLS AND STRATEGIES = 0.43

Social learning intentions allow teachers to develop and leverage social and sociomathematical norms within their classroom culture. **Social learning intentions** answer the question "How should I interact with my learning community today?"

Ms. Rios chooses to communicate the daily learning she intends for her students through these content, language, and social lenses, as she finds it gives her the flexibility to target different areas of growth for different students. She also suggests that this dynamic approach helps ensure she is addressing the bigger picture of learning—like how we communicate and compare our thinking to others so we can grow further. Her learning intentions for this lesson are as follows:

> *Content Learning Intention:* To use our understanding of systems of linear equations to make informed decisions about a real-world problem.
>
> *Language Learning Intention:* To construct viable financial arguments based on mathematical reasoning and communicate them verbally and in writing.
>
> *Social Learning Intention:* To work toward mathematical and logical consensus with our collaborative teams.

Ms. Rios always starts her day by reviewing the learning intentions, briefly discussing them, and then referring to them throughout the lesson to keep students progressing. She is careful not to simply use the content standard as her learning intention. Instead, she unpacks the standard and presents the learning intention in student-friendly language.

Ms. Rios provides learners with success criteria in the form of *I can* statements so that they may self-assess their progress toward today's learning intentions. Today, she has integrated the success criteria into the structure of the application task itself so that students may monitor both

> **Social learning intentions:** How should I interact with my learning community today?

> **Teaching Takeaway**
>
> Although the learning intention and success criteria are derived from the content standard, they are not simply copied and pasted. These statements should be unpacked and presented in student-friendly language.

Video 4
Learning Intentions and Success Criteria in an Application Lesson

https://resources.corwin.com/vlmathematics-9-12

their learning progress and their progress toward task completion. The four success criteria of the day are as follows:

> ☐ I can mathematically model a situation with a system of linear functions.
> ☐ I can solve a system of linear equations using my preferred method (algebraically or graphically).
> ☐ I can use my math as evidence to collaboratively construct a claim about a real-world situation.
> ☐ I can logically communicate how my mathematical evidence supports my claim to my peers.

EFFECT SIZE FOR METACOGNITIVE STRATEGIES = 0.60

When applying mathematics concepts and thinking skills, it is important for students to be mindful of *what* mathematical knowledge they are drawing on and *why* they are using those concepts and procedures. This metacognitive process serves as a means of grounding thinking and provides a lasting sense of direction when solving complex problems.

Ms. Rios thinks of this process as a system of checks and balances between the specific context and the abstract mathematics. This fluid "back and forth" between the mathematics and the context is apparent in Ms. Rios's criteria for success. The first two criteria call on a conceptual understanding of linear functions and their structure, as well as procedural fluency with their manipulation. The last two criteria, however, are clearly asking students to investigate their ability to transfer their abstract skillset to the concrete and communicate *how* their mathematical understanding applies to this situation. By providing students the means to self-assess against these measures, Ms. Rios is providing students a scaffold toward metacognition. In addition, the criteria for success align with the learning intentions to offer learners an opportunity to engage in content, language, and social learning.

Guiding and Scaffolding Student Thinking

Video 5
Modeling a Close Read

https://resources.corwin.com/vlmathematics-9-12

In this application lesson where students will be consolidating previously learned material, Ms. Rios intends to jump directly into guided practice with a structured close reading. She begins her day by distributing the task (*Are hybrid cars really worth the price?*) to each group and instructing them to "read with a pencil" as they try to answer the question "What is the big idea of the text?" Her students recognize this sense-making protocol as one of annotating the text in search of the overarching theme, identifying phrases or words they do not yet understand, and locating key details that might help them in their work.

This strategy of *text-dependent questioning* is intended to guide students from the broad peripherals of a text, where a general understanding can be gained, down to specific sections and key details where inferences can be drawn.

TEXT-DEPENDENT QUESTIONS

- ☐ What is the big idea of the task/text? What are we doing?
- ☐ What is a hybrid car? What is a non-hybrid car? Why is this difference important, according to the task?
- ☐ What information is provided in the table? What does each column mean? What does each row mean?
- ☐ What exactly *is* MPG? Why is this information important to the task?
- ☐ What are some initial ideas about how we might use math to approach this task?
- ☐ How might a system of linear equations help us?
- ☐ How can we use the information in the table to create linear equations?
- ☐ How can we determine the *average yearly gasoline cost* for each model?

You will notice that Ms. Rios employs both **focusing** and **funneling** types of text-dependent questions (Herbel-Eisenmann & Breyfogle, 2005; Wood, 1998).

Her general strategy is to start with a prompting focus question and then cue her students with a funneling question if they need an extra boost or are not quite getting where she intends for them to go. Again, her goal is to maintain the maximum rigor for each student while ensuring access for all. Ms. Rios reflects,

> **Teaching Takeaway**
>
> Text-dependent questioning can guide students to identify key details and make inferences in mathematics.

> **Focusing questions** allow students to do the cognitive work of learning by helping to push their thinking forward.

> **Funneling questions** guide students down the teacher's path to find the answer.

> **Teaching Takeaway**
>
> Providing opportunities for learners to take ownership of their learning is essential in building assessment-capable visible learners in mathematics.

> EFFECT SIZE FOR CLASSROOM DISCUSSION = 0.82

> EFFECT SIZE FOR SMALL-GROUP LEARNING = 0.47

> EFFECT SIZE FOR SCAFFOLDING = 0.82

When I was a beginning teacher, I would read these problems, do all of the setup for my students, and point out what the problem was asking of them so that they could just "get to the math." I eventually realized that I was the one doing all the work and all of the thinking! All my students were left with was a procedural exercise, which entirely defeated the purpose of the task.

Now, she has learned to scaffold—rather than eliminate—the complexity of inferencing mathematics from a situation.

As her students finish their close reading and embark on the rest of the task in their groups, Ms. Rios circulates through the room, eavesdropping on conversations and listening carefully to make sure students are on the right track. Collaborative groups have been constructed so that students early in their English development have been paired with others who are bilingual in English and their first language (when available) so that all students may thoroughly discuss the task.

Her years of experience have helped her develop a tolerance for allowing students to struggle, largely because she has learned to differentiate between productive and unproductive failure and success (see Figure 2.1).

She notices one group trying to make sense of how to generate a slope out of the given miles per gallon, average yearly miles driven, and the average cost of gasoline. Even though she overhears some group members making inaccurate suggestions, she recognizes that one group member is respectfully disagreeing (for the right reasons) and silently nods to him approvingly. She is confident that this silent approval will empower the young man to keep advocating for his (accurate) perspective.

As she listens in on another group, however, she notices something different. This second group's conversation is notably mum compared to other groups, and they seem to be stalled out. With a quick group interview, she discovers that the only suggestion they have for how to mathematically model the cost of their vehicle over time is to use the average miles per gallon as the slope of a linear function. The trouble, of course, is that their vehicle's fuel economy is going to indirectly affect the cost over time, not directly. Since this group seems to be struggling more seriously with the concept of mathematically modeling this situation and

FOUR POSSIBLE LEARNING EVENTS

	Unproductive Failure	Unproductive Success	Productive Success	Productive Failure
Type of learning event	Unguided problem solving without further instruction	Rote memorization without conceptual understanding	Guided problem solving using prior knowledge and tasks planned for success	Unsuccessful or suboptimal problem solving using prior knowledge, followed by further instruction
Learning outcome	Frustration that leads to abandoning learning	Completion of the task without understanding its purpose or relevance	Consolidation of learning through scaffolded practice	Learning from errors and ensuring learners persist in generating and exploring representations and solutions
Useful for . . .			Surface learning of new knowledge firmly anchored to prior knowledge	Deep learning and transfer of knowledge
Undermines . . .	Agency and motivation	Goal setting and willingness to seek challenge		
Promotes . . .			Skill development and concept attainment	Use of cognitive, metacognitive, and affective strategies

Source: Frey, N., Hattie, J., & Fisher, D. (2018).

Figure 2.1

 This figure is available for download at resources.corwin.com/vlmathematics-9-12.

the subsequent procedure that supports it, Ms. Rios decides to provide them some preprinted scaffolds specific for this part of the task, saying, "I notice that you have encountered a challenge with your conversions. How could you use this information to get around this apparent impasse?"

On these printed scaffolds, the group finds a similar problem that contains a detailed procedure for converting *miles per gallon, average yearly miles driven*, and *average cost of gasoline per gallon* into the *average yearly gasoline cost*. With this helping hand, the group is now able to access the task and begins mirroring the procedure with their own values.

Teaching Takeaway

An effective means for formatively evaluating learners is through observations and student interviews

Before she moves on, Ms. Rios overhears the group start to make predictions about which car is going to be less expensive over time, based on their in-progress calculations. She recognizes their prediction as a resurfacing of their conceptual understanding of the underlying mathematics and is confident they will continue to make progress without her. To document learning, Ms. Rios uses her observation recording tool (see Figure 2.2). This allows her to document progress and track whom she has observed during the lesson.

Teaching for Clarity at the Close

The class periods at Ms. Rios's school are only a short 48 minutes in duration. Therefore, she is comfortable scheduling rich application tasks over multiple class periods. This particular task is slated to take two periods, and Day 1 ends right on schedule—students are almost done with their posters. As a quick exit ticket, she asks her learners to summarize the day on an index card using the following questions: What it is that we are learning? How did today move your learning forward? What did you do, and what did you learn?

Taking note of where her learners are in their progress toward the learning intentions and success criteria, Ms. Rios knows where to begin on Day 2 of this application task. She launches it with a brief set of questions designed to quickly refresh students' thinking and get them back up to speed with the context and goal of the task. These questions are similar to yesterday's exit ticket: "With your neighbors, review what it is that we are learning. How did yesterday move your learning forward? What did you do, and what did you learn? What is your plan for today?" Students then spend about 15 minutes completing their posters and displaying them on the classroom walls. Now they are ready for a gallery walk.

Gallery walks are an efficient way for students to review their peers' work, leave feedback, and gather talking points for whole-class discussions. Students move in groups from poster to poster, briefly discussing what they see, leaving comments for the authors on sticky notes, and recording notes of their own.

Teaching Takeaway

Having scaffolds available to learners, when needed, ensures all learners have access to mathematics concepts and thinking.

EFFECT SIZE FOR FEEDBACK = 0.70

EFFECT SIZE OF STRATEGY TO INTEGRATE WITH PRIOR KNOWLEDGE = 0.93

Gallery walks are an efficient way for students to review their peers' work, leave feedback, and gather talking points for whole-class discussions.

SMALL-GROUP LEARNING: IMPLEMENTATION AND RECORDING TOOL FOR OBSERVATIONS

Intent of the Observation	Brief Description/Comments	Observed?
Mathematics content		
Mathematical practices or processes		
Student engagement		
General comment:		
Feedback to students:		

Source: Fennell, F., Kobett, B., & Wray, J. (2015). Classroom-based formative assessments: Guiding teaching and learning. In C. Suurtamm (Ed.) & A. R. McDuffie (Series Ed.), *Annual perspectives in mathematics education: Assessment to enhance teaching and learning* (pp. 51–62). Reston, VA: National Council of Teachers of Mathematics. Republished with permission of the National Council of Teachers of Mathematics; reprinted with permission.

Figure 2.2

 This tool is available for download at resources.corwin.com/vlmathematics-9-12.

EFFECT SIZE FOR SUMMARIZATION = 0.79

As the students in Ms. Rios's class go about their rotations, she is thrilled to hear them making connections between their own work and the work of their peers. Groups end their rotations by revisiting their own posters and discussing the feedback from other groups. As before, Ms. Rios eavesdrops on these conversations and uses her observation recording tool to document the evidence.

Ms. Rios closes the task and application lesson by leading a discussion with her whole class. She revisits the learning intentions and success criteria to open the discussion and then begins asking questions. She strategically groups her questions and delivers them in a specific order, starting with a series of conclusion—or *what's the answer*—questions. Through these, she is able to formatively assess the overall impact of the task.

EFFECT SIZE FOR QUESTIONING = 0.48

Conclusion Questions:

- What did we discover? Are hybrid cars really worth the price?
- How does your math justify your claim?

She then moves on to process questions that assess students' ability to apply their mathematics. She wants to know if students are internalizing the "nuts and bolts" of how they came to their conclusions. Can they rejustify their claims, if needed? Students' answers to these structural questions hold implications for their ability to transfer this specific application to additional situations.

Process Questions:

- What did we need *mathematically* in order to investigate this situation?
- Why/how do these equations represent the cost of each vehicle over time?
- What was the point of solving a system of equations? What does the solution represent?
- How did your group decide to solve your system? Why?
- What other situations might lend themselves to this type of modeling?

She concludes with a set of reflection questions designed to make students extend their thinking beyond the rigidity of their calculations.

These questions are intended to help the task make a lasting impression on students and "keep them thinking" as they leave class. She is hoping to activate those checks and balances between the concrete context and the abstract mathematics within her students and generate a desire to "tinker" with their models, as this iterative process of refinement is truly the role of applied mathematicians.

> EFFECT SIZE FOR EVALUATION AND REFLECTION = 0.75

Reflection Questions:

- What possible inaccuracies exist in our assumptions/generalizations?
- Where is our math the weakest?
- Could anything change our claims (i.e., different yearly miles driven, different cost of gasoline, highway miles driven vs. city miles driven, etc.)?
- Overall, how confident are we in our claims?

This application task was the result of specific, intentional, and purposeful decisions about mathematics instruction critical for student growth and achievement. Although the outcome of these decisions is shared here, the process for arriving at this point originated from Ms. Rios's focus during the planning process. Figure 2.3 shows how Ms. Rios made her planning visible so that she could then provide an engaging and rigorous learning experience for her learners.

Moving from algebra to geometry, let us look at a different way of teaching the application of concepts and thinking skills in the Visible Learning classroom.

Ms. Rios's Teaching for Clarity PLANNING GUIDE

ESTABLISHING PURPOSE

1. What are the key content standards I will focus on in this lesson?

Content Standards:

A.REI.6. Solve systems of linear equations exactly and approximately (e.g., with graphs), focusing on pairs of linear equations in two variables.

A.REI.11. Explain why the x-coordinates of the points where the graphs of the equations $y = f(x)$ and $y = g(x)$ intersect are the solutions of the equation $f(x) = g(x)$; find the solutions approximately (e.g., using technology to graph the functions, make tables of values, or find successive approximations).

F.BF.1. Write a function that describes a relationship between two quantities.

a. Determine an explicit expression, a recursive process, or steps for calculation from a context.

Standards for Mathematical Practice:
- Make sense of problems and persevere in solving them.
- Use appropriate tools strategically.
- Model with mathematics.

2. What are the learning intentions (the goal and *why* of learning, stated in student-friendly language) I will focus on in this lesson?

Content: To use our understanding of systems of linear equations to make informed decisions about a real-world problem.

Language: To construct viable financial arguments based on mathematical reasoning and communicate them verbally and in writing.

Social: To work toward mathematical and logical consensus with our collaborative teams.

3 **When will I introduce and reinforce the learning intention(s) so that students understand it, see the relevance, connect it to previous learning, and can clearly communicate it themselves?**

Open the day with an overview to set the stage for this closing transfer task: We've gained all these tools; let's use them to solve real-world problems. As I introduce the task, I will refer to the learning intentions and make connections to activate students' prior knowledge (i.e., remind them about how they can model situations with linear functions when discussing the context of the task; remind them how they can solve systems of linear equations algebraically and graphically and how to interpret a solution given a context, etc.).

As students engage in the task, I will refer to the language intention to stimulate the use of academic and content language in their speaking and writing. I will refer to the social intention to remind students of our expectations of collaboration and building consensus based on mathematical evidence.

SUCCESS CRITERIA

4 **What evidence shows that students have mastered the learning intention(s)? What criteria will I use?**

I can statements:

- I can mathematically model a situation with a system of linear functions.
- I can solve a system of linear equations using my preferred method (algebraically or graphically).
- I can use my math as evidence to construct a claim about a real-world situation.
- I can logically communicate how my mathematical evidence supports my claim.

INSTRUCTION

5 **How will I check students' understanding (assess learning) during instruction and make accommodations?**

We will begin the day with a structured close read of the task itself to ensure all students come to a shared understanding of the context and what the problem is asking. Students will revoice the context and the end goal of the task with their groups, and each group will be asked to share with the whole class. This is where we will discuss any unclear content and academic language. This is especially important for our ELLs, who will be encouraged to use their personal electronic devices or school devices to help translate unfamiliar English words to their first language. Additionally, collaborative groups have been constructed with this in mind—students early in their English development have been paired with others who are bilingual in English and their first language (when available) so that all students may thoroughly discuss the task.

Once students start digging into the task collaboratively, I will scan the classroom, table to table, listening in on conversations and redirecting as needed. I will be careful not to interfere while students are productively struggling through the intended rigor of the task, but only step in when groups seem to be at a dead end. Based on the reason for their stalled production, I have a series of predesigned scaffolds at the ready.

6 **What activities and tasks will move students forward in their learning?**

Collaborative Task (Are hybrid cars really worth the price?), a close-reading application task that leads to a collaborative poster, followed by a gallery walk and whole-class discussion.

7 **What resources (materials and sentence frames) are needed?**

1. Printed copies of the task for each learner
2. Sticky poster paper for collaborative posters
3. Markers for posters
4. Printed copies of Scaffold 1: Parallel problem turning the given information (average monthly miles, average MPG, and average cost of gasoline) into the slope of a line and the cost of the vehicle into the y-intercept.
5. Printed copies of Scaffold 2: Review of solving systems of linear equations with references to prior class notes and examples.

8 **How will I organize and facilitate the learning? What questions will I ask? How will I initiate closure?**

1. Close Reading (Whole-Class)/Text-Dependent Questions

   What is the big idea of the task/text? What are we doing?

   What is a hybrid car? What is a non-hybrid car? Why is this difference important, according to the task?

   What information is provided in the table? What does each column mean? What does each row mean?

   What exactly is MPG? Why is this information important to the task?

   What are some initial ideas about how we might use math to approach this task?

   How might a system of linear equations help us?

   How can we use the information in the table to create linear equations?

   How can we determine the average yearly gasoline cost for each model?

2. Collaborative Work/Guided Practice

   Once the class as a whole is understanding the context and goal of the task via the close reading, I will release them to work collaboratively. This will be my opportunity to engage struggling groups in guided practice around the necessary computations to keep the task moving forward. This is also the time for formative scanning and eavesdropping.

3. Gallery Walk

   Completed posters will be displayed around the room. Groups will cycle through the room, poster to poster, leaving feedback on sticky notes and gathering talking points for the upcoming whole-class conversation.

4. Wrap-Up/Whole-Class Discussion (Backward Questioning)

   Conclusion:

   What did we discover? Are hybrid cars really worth the price?

   How does your math justify your claim?

   Process:

   What did we need mathematically in order to investigate this situation?

   Why/how do these equations represent the cost of each vehicle over time?

   What was the point of solving a system of equations? What does the solution represent?

   How did your group decide to solve your system? Why?

   Reflection:

   What other situations might lend themselves to this type of modeling?

> What possible inaccuracies exist in our assumptions/generalizations? Where is our math the weakest?
>
> Could anything change our claims (i.e., different yearly miles driven, different cost of gasoline, highway miles driven vs. city miles driven, etc.)?
>
> Overall, how confident are we in our claims?

 This lesson plan is available for download at resources.corwin.com/vlmathematics-9-12.

Figure 2.3   Ms. Rios's Systems of Linear Equations Application Lesson

Mr. Wittrock and Three-Dimensional Shapes

Mr. Wittrock is pleased with the temperate weather today because he will be spending about half of each class period outside with his students so they can get a closer look at the large water tower near their campus (see Figure 2.4).

Students have been studying trigonometric ratios and three-dimensional figures during the past two units, and Mr. Wittrock sees this mini-field study as the perfect opportunity to continue to build relevance in their work. He has a simple question for them that has anything but a simple solution path: How much water can the tower hold?

Mr. Wittrock's students have developed a deep understanding of the concepts of surface area and volume of three-dimensional objects. They built their conceptual understanding through hands-on lab experiences exploring shapes and their properties. They also built their procedural knowledge by learning (and in some cases, discovering) the formulas for surface area and volume and applying them to solve problems. Students have even started to transfer this learning by engaging in textbook word problems that require them to model real-world objects by viewing them as composites of common

Teaching Takeaway

Guiding questions can be used to provide an authentic context for learning intentions. This can increase student engagement and task value.

WATER TOWER AS COMPOSITE OF SEMI-SPHERE, CYLINDER, AND CONE

Source: Water Tower Image by pxhere. https://pxhere.com/en/photo/495060

CC0 1.0 Universal (CC0 1.0) Public Domain Dedication https://creativecommons.org/public domain/zero/1.0/

Figure 2.4

> **Deliberate practice** is the type of practice that is purposefully designed to either address particular learning gaps or refine high-level skills.

> **EFFECT SIZE FOR PRIOR ACHIEVEMENT = 0.55 AND PRIOR ABILITY = 0.94**

three-dimensional shapes. This **deliberate practice** has provided the foundation for today's application task: Mr. Wittrock carefully selected the word problems to target the learning intentions, success criteria, and gaps in student learning. Given this level of prior knowledge, Mr. Wittrock anticipates that students will not have too much trouble identifying what measurements they will need in order to solve the problem.

Additionally, Mr. Wittrock's students have demonstrated a strong understanding of trigonometric ratios and their (textbook) applications. For instance, students have completed word problems looking for the heights of trees by using the angle of inclination of a viewer's line of sight and that person's horizontal distance from the tree. Again, this was a *textbook* application, and Mr. Wittrock recalls the question coming from one of his students: "How do they know the angle of inclination? Your neck doesn't have a protractor!" This question and subsequent

DIGITAL INCLINOMETER MADE WITH A PERSONAL DEVICE

Source: iHandy Level App by iHandy Inc.

Figure 2.5

comment solidified Mr. Wittrock's decision to execute this application task. It was time to let his students *actually* apply their math. His learners will work in groups to answer the guiding question of the day: How much water can the tower hold?

While his students are conceptually and procedurally prepared for today's task, Mr. Wittrock knows that they are still at the surface level of learning hands-on measuring skills, especially with some of the new tools and strategies they will be using today. He recognizes that these are new skills for his students and that, up to this point, the textbook has provided most measurements. In this case, Mr. Wittrock will provide each group with a measuring tape, straws, and extra tape in case they want to use their personal devices as digital inclinometers (see Figure 2.5); a roll of string for measuring curved distances; a meter stick; and an inclinometer that students constructed the day before from protractors, yarn, and

EFFECT SIZE FOR DELIBERATE PRACTICE = **0.79**

paper clips. Other than lightly addressing inclinometers (for example) in a previous class, today will be students' first true use of these tools.

Mr. Wittrock therefore anticipates some increased *difficulty* in this part of the task, based on students' novice experience levels with the tools. He plans to scaffold by leading direct demonstrations for groups of how to use the tools, providing plenty of time for practice, encouraging multiple measurements to increase accuracy, and asking students to switch roles so they can gain a full understanding of the measuring process.

The sheer diversity of concepts discussed so far alludes to the fact that this task is highly complex. Mr. Wittrock thinks through the chain of events that would be required for successful completion: Students will need to use their understanding of composite shapes to recognize how to model geometrically a real-world object using pieces of familiar three-dimensional shapes. This model must then spur the need to collect specific measurements (height, radius, etc.), which will have to be conducted using knowledge of trigonometric ratios and tools new to the students. Mr. Wittrock is well aware of how much he is asking of his students, and he feels comfortable in doing so for two reasons. One, he has tremendous belief in his students and makes that well-known to them. "I keep raising the bar because you keep jumping over it," he tells them. Two, he knows where they are strong, he knows where they are still developing, and he has levels of questions prepared to scaffold the connecting between topics.

> EFFECT SIZE FOR TEACHER EXPECTATIONS = 0.43

> EFFECT SIZE FOR STUDENT FEELINGS OF EFFICACY = 0.92

What Mr. Wittrock Wants His Students to Learn

Get ready—Mr. Wittrock has lofty goals for his students. The following standards are addressed and indeed interwoven in this task, as follows:

> ### TEXAS ESSENTIAL KNOWLEDGE AND SKILLS (TEKS) GEOMETRY STANDARDS
>
> (9) **Similarity, proof, and trigonometry**. The student uses the process skills to understand and apply relationships in right triangles. The student is expected to

(A) determine the lengths of sides and measures of angles in a right triangle by applying the trigonometric ratios sine, cosine, and tangent to solve problems.

(10) **Two-dimensional and three-dimensional figures.** The student uses the process skills to recognize characteristics and dimensional changes of two- and three-dimensional figures. The student is expected to

(B) determine and describe how changes in the linear dimensions of a shape affect its perimeter, area, surface area, or volume, including proportional and nonproportional dimensional change.

(11) **Two-dimensional and three-dimensional figures**. The student uses the process skills in the application of formulas to determine measures of two- and three-dimensional figures. The student is expected to

(C) apply the formulas for the total and lateral surface area of three-dimensional figures (including prisms, pyramids, cones, cylinders, spheres, and composite figures) to solve problems using appropriate units of measure; and

(D) apply the formulas for the volume of three-dimensional figures (including prisms, pyramids, cones, cylinders, spheres, and composite figures) to solve problems using appropriate units of measure.

Mr. Wittrock is helping his learners develop the following TEKS Mathematical Process Standards:

- Use a problem-solving model that incorporates analyzing given information, formulating a plan or strategy, determining a solution, justifying the solution, and evaluating the problem-solving process and the reasonableness of the solution.

(Continued)

> (Continued)
>
> - Select tools, including real objects, manipulatives, paper and pencil, and technology as appropriate, and techniques, including mental math, estimation, and number sense as appropriate, to solve problems.
>
> - Analyze mathematical relationships to connect and communicate mathematical ideas.

Again, while interrelating so many concepts indeed makes today's task more authentic, it also drastically increases the complexity. Mr. Wittrock is prepared to scaffold this complexity by supporting students to make connections between each concept and recognize how this task links them.

Learning Intentions and Success Criteria

Much like Ms. Rios, Mr. Wittrock breaks his learning intentions down into content, language, and social subparts. As students walk into his classroom, he passes out clipboards for recording data and making calculations so that learners can complete the task outside. He has printed today's learning intentions and success criteria for the students. He uses them actively in his teaching by referring to them as students need a sense of direction, redirection, or prompting, or during scaffolding and questioning. This also allows students to monitor their own learning progression. Mr. Wittrock has provided the hands-on tools the students can use to complete the task.

> EFFECT SIZE FOR SELF-REGULATION STRATEGIES = 0.52

As they begin walking toward the water tower, Mr. Wittrock uses this time to introduce the task and review the learning intentions. "So we only have one problem to solve today," Mr. Wittrock begins. "It is just a single question: *How much water can the water tower hold?* Think about how you might go about answering that question as we read through the learning intentions." He then reads through the following learning

> EFFECT SIZE FOR PLANNING AND PREDICTION = 0.76

intentions and expands briefly on each, fielding questions from his students as they arise:

> *Content Learning Intention:* To apply our understanding of trigonometric ratios and three-dimensional shapes to measure volumes and surface areas of real-world objects.
>
> *Language Learning Intention:* To explain how to determine the volume and surface area of real-world objects using writing and labeled diagrams.
>
> *Social Learning Intention:* To help one another use appropriate tools—both physical and mathematical—to solve real-world problems.

By the time the day's learning is introduced and discussed, the students and Mr. Wittrock arrive at the water tower site. Mr. Wittrock explains the success criteria, which are printed directly below the learning intentions on the task sheet. "The success criteria today really guide you through the math skills you'll need to bring to bear in order to be successful in this task, along with the expectations of the task itself." He then reads the following success criteria and elaborates on the requirements of the task:

> ☐ I can accurately measure angles of inclination with an inclinometer.
> ☐ I can measure heights of tall objects using trigonometry.
> ☐ I can model composite shapes using common 3-D shapes.
> ☐ I can apply my knowledge of surface area and volume to composite shapes.
> ☐ I can demonstrate my problem-solving process in writing.

Video 6
Collaborative Learning in an Application Task

https://resources.corwin.com/ vlmathematics-9-12

He uses this introduction of success criteria as a transition into the planning phase of the task.

Guiding and Scaffolding Student Thinking

First, Mr. Wittrock instructs students, "So before we just jump into calculations, we need to make some sense of the structure of the problem itself. What information do we have?"

"Well, we have the water tower, but that's it," one of the students comments.

"That we do!" Mr. Wittrock tilts his head up to look at the top of the tower. "What does it remind us of? What does it *kind* of look like?"

"It reminds me of a water tower and it kind of looks like a water tower," another student sarcastically says, which gets a laugh out of the rest of the students. Mr. Wittrock laughs along with them and decides to clarify. This time he directs his question at the student who made the joke.

"Good stuff . . . I agree!" Mr. Wittrock knows that acknowledging the student's humor will go further than taking offense and pursuing a confrontation. "Let me ask my question a better way," he says and chooses his phrasing to give the student the opportunity to reengage while remaining socially unscathed. Again, his focus is on the learning. "If this thing were made out of giant Legos, what are the pieces you would need?"

"A cylinder," the student claims.

"OK, why and where?" Mr. Wittrock follows up.

"The middle is shaped basically like a cylinder, even though it is kind of bumpy."

"Absolutely right! What other Legos—or three-dimensional figures—would we need to model its shape?" Mr. Wittrock smoothly transitions the discussion from the informal space of "giant Legos" back to formal academic language after he is confident that he has reactivated his students' prior conceptual knowledge. Students go on to identify the semi-spherical shape of the tower's base and the conic top. "So why don't you all take a minute to brainstorm how you might go about calculating the volume, based on this discussion." Mr. Wittrock uses this opportunity to listen in on each discussion and make sure that students are generally on the right track.

This is a **direct/deliberate instruction** approach to teaching and learning mathematics.

Teaching Takeaway

Learners' responses to our questions are feedback on both the quality of the question and their level of understanding.

"OK, so this brings us to the next question," Mr. Wittrock gets everyone's attention. "What information do we need?" Much like the last guiding question, Mr. Wittrock uses this question to generate discussion about various dimensions that might need to be measured in order for students to be able to make their desired calculations. He elicits terms such as *height, lateral height, radius, diameter, area of the base,* and others from his students before moving on.

"Finally, how are we going to use the tools we have to get these measurements?" he asks. This part of the discussion is a little more chaotic, as it necessitates a bit of "play" as students start to practice with inclinometers, extend measuring tapes, and the like. Mr. Wittrock decides that any semblance of whole-group instruction will be ineffective at this point and prompts students to just "go for it" as the measuring phase begins. He cycles from group to group, scaffolding the use of the measuring tools as needed.

> **Teaching Takeaway**
>
> We must use feedback from our students—in this case the learners' conversations and actions—to adjust instruction and where we are going next.

Modeling Strategies and Skills

Throughout the task, Mr. Wittrock is monitoring his students' learning. As anticipated, learners are not equally proficient at measuring angles using the inclinometers. Specifically, one group seems to be struggling, as evidenced by their conflicting results (some negative angles and some positive), so Mr. Wittrock steps in to model proper use. This group is using a digital inclinometer as shown in Figure 2.5. Mr. Wittrock talks through his goal of controlling the tilt of the device until his line of sight through the straw is "just barely" in line with the top of the height he is trying to measure. Once he communicates that he is satisfied with the position—along with why he feels this way—he asks another student to read the device. Afterward, he switches roles with the student so that he can model how to read the device and what he is thinking about critically to determine whether or not the readings are accurate.

This form of teacher modeling helps provide students a sense of direction as they develop new skills. It helps scaffold the question "Am I doing this right?" by instead answering the question "How will I know if I am doing this right?"

> **EFFECT SIZE FOR RECIPROCAL TEACHING = 0.74**

Mr. Wittrock then provides time for his learners to engage in strategic planning. Individually, with a partner, or in a small group, students plan what they are going to measure and how they are going to make those measurements. In some cases, learners developed their own plans first before sharing each plan with their groups. This allows them to evaluate several strategic plans before finalizing the group's plan. Once students have agreed on their measurement approach, they are free to make those measurements and record them on their task sheets.

"Remember, having more data than you need is a better problem to have than not having everything. If you think you might need it, measure it." Mr. Wittrock brings the measurement phase of the task to a close with this advice to students before asking them to pack up their tools and head back to class.

After the students get settled back at their tables in their classroom, Mr. Wittrock directs them toward the consolidating phase of this task:

> So far you have made a plan and started executing that plan by taking lots of measurements. Now it is time to bring it all together and start solving the problem. How can we use these measurements and our knowledge of composite shapes to calculate the volume of the water tower? Also, how can drawing a diagram help? Please discuss at your tables before starting your calculations.

This reiterative line of questioning is intended to further scaffold the complexity of the task by asking students to make connections between each step students have taken and those they are about to take. This is also a strategy to slow down the process slightly so that all group members can process the chain of events required to make sense of the task.

After groups come to consensus about what they have done and where they are going, they begin collaboratively drawing diagrams of the water tower and making calculations using their own measurements. Mr. Wittrock is pleased that all students appear onboard and are actively contributing.

Teaching for Clarity at the Close

Mr. Wittrock directs students' attention to the learning intentions—specifically, the language learning intention, which includes explaining how to determine the volume and surface area of real-world objects using writing and diagrams, as well as demonstrating the problem-solving process in writing. He instructs them, "Write a claim supported by mathematical evidence and further justified by logical reasoning. I have some sentence frames for you if you get writer's block, but try to add your own style to this."

Mr. Wittrock then writes the following three questions on the board and continues, "As you write, continually ask yourself these questions":

- Is your solution clearly stated for the reader?
- How can you organize the explanation of your process so that the reader could replicate it if he or she wanted?
- How can the use of visuals help the reader make sense of your thinking and process?

Some students self-select a printout of sentence frames as a scaffold for this portion of the task, as shown in Figure 2.6 on the next page.

Timing was as important as any other element of planning when Mr. Wittrock was designing this task. He knows that this task constitutes problem-based learning (PBL), which has a very low effect size when used as a sole means of instruction. This is because PBL is best used as a strategy for teaching for transfer, where it has a higher effect size—which is exactly where his students are in their learning at this point. However, if students are still developing a surface-level understanding of concepts and procedures, they likely won't have access to a task such as this. The increased difficulty of each individual step could blind them from the complex connectivity between concepts.

Figure 2.7 shows how Mr. Wittrock made his planning visible so that he could then provide an engaging and rigorous learning experience for his learners.

> EFFECT SIZE FOR PROBLEM-BASED LEARNING = **0.26** (WHEN USED AS SOLE MEANS OF INSTRUCTION)

> EFFECT SIZE FOR PROBLEM-BASED LEARNING = **0.61** (WHEN USED FOR TRANSFER LEARNING)

Teaching Takeaway

Using the right approach at the right time increases our impact on student learning in the mathematics classroom.

SENTENCE FRAMES FOR WATER TOWER TASK

CLAIM:

The volume of the water tower is _____.

EVIDENCE:

Draw a diagram of the water tower and label each component with your measurements.

The water tower can be modeled as a composite shape that is part _____, part _____, and part _____. The volume of each of these parts, based on our measurements, is _____, _____, and _____. [Include calculations and relevant formulas.]

REASONING:

Therefore, the total volume is found by _____ and is _____

The way that my team measured _____ was _____

We also measured _____ by _____

Figure 2.6

 This tool is available for download at resources.corwin.com/vlmathematics-9-12.

Mr. Wittrock's Teaching for Clarity PLANNING GUIDE

ESTABLISHING PURPOSE

1

What are the key content standards I will focus on in this lesson?

Content Standards:

TEKS Geometry Standards

(9) Similarity, proof, and trigonometry. The student uses the process skills to understand and apply relationships in right triangles. The student is expected to:

  (A) determine the lengths of sides and measures of angles in a right triangle by applying the trigonometric ratios sine, cosine, and tangent to solve problems; and

(10) Two-dimensional and three-dimensional figures. The student uses the process skills to recognize characteristics and dimensional changes of two- and three-dimensional figures. The student is expected to:

  (B) determine and describe how changes in the linear dimensions of a shape affect its perimeter, area, surface area, or volume, including proportional and non-proportional dimensional change.

(11) Two-dimensional and three-dimensional figures. The student uses the process skills in the application of formulas to determine measures of two- and three-dimensional figures. The student is expected to:

  (C) apply the formulas for the total and lateral surface area of three-dimensional figures, including prisms, pyramids, cones, cylinders, spheres, and composite figures, to solve problems using appropriate units of measure; and

  (D) apply the formulas for the volume of three-dimensional figures, including prisms, pyramids, cones, cylinders, spheres, and composite figures, to solve problems using appropriate units of measure.

TEKS Mathematical Process Standards

- Use a problem-solving model that incorporates analyzing given information, formulating a plan or strategy, determining a solution, justifying the solution, and evaluating the problem-solving process and the reasonableness of the solution.
- Select tools, including real objects, manipulatives, paper and pencil, and technology as appropriate, and techniques, including mental math, estimation, and number sense as appropriate, to solve problems.
- Analyze mathematical relationships to connect and communicate mathematical ideas.

2 **What are the learning intentions (the goal and *why* of learning, stated in student-friendly language) I will focus on in this lesson?**

Content: To apply our understanding of trigonometric ratios and three-dimensional shapes to measure volumes and surface areas of real-world objects.

Language: To explain how to determine the volume and surface area of real-world objects using writing and diagrams.

Social: To help one another use appropriate tools—both physical and mathematical—to solve real-world problems.

3 **When will I introduce and reinforce the learning intention(s) so that students understand it, see the relevance, connect it to previous learning, and can clearly communicate it themselves?**

The learning intentions will be introduced as we walk outside to our learning site. Students will have them printed, along with the success criteria, on their task sheet so we can multitask our talking/reading/walking. We will converse about the goal, the tools we have, and some potential ideas. I'll loop back to the social intention as we engage in the measurement portion of the task outside. I'll revisit the language purpose as we conduct our write-up at the end of the day.

CHAPTER 2. TEACHING FOR THE APPLICATION OF CONCEPTS AND THINKING

SUCCESS CRITERIA

4

What evidence shows that students have mastered the learning intention(s)? What criteria will I use?

I can statements:

- I can accurately measure angles of inclination with an inclinometer.
- I can measure heights of tall objects using trigonometry.
- I can model composite shapes using common 3-D shapes.
- I can apply my knowledge of surface area and volume to composite shapes.
- I can demonstrate my problem-solving process in writing.

5

How will I check students' understanding (assess learning) during instruction and make accommodations?

I will check in with the groups throughout the measurement portion of the task and assess through regular conversation. I will help students make sense of the inclinometers (digital or analog) and their readings as they practice with them.

We will also engage in a "planning phase" outside at the learning site before we jump into collecting measurements. During this phase, I will facilitate conversations within and between groups as we develop a collective understanding of which measurements we might need. I will emphasize the overcollection of data as being a better problem to have than the undercollection of data (i.e, if you think you might need it, measure it).

INSTRUCTION

6

What activities and tasks will move students forward in their learning?

Planning: During this phase, students will begin organizing their understanding of the problem itself and possible solution paths.

Additionally, they will start to determine which measurements they need to collect and which tools they should use for their collection. I expect students to experiment with measuring during this phase as well to see how various tools work.

Measuring: Students will use tape measures, inclinometers (both analog with protractors and digital with their phones), meter sticks, and string to determine various dimensions of the water tower they will be investigating.

Consolidating: Students will use their measurements and their knowledge of composite shapes to calculate the surface area and volume of the water tower.

Write-Up: In this phase, students will do a formal write-up of their work, explaining their process and solutions in words and with the help of diagrams they will generate.

7 **What resources (materials and sentence frames) are needed?**

1. Straws to attach to cell phones or tablets to make digital inclinometers
2. Level app that shows degree of tilt
3. Protractors, string, and weights to make analog inclinometers
4. Meter sticks
5. Measuring tape
6. String for measuring
7. Clipboards for outside work
8. Printed task sheets

> **How will I organize and facilitate the learning? What questions will I ask? How will I initiate closure?**

The day will be organized in a linear fashion through the four phases previously listed:

1. Planning
   a. What are some dimensions of this water tower we might want to measure for future calculations?
   b. How might we go about measuring? Which tools should we use?

2. Measuring
   a. How does the inclinometer work?
   b. Have you taken multiple measurements of the same thing to check for accuracy?
   c. Are there any measurements you think you might need later, even if you aren't sure?

3. Consolidating
   a. How can we put all this together to start calculating surface area and volume?
   b. How can drawing a diagram help?

4. Write-Up
   a. Is your solution clearly stated for the reader?
   b. How can you organize your explanation of your process so that the reader could replicate it if he or she wanted?
   c. How can the use of visuals help the reader make sense of your thinking and process?

 This lesson plan is available for download at resources.corwin.com/vlmathematics-9-12.

Figure 2.7 Mr. Wittrock's Three-Dimensional Shapes Application Lesson

Ms. Shuzhen and Statistical Reasoning

As previously mentioned, teaching mathematics in the Visible Learning classroom requires helping mathematics learners to see themselves as their own teachers. This is the penultimate goal for Ms. Shuzhen. Her approach to teaching statistics strives to prepare learners to engage in the lifelong pursuit of mathematics or develop strong mathematical literacy in their everyday lives. Her classroom is set up in such a way that learners can see the relevance of statistics all around them. From weather forecasts to political polls, her learners have access to a vast array of applications of concepts and thinking in statistics.

Over the past several weeks, students have engaged in challenging tasks that build surface and deep learning in conceptual understanding around independent and conditional probability, as well as the procedural knowledge in calculating these probabilities. Ms. Shuzhen recognizes that transfer of that knowledge requires intentional and purposeful tasks that support learners in their application of statistics concepts and statistical thinking. As she plans for today's lesson, she seeks to offer learners multiple opportunities for this application through a menu of tasks—authentic problem-solving scenarios—that align with students' interests. She believes that incorporating student interest into application tasks is a necessary condition for engaging learners in the task and their willingness to take risks with both complex and difficult tasks. Ms. Shuzhen thinks of this as an exit task—a capstone task in which students demonstrate their ability to apply all of their previously learned knowledge (see Fennell, Kobett, & Wray, 2017).

What Ms. Shuzhen Wants Her Students to Learn

The menu of tasks that Ms. Shuzhen has selected for her learners asks them to apply multiple concepts and skills related to probability.

> 1. How do the dimensions of a baseball field affect batting statistics?
> 2. Is there such a thing as streakiness in baseball?

3. How do combinatorial games work? What are several examples?

4. What are theoretical solutions and Monte Carlo simulations? What are several examples?

5. Determine if the Monty Hall theory is mathematically correct.

6. Prove the best strategy for playing hi-lo using probability.

7. Determine if it is reasonable in blackjack to act differently with a two-card 16 than with a three-card 16 against a dealer's 10. Alternatively, come up with your own blackjack scenario.

8. Test the probabilities of rolling certain combinations of dice in role-playing games.

9. Determine if the probability of picking the right object is better by switching your initial choice with a variant shell game, where one choice that is for sure wrong is removed by the person in charge and shown to you after you make your first guess.

The common thread across each task is the use of those concepts to make decisions—the specific of the standard. The overarching idea is that learners will use probability and statistical reasoning to make decisions.

MATHEMATICS CONTENT AND PRACTICE STANDARDS

S-MD.B.7

Analyze decisions and strategies using probability concepts (e.g., product testing, medical testing, pulling a hockey goalie at the end of a game).

Ms. Shuzhen is helping her learners develop the following Standards for Mathematical Practice:

- Make sense of problems and persevere in solving them.
- Reason abstractly and quantitatively.
- Construct viable arguments and critique the reasoning of others.

Ms. Shuzhen will structure the learning tasks so that each student has the opportunity to relate the decisions and strategies of independent and conditional probability, as well as the rules of probability.

Learning Intentions and Success Criteria

Ms. Shuzhen is very purposeful about her learning intention. What is it that she wants her students to learn from this particular experience? Aligned with her approach to teaching high school statistics, she wants her learners to understand how statistics and probability can and do inform our decision making. Thus, she displays learning intentions that reflect this goal, making them visible to each of the students in her classes:

> *Content Learning Intention:* To apply our understanding of probability and statistical reasoning to make decisions.
>
> *Language Learning Intention:* To explain how to make decisions using independent probability, conditional probability, and the rules of probability.
>
> *Social Learning Intention:* To engage in productive discussions about how my peers made their decisions, including their reasoning and modeling of the scenario.

EFFECT SIZE FOR LEARNING GOALS = 0.68

At this point in her students' learning progressions, they have devoted significant time to different types of conceptual understanding and procedural knowledge in dependent and conditional probability. At this point in the unit, learners have engaged in many checks for understanding, as well as tasks that assess for mastery around each of these concepts and associated procedures for calculated dependent and conditional probability. Furthermore, Ms. Shuzhen has consistently modeled the role of success criteria in helping her learners know where they are in their own understanding and where they are going next.

Teaching Takeaway

Co-constructing success criteria with learners is a way to engage them in their learning.

As learners have used success criteria to monitor their own learning, she hopes to have them co-construct their own success criteria for today's tasks (Moss & Brookhart, 2012; O'Connell & Vandas, 2015). Co-constructing success criteria is more than handing them a list of what they must complete; rather, it is building a shared understanding of learning expectations and a pathway to make progress (Almarode & Vandas, in press).

LEARNER SUCCESS CRITERIA MONITORING SHEET

SUCCESS CRITERIA	EVIDENCE
I CAN	
I CAN	
I CAN	
I CAN	

Figure 2.8

 This figure is available for download at resources.corwin.com/vlmathematics-9-12.

Students will generate their own success criteria for this task. Ms. Shuzhen's learners are very familiar with this process. They have analyzed Ms. Shuzhen's learning intentions and success criteria in the past and built up to this moment. In addition, Ms. Shuzhen has the Standards for Mathematical Practice posted in the room. Learners know they are to include them in their success criteria as well. However, we must point out that Ms. Shuzhen's decision to use choice in the task does not automatically mean that students create their own success criteria. There are many times throughout the year that her learners have had choice but have all worked toward a common set of learning intentions and success criteria.

To generate their own success criteria, learners explored the options on their choice boards, deciding which ones they would tackle during the day's class. In addition to selecting one of the options, students had to decide how they would present the problem to their peers (e.g., presentation, demonstration, written solution, etc.). This makes the process of developing two or three *I can* statements easier and the learning visible to both Ms. Shuzhen and themselves. These success criteria will be documented in their interactive notebooks and referenced during one-on-one student conferences using a monitoring sheet (see Figure 2.8).

Modeling Strategies and Skills

In addition to Ms. Shuzhen's use of this lesson as an exit task, as learners engage in the task of their choosing she plans to constantly check for

> **Teaching Takeaway**
>
> Offering students choices in their learning promotes buy-in. The student voice inherent in both task choice and co-constructing success criteria allows learners to take ownership of their learning.

EFFECT SIZE FOR SETTING STANDARDS FOR SELF-JUDGEMENT = 0.62

> **Teaching Takeaway**
>
> Effective formative assessment can include observations, interviews, "show-me" moments that ask learners to show what they know, hinge questions, and exit tasks (Fennell et al., 2017).

> **EFFECT SIZE FOR STRATEGY MONITORING = 0.58**

> **EFFECT SIZE FOR STUDENT-TEACHER RELATIONSHIPS = 0.52**

understanding through observations, interviews (student conferencing), and asking students to show what they know (see Fennell et al., 2017).

To help her learners focus on the *why* behind these authentic problem-solving tasks, Ms. Shuzhen will use a guiding question—something learners are familiar with in her classroom: "Remember, ladies and gentlemen, as you embark on your problem-solving adventure, you must be able to extrapolate the answer to our guiding question—'How can probability and statistical reasoning help me make decisions?'"

Ms. Shuzhen is excellent at monitoring learning through checks for understanding that identify any areas that need more focused learning around particular content. For example, individual students may need remediation around prior knowledge, skills, and understandings needed for their problem-solving tasks. In addition, the choices available to students will differ based on learners' levels of readiness. Although all learners will engage in the application of concepts and thinking, Ms. Shuzhen will make sure all students have access to this application by accommodating the needs of each student. She adjusts the content through different modalities—for example, she will translate it into Spanish for some students, provide video clips and worked examples for some learners, and offer graphic organizers to assist with problem solving. This way, all learners will have access to the type of thinking expected in this application task.

As learners prepare to start the day, Ms. Shuzhen gets their attention and presents the day's learning intention. "Today, we are going to bring together the procedures and concepts from the past two weeks and use this learning to explore different contexts related to statistics and probability." She tells them their role is to answer the question "How can probability and statistical reasoning help me make decisions?" She directs their attention to the learning intention on the board. Without much hesitation, Brock pipes up and says, "Hey, what are the success criteria? What I am supposed to get out of this?" This prompts much laughter from both Ms. Shuzhen and Brock's peers.

Ms. Shuzhen also uses this question to introduce the day's tasks:

> Ladies and gentlemen, in just a few moments I will hand you a choice board. You will have four different problem-solving tasks on that choice board. After you have a few moments to

read each problem-solving task, I am going to ask you to pick the one that you will tackle today. Realize that this task may take more than one class period, so do not worry about the time component.

Ms. Shuzhen distributes the choice boards to her students. Each of the choice boards has four of the following nine problem-solving scenarios (also outlined on pages 80–81):

1. How do the dimensions of a baseball field affect batting statistics?
2. Is there such a thing as streakiness in baseball?
3. How do combinatorial games work? What are several examples?
4. What are theoretical solutions and Monte Carlo simulations? What are several examples?
5. Determine if the Monty Hall theory is mathematically correct.
6. Prove the best strategy for playing hi-lo using probability.
7. Determine if it is reasonable in blackjack to act differently with a two-card 16 than with a three-card 16 against a dealer's 10. Alternatively, come up with your own blackjack scenario.
8. Test the probabilities of rolling certain combinations of dice in role-playing games.
9. Determine if the probability of picking the right object is better by switching your initial choice with a variant shell game, where one choice that is for sure wrong is removed by the person in charge and shown to you after you make your first guess.

Ms. Shuzhen provides varying degrees of difficulty and complexity depending on the level of readiness for each student by selecting four options to appear on specific learners' choice boards. She asks them to partially solve some of the problems to understand the nature of the problems and envision a plan and product before making a decision about which of the scenarios they would like to tackle. She then walks the students through the development of their own personal success

EXAMPLE OF A LEARNER SUCCESS CRITERIA MONITORING SHEET

SUCCESS CRITERIA	EVIDENCE
I can create four different scenarios that have different probabilistic outcomes.	I will calculate the probability of the player winning against the dealer in each scenario.
I can identify and model the rules of probability in each scenario.	I will present this information in my Prezi.
I can explain my reasoning and calculations to my classmates.	I will get feedback from my peers and ask them to try a problem on their own.

Figure 2.9

criteria and evidence necessary to show progress toward the success criteria. This is where each learner determines the specific product or approach for his or her particular problem. You can see an example of one learner's approach in Figure 2.9. Jackson decides to select Option 7 and create four different blackjack scenarios to analyze. He wants to develop a Prezi that walks his peers through the decision-making process at the gambling table.

Using a hinge question, Ms. Shuzhen asks her learners to "give her five" based on the *I can* statements they have created. "Give me five if you are confident or one finger if you are in need of additional assistance with your *I can* statements." Looking around to see how many students are holding up five fingers versus those holding up one finger, she can provide additional support to those learners who indicate they are not quite there with their *I can* statements. Once she and the students agreed on the success criteria, she released the learners to tackle their problem-solving scenario.

As each student works on his or her task, Ms. Shuzhen moves around the room, asking specific questions and watching students work. At the same time, she checks for their understanding by asking questions and interviewing them about their progress. She is constantly reflecting on the learning in her classroom: Where did learners struggle in the task?

Were there gaps in their learning that needed to be addressed at this point in the learning progression? She did not want to miss opportunities to provide feedback to students as they applied their concepts and thinking to these problem-solving scenarios.

Teaching for Clarity at the Close

As learners complete the task, they compile their evidence associated with each success criterion. This evidence, along with the answer to their authentic scenario, will be submitted for tomorrow's peer review. Learners will present their responses and engage in productive discussions about how peers made decisions, including their reasoning and modeling of the scenario. Until then, Ms. Shuzhen collects their progress so that she can review student work this evening and make adjustments, where needed, for tomorrow.

Figure 2.10 shows how Ms. Shuzhen made her planning visible so that she could then provide an engaging and rigorous learning experience for her learners.

Ms. Shuzhen's Teaching for Clarity PLANNING GUIDE

ESTABLISHING PURPOSE

1. What are the key content standards I will focus on in this lesson?

Content Standards:

S-MD.B.7

Analyze decisions and strategies using probability concepts (e.g., product testing, medical testing, pulling a hockey goalie at the end of a game).

Standards for Mathematical Practice:

- Make sense of problems and persevere in solving them.
- Reason abstractly and quantitatively.
- Construct viable arguments and critique the reasoning of others.

2. What are the learning intentions (the goal and *why* of learning, stated in student-friendly language) I will focus on in this lesson?

Content: To apply our understanding of probability and statistical reasoning to make decisions.

Language: To explain how to make decisions using independent probability, conditional probability, and the rules of probability.

Social: To engage in productive discussions about how my peers made their decisions, including their reasoning and modeling of the scenario.

3 **When will I introduce and reinforce the learning intention(s) so that students understand it, see the relevance, connect it to previous learning, and can clearly communicate it themselves?**

The learning intentions will be introduced as learners enter the classroom and prepare for the day. I will also reinforce the learning intentions when students present their products and success criteria. This will allow me to make explicit connections between the learning intentions, success criteria, and student products.

SUCCESS CRITERIA

4 **What evidence shows that students have mastered the learning intention(s)? What criteria will I use?**

I can statements:

Learners will co-construct their success criteria based on the scenario they select. I will first ask them to make a decision about which of the scenarios they would like to tackle. I will walk the students through the development of their own personal success criteria and evidence necessary to show progress toward the success criteria. This is where each learner will describe the specific product or approach for his or her particular problem. Once the students and I agree on the success criteria, they will be released to tackle their problem-solving scenario.

5 How will I check students' understanding (assess learning) during instruction and make accommodations?

I will move around the room, asking specific questions and watching students work. At the same time, I will be checking for their understanding by observing students, asking questions, and interviewing them about their progress. I will constantly reflect on the learning in the classroom by asking where did learners struggle in the task and were there gaps in their learning that needed to be addressed at this point in the learning progression. I will provide feedback to all students as they apply their concepts and thinking to these problem-solving scenarios.

INSTRUCTION

6 What activities and tasks will move students forward in their learning?

I will distribute the choice boards to the students. Each of the choice boards has four of the following problem-solving scenarios:

1. *How do the dimensions of a baseball field affect batting statistics?*
2. *Is there such a thing as streakiness in baseball?*
3. *How do combinatorial games work? What are several examples?*
4. *What are theoretical solutions and Monte Carlo simulations? What are several examples?*
5. *Determine if the Monty Hall theory is mathematically correct.*
6. *Prove the best strategy for playing hi-lo using probability.*

7. Determine if it is reasonable in blackjack to act differently with a two-card 16 than with a three-card 16 against a dealer's 10. Alternatively, come up with your own blackjack scenario.

8. Test the probabilities of rolling certain combinations of dice in role-playing games.

9. Determine if the probability of picking the right object is better by switching your initial choice with a variant shell game, where one choice that is for sure wrong is removed by the person in charge and shown to you after you make your first guess.

---

7. What resources (materials and sentence frames) are needed?

1. Choice boards
2. Success criteria and evidence charts
3. Calculators
4. Manipulatives (e.g., deck of cards, dice, various objects for modeling)
5. Computer simulation software on Chromebooks

---

8. How will I organize and facilitate the learning? What questions will I ask? How will I initiate closure?

I will organize today's class into the following blocks of time:

1. Introduction of the learning intentions and tasks (whole-group)
2. Selection of the tasks from the choice boards (independent)
3. Development of the product and success criteria (conferencing with me)

> 4. Work toward the task and the gathering of evidence (independent)
>
> 5. Feedback and closure
>
> Due to the independent nature of this task, learners will be responsible for organizing a portion of the day. For these specific chunks of time, they will have the option to work in the classroom or go to the library to secure additional resources or space to model the specific scenario. As learners complete the task, I will help them compile the evidence and their response to prepare for tomorrow's peer review.

 This lesson plan is available for download at resources.corwin.com/vlmathematics-9-12.

Figure 2.10 Ms. Shuzhen's Statistical Reasoning Application Lesson

Reflection

The three examples from Ms. Rios, Mr. Wittrock, and Ms. Shuzhen exemplify what teaching mathematics for application of concepts and thinking skills in the Visible Learning classroom looks like. Using what you have read in this chapter, reflect on the following questions:

1. In your own words, describe what teaching for the application of concepts and thinking skills looks like in your mathematics classroom.

2. How does the Teaching for Clarity Planning Guide support your intentionality in teaching for the application of concepts and thinking skills?

3. Compare and contrast the approaches to teaching taken by the classroom teachers featured in this chapter.

4. How did the classroom teachers featured in this chapter adjust the difficulty and/or complexity of the mathematics tasks to meet the needs of all learners?

TEACHING FOR CONCEPTUAL UNDERSTANDING 3

CHAPTER 3 SUCCESS CRITERIA:

(1) I can describe what teaching for conceptual understanding in the mathematics classroom looks like.

(2) I can apply the Teaching for Clarity Planning Guide to Teaching for Conceptual Understanding.

(3) I can compare and contrast different approaches to teaching for conceptual understanding with teaching for application.

(4) I can give examples of how to differentiate mathematics tasks designed for conceptual understanding.

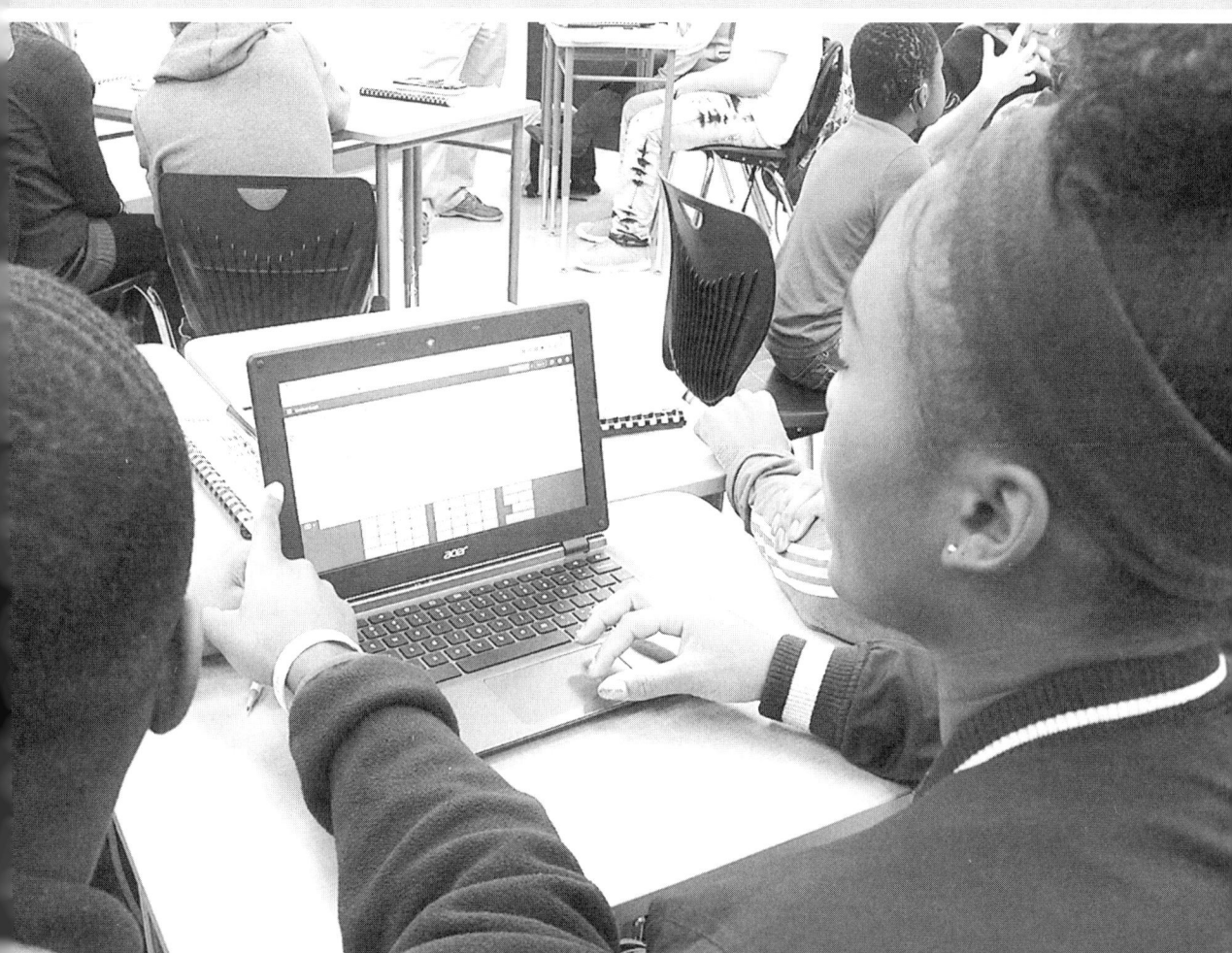

In Chapter 2, we visited the three classrooms as they engaged in the application of concepts and thinking skills. As you recall, this application of mathematics to purchasing a car, determining the volume of water in a water tower, and making decisions using the rules of probability required learners to have foundational knowledge in conceptual understanding and procedural knowledge. In this chapter, we will turn back time to see how each of the three teachers supported their learners as they developed conceptual understanding in their mathematics learning. We will also share videos of what conceptual learning looks like in a geometry classroom.

If learners are to see mathematics as more than algorithms and mnemonics, we must provide learning experiences that focus on the underlying properties and principles. For Ms. Rios, Mr. Wittrock, and Ms. Shuzhen, the end goal is to understand, conceptually, systems of equations, the volume of three-dimensional shapes, and independent and dependent probability, respectively. All three teachers expect their learners to understand the meaning behind mathematical procedures rather than relying on shortcuts and memory jingles. As in Chapter 2, each of these classrooms will differentiate the mathematics tasks by providing varying degrees of complexity and difficulty to their learners. Although every learner will be actively engaged in a challenging mathematical task that builds conceptual understanding of key concepts, Ms. Rios, Mr. Wittrock, and Ms. Shuzhen will adjust the complexity and difficulty of the task to ensure all learners have access to these concepts.

Ms. Rios and Systems of Linear Equations

EFFECT SIZE FOR PRIOR ABILITY = 0.94

EFFECT SIZE FOR STRATEGIES TO INTEGRATE WITH PRIOR KNOWLEDGE = 0.93

In a previous unit, students in Ms. Rios's algebra class dove deep into linear functions. They calculated rates of change and predicted points (including x- and y-intercepts) from given values, graphed lines, and mathematically modeled real-world scenarios with linear functions. As she begins this next unit on systems of equations, she intends to leverage their understanding of graphing to introduce the concept of *solving* systems of equations. Her students developed proficiency at interpreting graphs of single linear functions, including extracting explicit functions from simple graphs by locating the y-intercept and identifying the slope. So she decides she will start this day of conceptual understanding there.

What Ms. Rios Wants Her Students to Learn

Ms. Rios wants to dedicate the bulk of this class period to the *concept* of a solution of a system of equations so that she can later build procedural knowledge that is grounded and has meaning for students. Essentially, by building a new conceptual understanding today, she is sowing the seeds and building the need for additional procedural knowledge tomorrow. This is why she will be focusing on the following single standard:

> ### MATHEMATICS CONTENT AND PRACTICE STANDARDS
>
> A.REI.D.11.
>
> Explain why the x-coordinates of the points where the graphs of the equations $y = f(x)$ and $y = g(x)$ intersect are the solutions of the equation $f(x) = g(x)$; find the solutions approximately (e.g., using technology to graph the functions, make tables of values, or find successive approximations).
>
> **Ms. Rios is helping her learners develop the following Standards for Mathematical Practice:**
>
> - Reason abstractly and quantitatively.
> - Construct viable arguments and critique the reasoning of others.
> - Look for and make use of structure.

Conceptual understanding is at the heart of this standard. Notice that the key verb in this standard (and first word) is *explain*. Only concepts that are understood can be meaningfully explained. This further supports the need for spending the time and designing specific tasks to develop students' conceptual understanding of solutions of systems of equations.

Learning Intentions and Success Criteria

As mentioned in the previous chapter, Ms. Rios uses the *content*, *language*, and *social* varieties of learning intentions so that she can focus on

---

Teaching Takeaway

We must be clear on the expectations of the content standards to ensure teaching and learning are aligned with this standard.

EFFECT SIZE FOR STUDENT FEELINGS OF EFFICACY = 0.92

EFFECT SIZE FOR STUDENT–TEACHER RELATIONSHIPS = 0.52

EFFECT SIZE FOR TEACHER CREDIBILITY = 0.90

specific areas of growth for each category. Her learning intentions for this lesson are as follows:

> *Content Learning Intention:* To understand that a system of equations is a set of two or more equations with the same unknowns.
>
> *Language Learning Intention:* To articulate the meaning of solutions of systems of equations both abstractly and within a context.
>
> *Social Learning Intention:* To communicate our thinking to our peers even before we completely understand a topic.

Ms. Rios begins her day by introducing these learning intentions and using their language as a means of communicating her expectations:

> Today is about using the tools we already have to think about something new. It's a new unit, so we haven't talked about these things before. But don't let that stop you from thinking out loud with your partners. This is why our social learning intention today is to communicate our thinking to our peers even before we completely understand a topic. Remember, you deserve to know this stuff—so let's talk it out.

Ms. Rios finishes her introduction by asking, "Whose math is this?" The students chorally respond, "Our math!" Just as she wishes her students to be unafraid when "putting themselves out there," Ms. Rios models this behavior by showing her passion for the subject and for her own students' learning. She knows that student–teacher relationships have a high effect size, and she uses these displays of advocacy to further those relationships. Students are more likely to take risks for teachers they trust.

Ms. Rios is laser-focused on the standard's use of the verb *explain* as a means of measuring what conceptual understanding looks like in this context, which is why you will find that this verb shows up so frequently in her success criteria for this lesson. Rather than simply rewriting the standard with the words *I can* in front of it, Ms. Rios put a great deal of thought into what it means for students to be able to explain *why* the x-coordinates of the points where the graphs of the equations $y = f(x)$ and $y = g(x)$ intersect are the solutions of the equation $f(x) = g(x)$. She asked herself what progress along the path to mastering this standard looks

Teaching Takeaway

Teacher credibility includes three constructs: perceived competence, trustworthiness, and caring.

Teaching Takeaway

Success criteria should provide a clear path toward mastery of the learning intention.

like for her learners. What underlying mathematics are required in service of this standard? What are some mile markers that indicate partial progress toward mastery? Ultimately, she broke it into four categories:

> ☐ I can explain the meaning of graphs and tables by analyzing their labels, units, values, and behavior.
> ☐ I can explain how to locate a solution to a system of equations by examining a graph.
> ☐ I can explain how to locate a solution to a system of equations by generating and analyzing a table of values.
> ☐ I can explain the meaning of a solution to a system of equations mathematically and within a context.

The first criterion addresses some prior knowledge that her students will bring to bear when mastering this standard—they need to be able to read and explain graphs and tables if they are going to use them to find and explain solutions. The second and third criteria build on the first by splitting the concepts of representing systems graphically or numerically and the solving methods associated with both. These two address the process. The fourth criterion gets at the interpretation of a solution—both abstractly and in the concrete. Ms. Rios unpacked the standard's expectation of an explanation into three subparts: explain the representation, explain the process, and explain the result.

Breaking success criteria down in this fashion also allows students to identify specifically where their learning might be stalling. Maybe they are able to explain how to locate solutions using graphs but cannot do the same with a table of data, for example. These formative data should elicit different responses from the teacher. This method also gives teachers a natural response to the vague "I-don't-get-it" types of responses. Ms. Rios likes to respond simply, "What don't you get?" as she prompts students to refer to their *I can* statements. She will continue, "Can you . . .?" as she reads off each success criterion. Admittedly, this can feel frustrating for students if they are new to this type of classroom culture. Many students arrive trained to simply seek out "right answers" and the "right way to do problems." Building an expectation of metacognition, self-assessment, and critical thinking can be a challenging culture shock for these students. Ms. Rios likes to address this by grabbing the bull by the horns. She often tells students,

Teaching Takeaway

Conceptual understanding can be at the deep phase of learning. This occurs when learners are making connections between concepts.

Teaching Takeaway

Through collaborative planning, we must spend time unpacking standards to ensure we have clarity about what our learners are expected to know, understand, and be able to do.

Video 7
Setting the Stage for Conceptual Learning

https://resources.corwin.com/vlmathematics-9-12

> **EFFECT SIZE FOR COGNITIVE TASK ANALYSIS = 1.29**

I know this can be uncomfortable, struggling with something new. Trust me, the easiest thing I could do right now is just give you the answer. The reason I choose not to take the easy road, however, is because I care about you becoming an independent learner. Sometimes—especially in college—you'll find yourself in a situation where you have to be your own teacher. I know I did. You have to understand what you know and, more importantly, what you don't know so that you can find the help you need and do something about it. I want to practice that now, while we are here where it is safe.

She believes in taking the time to invest in student–teacher relationships—again, a 0.52 effect size. She also feels an obligation to further her students down their own paths to becoming assessment-capable visible learners.

Instructional Approaches That Promote Conceptual Understanding

> **EFFECT SIZE FOR DIALOGIC INSTRUCTION = 0.82 AND DIRECT/DELIBERATE INSTRUCTION = 0.60**

Ms. Rios is truly hybridizing dialogic and direct/deliberate instructional approaches in this lesson by engaging in a back-and-forth with students. She plans to prompt students to discuss a series of questions using the think–pair–share protocol, whereby students first take time to individually think about their responses before discussing with a partner and ultimately sharing with the whole class. Her goal with this dialogic approach is to allow students the opportunity to activate their prior knowledge, experience the perturbation required for new learning to occur, and begin to construct their own understanding of the concept. After facilitating a discussion based on student responses, she will model her own thinking through a think-aloud. This direct approach gives students the ability to witness how an expert would approach a given situation or problem. Ms. Rios recognizes that the effect size for both dialogic instruction and direct/deliberate instruction are above the hinge point and that she doesn't need to choose *which* to use exclusively, but *when* to use each (and for what purpose).

> **Teaching Takeaway**
>
> Using the right approach at the right time increases our impact on student learning in the mathematics classroom.

She begins her think–pair–share by prompting students to look at a projected image of a graphed system of equations in a context (see Figure 3.1).

GRAPHED SYSTEM OF EQUATIONS IN A CONTEXT: PLANES LEAVING THE AIRPORT

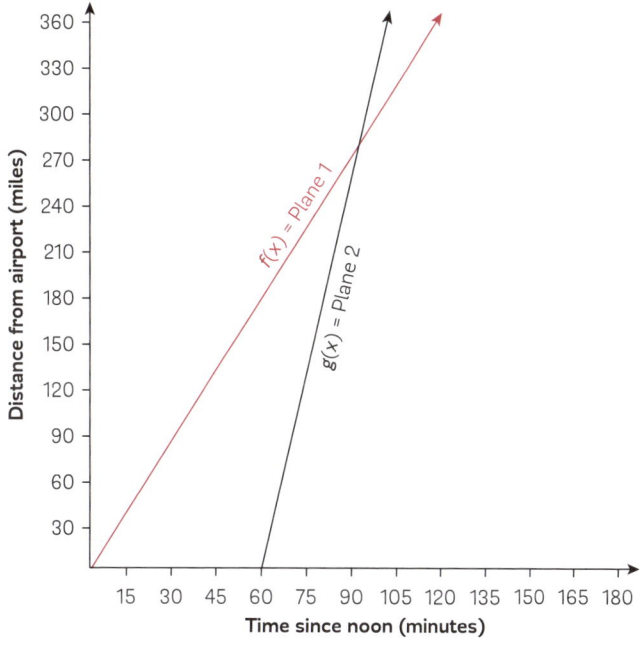

Figure 3.1

The context is not explicitly spelled out for students, but the graph is labeled in detail so that inferences may be drawn. For example, the *y*-axis is labeled *Distance From Airport* with the units marked in miles, the *x*-axis is labeled *Time Since Noon*, where the units are in 15-minute increments, and the graphs of each function are clearly labeled *Plane 1* and *Plane 2*. Without describing the image herself, Ms. Rios begins with, "Take a moment and think about the following question by yourself. No talking for this first part. What are the key features of this graph that will help communicate its meaning?" She repeats the question a second time as she notes her students' expressions while they look at the image and hear the question. After about 20 seconds of independent think time, Ms. Rios instructs her students, "OK, now turn to your partner and discuss your responses to the question."

While her students are buzzing with conversation, Ms. Rios is noting the engagement level of each pair. She is working to anticipate who will need

EFFECT SIZE FOR IMAGERY = 0.45

EFFECT SIZE FOR CLASSROOM DISCUSSION = 0.82

Video 8
Managing Student-Led Dialogic Learning

https://resources.corwin.com/vlmathematics-9-12

> **EFFECT SIZE FOR FEEDBACK = 0.70**

Teaching Takeaway

Our feedback to learners must be specific and constructive so that learners can assimilate the feedback into their thinking.

more support, be it academically, socially, or linguistically. She checks in with one pair that has ceased conversing and seems to be avoiding eye contact. "Hi, team," she begins. "What did we talk about here—what are the key features of this graph that will help communicate its meaning?" One student laughs nervously while the other shrugs. Ms. Rios tries again, "What does the y-axis tell us? What does it say?"

One of the students responds, "The distance from the airport."

"Distance from the airport? What does that mean—whose distance from the airport?" she questions.

"The plane's," the other student responds.

"The plane's?" she asks. "How many planes are there, and how do you know?"

The first student sits up in his chair and leans into the conversation, pointing at the projected image. "There are two planes because there are two lines called *Plane 1* and *Plane 2*. It says it right there!" Ms. Rios looks at the other student, who nods in agreement.

Seizing this opportunity to develop self-efficacy, Ms. Rios concludes this check-in with, "Awesome! Thank you both. What you're doing right now is explaining the meaning of graphs by analyzing their labels, units, values, and behavior. That's part of your first *I can* statement." She encourages them, saying, "Please see what else you can figure out about the graph as I check in with other tables."

Ms. Rios continues her scan briefly before bringing her students' attention back to the front of the class. "Welcome back, class. Who would like to share what your pair talked about? What does this graph tell us? How are you making sense of it?"

After taking a handful of responses and allowing students to openly converse and build off each other, Ms. Rios repeats this process with the following, planned focusing questions—all designed to build toward the first criterion for success:

- What are the key features of this graph that will help communicate its meaning?
- Which function, $f(x)$ or $g(x)$, is representing the following situation? This plane left the airport at noon and, traveling at a constant speed, traveled 90 miles in 30 minutes.

- Describe the situation represented by the other function. What key features made you describe it in that way?
- What does this point of intersection represent mathematically? What does the intersection mean in the context?
- In the context, what was happening before the intersection, and what happens after the intersection?

Some questions require longer think times and longer pair discussions than others do, and Ms. Rios is comfortable providing that time. She tries to gauge the quality of the conversations to determine when to move on. This is *their* time, after all, that she has set aside to develop a conceptual understanding.

Modeling Strategies and Skills

After completing each set of questions, Ms. Rios switches from the dialogic think–pair–share strategy to the deliberate strategy of expert modeling via a think-aloud. After the first set of questions aimed at developing students' abilities to conceptualize solutions of systems of equations graphically, Ms. Rios projects another labeled graph and requests that her students listen carefully while she models her thinking for them, using Figure 3.2.

She sets up the expectations of the think-aloud by asking them to simply watch and listen to how she thinks about and makes sense of the graph example and adds, "I want you to consider how this is similar to what we just did together and how maybe this can patch any holes in understanding you might have." She begins her explanation with,

> When I see this graph, the first thing that I notice is that the *y*-axis is labeled *Pounds of Fruit Harvested* and the *x*-axis is labeled *Year*. This tells me that I am looking at the weight of fruit harvested in a given year. I am also recognizing that my *x*-axis is counting by years, starting at the year 2000 and going to 2010. My *y*-axis is counting by thousands of pounds, starting at 1,000 and going up to 10,000. This tells me that the higher I go, the more fruit that is harvested, and the further to the right I go, the more time that has passed. Does everybody agree with this interpretation of the graph so far?

> **Teaching Takeaway**
>
> During our planning time, we must consider the types of questions we will ask our students and when we will ask them to promote their mathematics thinking and learning. This cannot always be effectively done in the moment.

GRAPHED SYSTEM OF EQUATIONS IN A CONTEXT: POUNDS OF FRUIT HARVESTED EACH YEAR

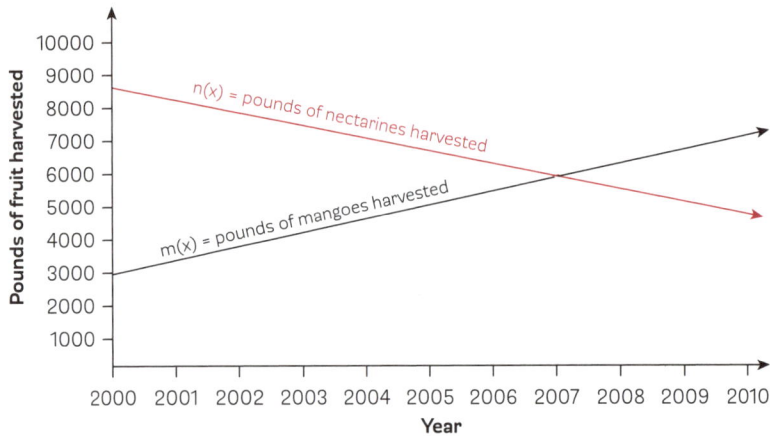

Figure 3.2

Ms. Rios pauses for a moment to allow students to ask clarifying questions. Then, she continues,

> Now, as I investigate these two functions and their labels, $m(x)$ and $n(x)$, I see that $m(x)$ is meant to represent the pounds of mangoes harvested each year, and $n(x)$ stands for the pounds of nectarines harvested. This makes me think that whoever made the graph chose good letters for his or her functions! I also recognize that the weight of nectarines harvested starts higher than the weight of mangoes in the year 2000.

Ms. Rios explicitly gestures to the part of the graph that she is interpreting as she describes it and then further animates the rest of her coming description with tracing motions.

> But then every year it seems that fewer and fewer nectarines are harvested and more and more mangoes are harvested. I know this because the slope of $n(x)$ is negative—it is going down—and the slope of $m(x)$ is positive—it is going up. I also see that in 2007 the two functions intersect—this is when they equal each other. This is the solution to $m(x) = n(x)$. This literally means that the weight of mangoes harvested was the

same as the weight of nectarines harvested in 2017. At every point in time before this solution, before this intersection, the weight of mangoes was less than the weight of nectarines. At every point in time after this solution, after this intersection, the weight of mangoes was greater than the weight of nectarines. This makes sense to me because the slope of the nectarine function is negative, which means it is decreasing, while the slope of the mango function is positive, which means that it is increasing. So at some point—apparently in 2007—mangoes should catch up to nectarines and then start outgrowing them. Does everybody agree with my claim? Are there any clarifying questions about how I've said this?

After allowing questions from her students, Ms. Rios concludes her think-aloud with, "Turn to your partners and tell them what makes the most sense about how I thought through this problem and what makes the least sense about my process."

> EFFECT SIZE FOR SUMMARIZATION = 0.79

Explicit teacher modeling is a difficult skill for many math teachers to build. As math students ourselves, we are often trained to become more efficient and begin pruning what feel like unnecessary steps and computational deadweight. The trouble with this path to efficiency is that these trimmings become expert blind spots when we run a classroom of our own. Many of us have lived through educational experiences in which we were taught to seek the right answers as quickly as possible. With a core shift to viewing mathematics as a *process* rather than a collection of *products*, it is important for us as educators to investigate our own problem-solving processes and regrow any trimmed blind spots. It helps to think about mathematics itself as an explanation, in which each individual step comes with purpose and justifiable legitimacy.

Ms. Rios continues this pattern of think–pair–share followed by explicit teacher modeling for a total of three rounds—each designed to address specific aspects of the learning intentions. (Questions for each round can be found in the Teaching for Clarity Planning Guide for this lesson.) She then provides her students some time to work on a collaborative task aligned to the day's success criteria.

Ms. Rios shows students another graph (Figure 3.3 at the top of the next page). Remaining in their pairs, students explain in writing what a graph means by referencing key details from the image itself. They locate the

GRAPHED SYSTEM OF EQUATIONS IN A CONTEXT: PRICE OF MOVIES

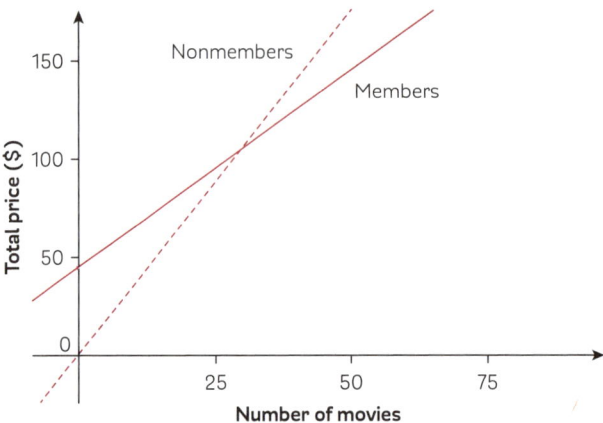

Figure 3.3

solution to the graphed system and explain their process and why it works, infer solutions to systems from datasets and explain their logic, and explain the contextual meaning of each solution. Students turn in this written task at the end of the day so that Ms. Rios may use the data formatively to provide feedback and plan the following day of learning.

Teaching for Clarity at the Close

Ms. Rios ends this day of conceptual understanding with a brief whole-class share-out. She asks students to journal each of the following questions in their notebooks before discussing each as a class:

- Explain what is meant by the "solution" of a system of equations.
- How does this relate to their graphs?
- How does this relate to tables of values?

She ends by asking her students to take a minute and reread through their *I can* statements and check the boxes that they are feeling confident about today. This feedback will provide valuable information for tomorrow's learning. Figure 3.4 shows how Ms. Rios made her planning visible so that she could then provide an engaging and rigorous learning experience for her learners.

EFFECT SIZE FOR ELABORATION AND ORGANIZATION = 0.75

Video 9
Making Learning Visible Through Learner Notebooks

https://resources.corwin.com/vlmathematics-9-12

Ms. Rios's Teaching for Clarity PLANNING GUIDE

ESTABLISHING PURPOSE

1. What are the key content standards I will focus on in this lesson?

Content Standards:

A.REI.11. Explain why the x-coordinates of the points where the graphs of the equations $y = f(x)$ and $y = g(x)$ intersect are the solutions of the equation $f(x) = g(x)$; find the solutions approximately (e.g., using technology to graph the functions, make tables of values, or find successive approximations).

Standards for Mathematical Practice:

- Reason abstractly and quantitatively.
- Construct viable arguments and critique the reasoning of others.
- Look for and make use of structure.

2. What are the learning intentions (the goal and *why* of learning, stated in student-friendly language) I will focus on in this lesson?

Content: To understand that a system of equations is a set of two or more equations with the same unknowns.

Language: To articulate the meaning of solutions of systems of equations both abstractly and within a context.

Social: To communicate our thinking to our peers even before we completely understand a topic.

3 **When will I introduce and reinforce the learning intention(s) so that students understand it, see the relevance, connect it to previous learning, and can clearly communicate it themselves?**

I will open the day with an explanation of the learning intentions and brief expansion of each. I really want to emphasize the social intention today so that students can practice thinking out loud as they problem solve. Transparent struggle is important for collaboration. I will also reiterate the language intention as we discuss and write stories for our graphs.

SUCCESS CRITERIA

4 **What evidence shows that students have mastered the learning intention(s)? What criteria will I use?**

I can statements:

- I can explain the meaning of graphs and tables by analyzing their labels, units, values, and behavior.
- I can explain how to locate a solution to a system of equations by examining a graph.
- I can explain how to locate a solution to a system of equations by generating and analyzing a table of values.
- I can explain the meaning of a solution to a system of equations mathematically and within a context.

5. How will I check students' understanding (assess learning) during instruction and make accommodations?

During direct/deliberate instruction, I will be using the think-pair-share protocol so students can process the concepts with a peer, and I can formatively assess their conversations and responses. This will also give me the chance to note who will need additional guided practice when we transition to collaborative work time. Finally, today's task comprehensively addresses and assesses each success criterion. I will collect the task at the end of the day and use the data to create tomorrow's study-group stations.

INSTRUCTION

6. What activities and tasks will move students forward in their learning?

Think-pair-share/direct/deliberate instruction combo: Students will be asked to process questions in think-pair-share format, and I will model specific skills and strategies based on their responses/need. I want to give them the chance to make discoveries and teach each other first.

Collaborative task: Analyzing systems

There are four questions aligned to success criteria. Students will continue to discuss and explain different representations of systems (graphs, tables, equations) while focusing on making meaning of their solutions.

7. What resources (materials and sentence frames) are needed?

1. Printed copies of the task for each learner
2. Chromebooks for Desmos online graphing calculator

How will I organize and facilitate the learning? What questions will I ask? How will I initiate closure?

1. Think-pair-share

    Organize students into pairs and instruct the learning intentions of the day. Have students record success criteria in their notebooks.

    a. Project an image of a graph of a system in a context and give students these questions:

    - What are the key features of this graph that will help communicate its meaning?
    - Which function, $f(x)$ or $g(x)$, is representing the following situation [read situation describing the behavior of one graph]?
    - Describe the situation represented by the other function. What key features made you describe it in that way?
    - What does this point of intersection represent mathematically?
    - What does the intersection mean in the context?
    - In the context, what was happening before the intersection, and what happens after the intersection?

    b. Project another image of a graph of a system in a different context. Model the sense-making process by answering the preceding questions again in a think-aloud. Explicitly link my think-aloud to Success Criteria 1, 2, and 4 when I model that behavior.

c. Project two sets of data within a table labeled in a context and have students answer the following questions:
   - How can we figure out what these data represent?
   - Which dataset represents the following situation [read situation describing the behavior of one dataset]?
   - Describe the situation represented by the other dataset. What key features made you describe it in that way?
   - How do these two datasets compare?
   - If these datasets were graphed, would they ever intersect? How can you tell?
   - In the context, what is meant by the x-value where they are equal?

d. Project another image of two sets of data within a table labeled in a context. Model the sense-making process by answering the preceding questions again in a think-aloud. Explicitly link my think-aloud to Success Criteria 1, 3, and 4 when I model that behavior.

e. Project two explicit functions, $f(x)$ and $g(x)$, and have students answer the following questions:
   - How can we determine if these two functions will ever equal each other?
   - How can graphing help?
   - How can making a table of values help?
   - At what approximate value of x will these two functions equal each other?

f. Project two more functions. Model the sense-making process of finding their solution(s) by answering and working through each of the preceding questions. Explicitly link my think-aloud to each success criterion when I model that behavior.

2. Pair Work: Analyzing Systems Task

Students work in their pairs to answer four questions aligned to each success criterion. The first question provides a labeled graph of a system of two functions and asks students to explain in writing what the graph means by referencing key details from the image itself. The second question asks them to locate the solution to the system and explain their process and why it works. The third question provides two datasets and asks students to infer the solution to this system and explain their logic. The final question asks students to explain the meaning of each prior solution within the context.

3. Closure: Share-Out

a. Explain what is meant by the "solution" of a system of equations.

b. How does this relate to their graphs?

c. How does this relate to tables of values?

d. Take a minute and reread through your I can statements and check the boxes that you are feeling confident about.

 This lesson plan is available for download at resources.corwin.com/vlmathematics-9-12.

Figure 3.4 Ms. Rios's Systems of Equations Conceptual Understanding Lesson

Mr. Wittrock and the Volume of Three-Dimensional Shapes

Mr. Wittrock's students just completed a unit of study where they had their first exposure to the concepts of trigonometry and applied these skills to finding areas of two-dimensional shapes. In this next unit, they will be expanding their surface understanding of trigonometry beyond the common 30–60–90 and 45–45–90 right triangles, as well as transferring their understanding of area to surface area and volume of three-dimensional shapes.

In this first lesson of their new unit of study, the students will also be reorganized into new learning groups. Mr. Wittrock likes to make sure that his students have the opportunity to work with as many different minds as possible throughout the year so they can develop a diverse interpersonal skillset. He doesn't just make his groups randomly, however. Mr. Wittrock is very strategic with his grouping because he knows that failing to properly mix students can have adverse effects. Grouping students in long-term homogeneous ability groups, for instance, has a small effect size, well below the hinge point.

As the department chair, he has fielded many concerns about this from parents and even other teachers regarding "the smart kids" and "gifted students." Labeling students frustrates Mr. Wittrock, but as a school leader, he knows that cultural shifts take time. In moments such as these, he relies on the facts and openly shares them with others: Ability grouping for gifted students has a relatively small effect. Furthermore, not labeling students has a relatively high effect size and accelerates learning for all. The reason for this is simple: Students are less likely to learn something if they believe they are "dumb" or less able than others in that subject. Likewise, if they bear the weighted burden of "special talent," "giftedness," or "brilliance," they are less willing to put that positive image on the line and take risks with challenging content. "Low" kids do not ask for help because they think they are hopeless, and "high" kids don't ask for help because they are ashamed and embarrassed, and don't want to admit to struggling. (For whom, then, are these labels working?)

This is not to say, though, that learners do not have differences. Every individual is at a different place in her or his learning at any given

> EFFECT SIZE FOR SMALL-GROUP LEARNING = **0.47**

> **Teaching Takeaway**
>
> Although small-group learning has an effect size > 0.40, whole-group learning is an important and necessary component of effective mathematics instruction.

> EFFECT SIZE FOR ABILITY GROUPING = **0.12**

> EFFECT SIZE FOR ABILITY GROUP WITH GIFTED LEARNERS = **0.30**

> EFFECT SIZE FOR NOT LABELING STUDENTS = **0.61**

> **Alternate group ranking** is based on assessment data and the specific learning needs for specific content.

> EFFECT SIZE FOR RESPONSE TO INTERVENTION = 1.29

moment in time. Mr. Wittrock has test scores from his last unit of study that support this idea. What he does with those data, however, is what decides how learning is propelled forward. Mr. Wittrock uses a heterogeneous grouping strategy called **alternate group ranking** (Frey, Hattie, & Fisher, 2018). In his class period with 32 students, for example, Mr. Wittrock wants to create groups of four students. To do this, he puts the stack of recent tests in descending order from highest score to lowest and starts sorting, one at a time, into eight stacks. This results in the groups seen in Figure 3.5.

These baseline groups are of heterogeneous *current* abilities and provide Mr. Wittrock an excellent starting point. He often makes adjustments based on the language needs of his students, specific pairings he knows to be productive, and social concerns (he tries to dodge grouping couples together, for example). The concept here is that no two students within a given group are "too far apart" to communicate productively. Anecdotally, Mr. Wittrock also notices that the students ranked in the middle tend to rise to the leadership roles in most groups, as they are close enough in current ability to communicate effectively with all members.

Keeping these new groupings in mind, Mr. Wittrock has designed this day of developing conceptual understanding to be conversational and collaborative. He wants to provide these students opportunities to develop productive working partnerships right out of the gate. As students walk into the classroom during their passing period, Mr. Wittrock has the new groups displayed on his projector, along with a new seating chart.

What Mr. Wittrock Wants His Students to Learn

The geometry standards call for students to apply volume formulas to solve problems and describe how changes in dimensions affect volume overall. Mr. Wittrock recognizes the algebraic linkage between these concepts and the precursory role these skills play to parametrization and integration in calculus and beyond. For these reasons, he finds it imperative to invest the time to build a strong conceptual foundation in volume itself.

ALTERNATE GROUP RANKING

Group 1	Group 2	Group 3	Group 4	Group 5	Group 6	Group 7	Group 8
Student 1	Student 2	Student 3	Student 4	Student 5	Student 6	Student 7	Student 8
Student 9	Student 10	Student 11	Student 12	Student 13	Student 14	Student 15	Student 16
Student 17	Student 18	Student 19	Student 20	Student 21	Student 22	Student 23	Student 24
Student 25	Student 26	Student 27	Student 28	Student 29	Student 30	Student 31	Student 32

Figure 3.5

"Anyone can plug stuff into a formula and pop out an answer," he tells his students while he introduces the new unit to them. "I am fully confident in your abilities to multiply and square things—congratulations, you are all able to use these formulas." He uses his dry sense of humor to try to deemphasize the computational aspect of the content:

> Today is not about that, however. Today, we are going to develop and dissect volume formulas so that we can truly own them. Once we own them, we can do more than just use them; we can manipulate them to design objects to have specific properties—soda cans that hold the most soda for the least aluminum; rocket boosters that have the most thrust for the least weight; houses with the most square footage and maximum energy efficiency, for example. I can't wait to see what your generation does with this math!

EFFECT SIZE FOR MOTIVATION = 0.42

Teaching Takeaway

Teaching mathematics in the Visible Learning classroom is possible regardless of your state's specific standards. Standards tell us what to teach, not how.

TEXAS ESSENTIAL KNOWLEDGE AND SKILLS (TEKS) GEOMETRY STANDARDS

(10) **Two-dimensional and three-dimensional figures.** The student uses the process skills to recognize characteristics and dimensional changes of two- and three-dimensional figures. The student is expected to

(Continued)

> **Teaching Takeaway**
>
> We do not have to start each day or class period with the learning intentions and success criteria. We can provide an engaging hook or introduction to the learning and then share the intentions and criteria for success.

> (Continued)
>
> (B) determine and describe how changes in the linear dimensions of a shape affect its perimeter, area, surface area, or volume, including proportional and nonproportional dimensional change.
>
> (11) **Two-dimensional and three-dimensional figures.** The student uses the process skills in the application of formulas to determine measures of two- and three-dimensional figures. The student is expected to
>
> (D) apply the formulas for the volume of three-dimensional figures, including prisms, pyramids, cones, cylinders, spheres, and composite figures, to solve problems using appropriate units of measure.
>
> **Mr. Wittrock is helping his learners develop the following TEKS Mathematical Process Standards:**
>
> - Use a problem-solving model that incorporates analyzing given information, formulating a plan or strategy, determining a solution, justifying the solution, and evaluating the problem-solving process and the reasonableness of the solution.
>
> - Analyze mathematical relationships to connect and communicate mathematical ideas.
>
> - Display, explain, and justify mathematical ideas and arguments using precise mathematical language in written and oral communication.

Neither one of these standards will be addressed in its entirety today. In fact, the top standard will not even be addressed today. However, Mr. Wittrock took a long-range view of these standards, as he indicated, and planned this conceptual lesson with both of these standards in mind. He recognizes that a conceptual understanding of volume itself is in service of each of these standards.

Learning Intentions and Success Criteria

Mr. Wittrock introduces the following learning intentions as a capstone on his lesson introduction:

> *Content Learning Intention:* To understand how the features of a three-dimensional shape are related to the volume of that shape.
>
> *Language Learning Intention:* To explain why volume formulas work by describing their components.
>
> *Social Learning Intention:* To get acclimated to our new groups by asking for and offering assistance when needed.

He chooses to elaborate on the language learning intention by telling his students,

> This is really about what algebraists call *chunking*. We want to know what each component in the formula represents and why it is there. If we can understand that, we can start to understand what happens to the volume overall if we alter one component. We can also recall formulas better—or rediscover them if we need to—if we think about them categorically. Instead of trying to memorize the nitty-gritty details of each volume formula, we can instead think about the components that make up a volume formula.

Mr. Wittrock introduces the success criteria with an interlude from the learning intentions that the students are used to hearing, "You will know you have successfully achieved the intended learning of the day when you can say with confidence 'I can do the following . . .'"

> ☐ I can identify the volume formulas for various types of prisms and cylinders and explain their meaning.
>
> ☐ I can identify the volume formulas for various types of pyramids and cones and explain their meaning.

These criteria are directly in line with Mr. Wittrock's learning intentions for the day. He wants his students to be able to recognize volume

> **Teaching Takeaway**
>
> Student interviews or conferences are ways to formatively evaluate learning.

formulas and explain how they know what each formula represents. This is the evidence of conceptual understanding he is looking for from his students.

Instructional Approaches That Promote Conceptual Understanding

Mr. Wittrock instructs students that they will be conducting two investigatory labs today: the first focused on prisms and cylinders and the second on pyramids and cones. As they start the first, he begins activating his students' prior knowledge by asking groups to discuss and share their thinking about a series of questions. To set the stage, he asks students to discuss this topic: *A cube has a side length of 2 cm. What is its width? What is its height?* This low-floor question allows the new groups a low-risk opportunity to start collaborating, as well as something to agree about early on. He follows up with, "What is the volume of that cube?" and "How did you calculate this?" In addition to those previously stated, his goal with this early line of questioning is to give students the opportunity to start structurally dissecting the most basic volume formula in order to recognize its key components—namely, length × width × height. He tries to solidify this by asking, "Why are the units cubic centimeters, or cm^3?" He wants students to explicitly recognize that three linear measurements must be multiplied together to generate a cubic unit, as this will further scaffold their ability to recognize components of formulas.

> **EFFECT SIZE FOR TRANSFER STRATEGIES = 0.86**

Once he is confident that the questioning bore the fruit he intended and that all students are contemplating volume as structured multiplication, Mr. Wittrock passes out a task sheet to guide them through the rest of this first lab. The task walks students through a line of light calculations and discussion questions, building from those they already answered.

As students work through this first lab assignment, Mr. Wittrock sits in with each group and conducts conferences. He checks for understanding of the task, listens for misconceptions of the content, highlights valuable insights, and encourages productive group work by referring back to the day's social learning intention. In his mind, he knows that he is asking for a lot of near transfer within mathematics from this task and that this type of transfer is something that can happen only if

Prism and Cylinder Lab

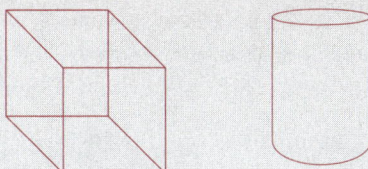

Introduction

1. A cube has a side length of 2 cm. What is its width? What is its height?
2. What is the volume of this cube?
3. How did you calculate this?
4. Why are the units cubic centimeters, or cm³?

Extension 1: Rectangular Prisms

5. What is the volume of a rectangular prism with length 2 cm, width 2 cm, and height 5 cm?
6. How is this the same as the original cube, and how is this different?
7. What is the area of the base of this prism? Does this show up anywhere in the volume calculation?

Extension 2: Triangular Prisms

8. Draw a picture of the triangular prism formed by cutting the rectangular prism above across the diagonal of its base.
9. How does the volume of this triangular prism with the same dimensions compare to the volume of the rectangular prism?
10. What is the area of the base of *this* prism? Does this show up anywhere in the volume calculation?

Conclusion: Prisms and Cylinders

11. What seems to be the general truth about volumes of prisms in terms of their bases and heights?
    a. Write formulas for the volumes of the following shapes. Label each component and explain its significance.
        (i) Cubes
        (ii) Rectangular prisms
        (iii) Triangular prisms
12. How might this apply to cylinders?

> **Teaching Takeaway**
>
> Conceptual understanding can also be at the transfer phase of learning. This occurs when learners independently apply those concepts to new or novel situations.

students possess the necessary prior knowledge. This is why he makes sure to conference with each group on a repeated basis, trying to prevent any from becoming dead in the water. Mr. Wittrock knows that there is a time and a place for productive, intentional struggle. For his learners today, he decides that the introduction to a new unit when conceptual understanding is just beginning to take root, however, is neither that time nor that place.

As individual groups finish their first lab activity, Mr. Wittrock reviews their work and conferences with them yet again to confirm that they have a basic conceptual understanding of volume of prismatic objects being equal to the area of their base × their height. This is the conceptual understanding that students will need to transfer to the next task. After each group defends its understanding of the first lab, Mr. Wittrock provides them with a second task sheet along with a plastic bin full of sand and various hollow, three-dimensional solids.

Pyramid Sand Lab

1. How are the following shapes related to one another?
    a. pyramids and prisms
    b. cones and cylinders
    c. pyramids and cones
    d. prisms and cylinders
2. What is the volume of a pyramid?
3. What is the volume of a cone?

The solids include a number of prisms with different bases and corresponding pyramids with identical bases and heights. There is also a cylinder and matching cone. Mr. Wittrock instructs students, "Go play in the sandbox. Compare the shapes to each other and see what they have in common. Then, start comparing their volumes by comparing how much sand each one holds."

Mr. Wittrock is careful not to overscaffold and give away the punchline to this task, though he definitely gets excited when he sees students on the precipice of discovery. He watches some groups try to separate piles of sand to compare volumes until they realize that they can conceptualize one of their objects into its own unit of measure. How many square pyramids full of sand, for instance, fit into a cube? Once students start viewing the task through this lens, they start bringing their algebra to bear and creating and solving equations such as the following:

$$3\,Cones = 1\,Cylinder$$

$$1\,Cone = \frac{1}{3}\,Cylinder$$

$$Volume_{Cone} = \frac{1}{3} \times area\,of\,circle\,base \times height$$

$$Volume_{Cone} = \frac{1}{3} \times \pi r^2 \times h$$

This is clear evidence of progress toward the day's success criteria, as students are substituting multiple representations of each component of the formula as they see fit.

Teaching for Clarity at the Close

As the day comes to a close, Mr. Wittrock passes out homework assignments to students in the form of a peer-assisted reflection task (Reinholz, 2015) (see Figure 3.6). Homework should focus on processing, elaborating, and reflecting on the day's learning.

Teaching Takeaway

Learners will always be moving from transfer to surface to deep to transfer to surface to deep to transfer . . . because learners will always bring valuable prior knowledge with them and do near-transfer work when they begin surface-level learning in a new unit. The cyclical nature and the importance of near-transfer work at surface level is critical. This demonstrates how surface level is not superficial.

EFFECT SIZE FOR COOPERATIVE LEARNING = 0.40

EFFECT SIZE FOR INQUIRY-BASED TEACHING = 0.40

PEER-ASSISTED REFLECTION FOR VOLUME FORMULAS

Peer-Assisted Reflection   Name: Period: Date:

Write your solution in the left column. The right column is used for annotations. If you provide feedback to your peer, you will annotate their solution. After class, you will annotate your own solution as well. In your submission, use the annotation column to explain how you did (or didn't) respond to peer feedback.

PAR 4.1: Volume Formulas

Success Criteria

☐ I can identify the volume formulas for various types of prisms and explain their meaning.

☐ I can identify the volume formulas for various types of pyramids and explain their meaning.

1. Write a formula that can be used to find the volume of the object that follows. Label each component and explain why it is necessary.

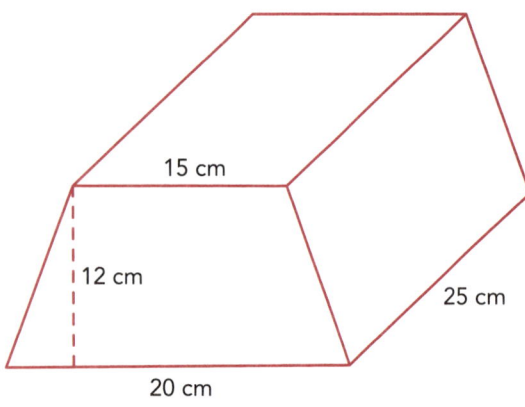

2. Calculate the volume using your formula.

3. Write and label a volume formula for this object as if it had the same base and height, but instead came to a point on one end. Justify your reasoning.

Reviewed by: _____

Rate your peer's mastery of the success criterion (this is the *last* thing you do):

☐ I can identify the volume formulas for various types of prisms and explain their meaning.

0—DO NOT check that box	1—ALMOST check that box	2—CHECK that box
Many mathematical errors and/or incomplete or unclear annotations	Few mathematical errors and/or somewhat incomplete or unclear annotations	No mathematical errors and perfectly complete and clear annotation

☐ I can identify the volume formulas for various types of pyramids and explain their meaning.

0—DO NOT check that box	1—ALMOST check that box	2—CHECK that box

DRAFT SOLUTION	ANNOTATIONS (author's *and* peer's)
REVISED SOLUTION	ANNOTATIONS (author only)

Figure 3.6

 This peer-assisted reflection task is available for download at resources.corwin.com/vlmathematics-9-12.

> **Teaching Takeaway**
>
> Although homework has an overall effect size of 0.29, in the secondary classroom the effect size is 0.64.

Peer-assisted reflection (PAR) is a collaborative protocol that requires students to

1. Work on meaningful problems
2. Reflect on their own work
3. Analyze a peer's work and exchange feedback
4. Revise their work based on insights gained throughout this cycle

(Reinholz, 2015)

> **Teaching Takeaway**
>
> Once students have the foundational knowledge about specific mathematics content, inquiry-based teaching supports the making of connections between concepts and ideas.

> EFFECT SIZE FOR PEER TUTORING = 0.53

> EFFECT SIZE FOR SPACED PRACTICE VERSUS MASS PRACTICE = 0.60

Mr. Wittrock accompanies every new lesson with a PAR task aligned to the day's success criteria as part of a formative assessment cycle. His intent is to transfer his teacher clarity into student clarity through this iterative feedback cycle. Over the course of the next few days, students will revisit these success criteria multiple times through the problems assigned in the PAR task. As their homework tonight, they must complete a draft solution—along with annotations explaining their thought process (not just *what* they did, but *why* they did it)—that is ready to be reviewed at the start of class tomorrow.

Tomorrow, they will exchange drafts with a peer and offer feedback in two phases. First, peers provide each other written feedback in the form of annotations and a rating toward mastery of each success criterion during a silent review phase. Mr. Wittrock likes to justify this phase by telling students, "We need to get to the point where our work speaks for itself. We want to make sure that the grader has no choice but to interpret our work the way we intend." Second, peers discuss the written feedback they provided and ask any clarifying questions they might have. The final step for students is to revise their draft solution into a final submission and include a reflection of how their thinking changed throughout this process. Mr. Wittrock scores these final submissions, collects the formative data they provide, and responds based on the results.

There are a number of benefits baked into this practice Mr. Wittrock uses. One is that students become greater academic risk takers because of the iterative nature of PAR assignments from draft to feedback to revision.

As one student put it, "How does one fail a draft?" Another benefit is the metacognitive process of students annotating their own work, receiving feedback, and then revisiting that same work. Yes, this is spaced practice of content as students revisit the same problems multiple days in a row; but it is also spaced practice in service of deeper thinking about one's own thinking as students work to revise and solidify their own understanding and thought processes. The formative data generated by the process is also very valuable for Mr. Wittrock. By the end of each PAR cycle, he has specific data about which students have met which success criteria. He can use this to design rotation stations, small-group instruction opportunities, whole-class reviews, or whatever else might be called for by the data.

The most important reason that Mr. Wittrock uses the PAR system, however, is to provide students actionable feedback (often delivered by peers) that they can use to further take control of their own learning and develop into assessment-capable visible learners. Student self-efficacy garnered through the process is priceless, as it truly puts them *in the know* about their own learning. The PAR cycle gives students the opportunity to compare and contrast: *This is what I used to be able to do; this is what I can do now. This is how I used to think about this problem; this is how I think about it now. This is what I used to know; this is what I know now.*

In addition to these before-and-after snapshots, the feedback and annotation components of PARs can collect much of the connective tissue that bridged students from where they were to where they are. In other words, not only does growth as an outcome become blatant to students, but students become aware of their own growth process as well. Figure 3.7 shows how Mr. Wittrock made his planning visible so that he could then provide an engaging and rigorous learning experience for his learners..

Video 10
Feedback Through Peer-Assisted Reflection

https://resources.corwin.com/vlmathematics-9-12

EFFECT SIZE FOR METACOGNITIVE STRATEGIES = **0.60**

EFFECT SIZE FOR ASSESSMENT-CAPABLE VISIBLE LEARNERS = **1.33**

Teaching Takeaway

Conceptual understanding can also be at the surface phase of learning. This occurs when learners are initially developing conceptual understanding.

Mr. Wittrock's Teaching for Clarity PLANNING GUIDE

ESTABLISHING PURPOSE

1

What are the key content standards I will focus on in this lesson?

Content Standards:

TEKS Geometry Standards

(10) Two-dimensional and three-dimensional figures. The student uses the process skills to recognize characteristics and dimensional changes of two- and three-dimensional figures. The student is expected to:

- (B) determine and describe how changes in the linear dimensions of a shape affect its perimeter, area, surface area, or volume, including proportional and nonproportional dimensional change.

(11) Two-dimensional and three-dimensional figures. The student uses the process skills in the application of formulas to determine measures of two- and three-dimensional figures. The student is expected to:

- (D) apply the formulas for the volume of three-dimensional figures, including prisms, pyramids, cones, cylinders, spheres, and composite figures, to solve problems using appropriate units of measure.

TEKS Mathematical Process Standards:

- Use a problem-solving model that incorporates analyzing given information, formulating a plan or strategy, determining a solution, justifying the solution, and evaluating the problem-solving process and the reasonableness of the solution.

- Analyze mathematical relationships to connect and communicate mathematical ideas.

- Display, explain, and justify mathematical ideas and arguments using precise mathematical language in written and oral communication.

2 **What are the learning intentions (the goal and *why* of learning, stated in student-friendly language) I will focus on in this lesson?**

Content: To understand how the features of a three-dimensional shape are related to the volume of that shape.

Language: To explain why volume formulas work by describing their components.

Social: To get acclimated to our new groups by asking for and offering assistance when needed.

3 **When will I introduce and reinforce the learning intention(s) so that students understand it, see the relevance, connect it to previous learning, and can clearly communicate it themselves?**

In addition to opening the day with the learning intentions, I will reinforce the language intention when asking students to summarize their discoveries and during our independent practice PAR assignment. The social intention will also be used to spur conversation and culture building within our new groups.

SUCCESS CRITERIA

4 **What evidence shows that students have mastered the learning intention(s)? What criteria will I use?**

I can statements:

- I can identify the volume formulas for various types of prisms and explain their meaning.
- I can identify the volume formulas for various types of pyramids and explain their meaning.

5 **How will I check students' understanding (assess learning) during instruction and make accommodations?**

Today is very lab-based, so I will be conducting a series of student conferences with each group. We will also end the day with a PAR assignment that will provide ongoing formative data for the next two days.

INSTRUCTION

6 **What activities and tasks will move students forward in their learning?**

Prism and Cylinder Lab: Students will infer the volume formulas for prisms and cylinders by discussing a series of guiding questions, starting with the area of a cube. Cubes→Rectangular Prisms→Triangular Prisms→Any Regular Prism → Cylinders $V = Bh$

Pyramid Sand Lab: Students will explore the relationship between the volumes of prisms and pyramids, along with cylinders and cones. In this lab, they will use hollow geometric solids with congruent bases and a bin of sand to compare volumes. The lab is designed to allow students to discover that pyramids and cones have one-third the volume of their congruent-base prism and cylinder counterparts.

Peer-Assisted Reflection (PAR): Students will complete a PAR aligned to the success criteria involving a trapezoidal prism and pyramid; will not be directly discussed in class.

7 **What resources (materials and sentence frames) are needed?**

1. Printout of lab sheets
2. Geometric solids kit for each group
3. Plastic bin of sand for each group
4. Printed PAR for each student

8 **How will I organize and facilitate the learning? What questions will I ask? How will I initiate closure?**

The day will be organized in this order:

1. Prism and Cylinder Lab
   a. What is the volume of a cube with a side length of 2 cm?
   b. How did you calculate this? ($l \times w \times h$)
   c. What is the volume of a rectangular prism with a length of 2 cm, width of 2 cm, and height of 5 cm?
   d. How is this the same? How is this different?
   e. What is the area of the base of this prism?
   f. What is the volume of a triangular prism with the same dimensions?
      i. Draw a picture for scaffold if needed.
      ii. Connect the area of the triangle to the area of the rectangle.
   g. What seems to be the general truth about volumes of prisms in terms of their bases and heights?
   h. How might this apply to cylinders?

2. Pyramid Sand Lab
   a. Which shapes seem to be related to one another?
      i. Pyramids and prisms have the same bases.
      ii. Cones and cylinders have the same bases.
      iii. Pyramids and cones both go from a base to a point.
      iv. Prisms and cylinders both go from a base to a base.
   b. What is the volume of a pyramid? Which shape might it be related to?
   c. What is the volume of a cone? Which shape might it be related to?

3. Peer-Assisted Reflection
   a. See attached PAR.

 This lesson plan is available for download at resources.corwin.com/vlmathematics-9-12.

Figure 3.7 Mr. Wittrock's Volume of Three-Dimensional Shapes Conceptual Understanding Lesson

Ms. Shuzhen and Independent Versus Conditional Probability

Ms. Shuzhen noticed that her students need additional *surface learning* in the *conceptual understanding* of the terminology in statistics and probability, specifically with understanding independent and conditional probability. Yesterday, her learners were asked to complete an exit ticket finding the probability of an event in the following scenario:

> EFFECT SIZE FOR PROVIDING FORMATIVE EVALUATION = 0.48

> The school leadership team is trying to gather data on student involvement in extracurricular clubs or activities. Out of 130 tenth graders, 35 are members of the speech and debate club, while 70 are members of various language clubs. There are 30 students in both clubs. What is the probability that a randomly chosen student from the sophomore class is involved in speech and debate as well as a foreign language club? What would your advice be to the school leadership team to ensure that as many different voices as possible are included in the data?

> EFFECT SIZE FOR RECORD KEEPING = 0.52

During a think–pair–share discussion and yesterday's exit ticket, learners demonstrated that they could provide a definition for the terms or vocabulary associated with these concepts, but they did not have a conceptual understanding of what these terms represent in specific situations. Working with their shoulder partners, learners struggled to apply the concepts and thinking to this exit ticket, suggesting they needed additional surface learning in these concepts. This vocabulary is a foundation for this unit of study and subsequent units in the class. Specifically, the vocabulary terms are *sample space, dependent events, independent events, mutually exclusive events*, and *conditional probability*. Therefore, today's lesson seeks to build that conceptual understanding and foundational learning in independent and conditional probability.

What Ms. Shuzhen Wants Her Students to Learn

For this particular class, Ms. Shuzhen will be focusing on the high school statistics and probability standard, S-CP.A.5. However, the learning progression for her students will start with conceptual understanding and the building of surface learning.

MATHEMATICS CONTENT AND PRACTICE STANDARDS

S-CP.A.5

Recognize and explain the concepts of independent and conditional probability in everyday language and everyday situations. For example, compare the chance of having lung cancer if you are a smoker with the chance of being a smoker if you have lung cancer.

Ms. Shuzhen is helping her learners develop the following Standards for Mathematical Practice:

- Construct viable arguments and critique the reasoning of others.
- Look for and make use of structure.
- Look for and express regularity in repeated reasoning.

Learning Intentions and Success Criteria

As with every unit and subsequent lessons, she provides a clearly stated learning intention for this week's learning. As students begin this multiday lesson, she wants them to learn the relationship between independent and conditional probability so they can interpret data, make inferences, and apply this understanding to authentic situations. She recognizes that this requires her learners to have a strong conceptual understanding of these ideas. Furthermore, she acknowledges that the preassessment, yesterday's think–pair–share discussion and exit ticket, indicates that her learners need additional surface learning with these foundational concepts:

> *Content Learning Intention:* To understand the specific conditions associated with independent and conditional probability.
>
> *Language Learning Intention:* To justify my inferences by interpreting and explaining data.
>
> *Social Learning Intention*: To ask probing questions that help my peers and me advance our thinking about probability.

Ms. Shuzhen has spent significant time thinking about the evidence she is looking for from her learners that would show they are moving toward mastery. This evidence—made visible to her learners through the *I can* statements—will guide her observations, questions, and other checks for understanding during today's lesson.

Teaching Takeaway

The language and social learning intentions are avenues for us to incorporate mathematical practice or process standards.

> ☐ I can describe what is meant by independent and conditional probability.
>
> ☐ I can give examples of independent and conditional probability.
>
> ☐ I can compare and contrast these two concepts using specific conditions or scenarios.

Modeling Strategies and Skills

As Ms. Shuzhen thinks about the checks for understanding and the tasks that will get her students to mastery, she draws from the standards for mathematical practice (© Copyright 2010. National Governors Association Center for Best Practices and Council of Chief State School Officers. All rights reserved.). During this lesson, she wants her learners to make sense of mathematical problems, construct viable arguments and critique the reasoning of others, and look for and make use of structure. To this end, she will engage her learners in reading mathematics content, writing about mathematics content, and justifying claims in specific conditions or scenarios. This will provide the foundation for applying these concepts and thinking to problem solving and modeling problems in statistics.

To guide and scaffold her learners' thinking, she will open the class with two guiding or probing questions:

> ***How is the probability of an event dependent upon whether the event is independent or conditional?***
>
> ***How are independent and conditional probability different?***

To support her learners, Ms. Shuzhen decides to use a combination of teacher-led dialogic and student-led dialogic instruction. She wants to be present initially during student discussions around independent and conditional probability so that she can scaffold the conversation and prepare her learners to take over and lead the discussion during the second half of the class. Of course, at all points during today's lesson, she will closely monitor learning using an observation recording tool similar to the one in Chapter 2 to identify any areas that need more focused learning around particular content (see Figure 2.2). For example, individual students, a small group of students, or, quite possibly, the whole group may need remediation around prior knowledge, skills,

Teaching Takeaway

Guiding or probing questions should be open-ended and require learners to synthesize their learning.

EFFECT SIZE FOR DIRECT/ DELIBERATE INSTRUCTION = **0.60**

and understandings (e.g., sample space, frequencies, intersections, and/or unions). At that point, Ms. Shuzhen would provide that support.

Instructional Approaches That Promote Conceptual Understanding

As her students enter the room, Ms. Shuzhen distributes grouping cards to each individual. The grouping cards have a mathematical symbol related to statistics on one side (e.g., union, factorial, different frequency distributions, etc.) and a mathematical formula on the other side of the card (e.g., standard deviation, variance, mean, etc.). Once everyone is in the classroom, Ms. Shuzhen instructs the learners to find their "symbol partners." She determined the symbol partners based on the responses to yesterday's exit ticket. For today's lesson, learners were paired with others of different levels of conceptual understanding. For example, Michael was able to define the concepts embedded in the previous day's exit ticket but did not know how that helped to answer the questions about after-school clubs. Zurita was able to calculate the probability but could not explain what her answer meant within the context of the exit ticket. Today, Michael and Zurita are paired together for this task.

> EFFECT SIZE FOR COOPERATIVE VERSUS COMPETITIVE LEARNING = 0.53

Once learners are seated with their symbol partners, Ms. Shuzhen shares the learning intention and success criteria for the day. She then distributes envelopes containing various situations that represent independent or conditional probability. She wants to be clear about the task and reiterates that they are not solving anything, but simply sorting these scenarios into two categories, based on whether they represent independent or conditional probability. "As you sort them, make sure you and your partner can make an argument for why you made your decision. If you disagree, critique each other's reasoning and come to an agreement," she explains. Some of these situations were as follows:

1. There is a 75% chance of measurable snow tonight if the cold front crosses the region before the moisture from the Gulf of Mexico arrives.

2. Joseph has 12 bow ties in his closet. Only four of the bow ties will match the outfit he has selected for today. What is the probability of him selecting a bow tie that matches?

3. The new F-150 pickup truck comes with several optional features. For example, buyers can select a "back-up" camera, a

> **EFFECT SIZE FOR INDUCTIVE TEACHING = 0.44**

> **Inductive teaching** uses several examples that require students to notice how a specific concept or concepts work.

> **EFFECT SIZE FOR CLASSROOM DISCUSSION = 0.82**

> **Teaching Takeaway**
>
> One way to scaffold student learning is to provide supports that reduce the difficulty of a task but maintain the complexity of the thinking.

Video 11
Consolidating Knowledge Through Direct/Deliberate Instruction

https://resources.corwin.com/vlmathematics-9-12

trailer hitch, or keyless entry. What is the probability of finding an F-150 with all three features?

4. Suppose you are on a game show and given the choice of three doors. Behind one door is a new car, but behind the others, cans of soup. You pick a door—say, Number 1—and the host, who knows what is behind the doors, opens another door—say, Number 3, which has cans of soup. He says to you, "Do you want to pick door Number 2?"

5. The official tosses the coin to determine who will kick and who will receive the football at the Super Bowl.

6. What is the probability of choosing a "face card" from a deck of cards, replacing the card, and then choosing an even-numbered card?

To support learners in this **inductive** task, she provides some groups with a "textbook" definition of *independent* and *conditional probability*. Although there are no examples with these definitions, this provides some partnerships with additional support in making sense of the problems. One group in particular received the same scenarios in Spanish (Hansen & Thunder, 2014). Ms. Shuzhen reminded them they had the option to select or use a graphic organizer from anchor charts throughout the room. In one case, learners opted for the Observe–Reflect–Question graphic organizer (Figure 3.8).

The partners sketched out the scenario (e.g., bow ties, cards, game show doors) in the *Observe* column then jotted down their thoughts about the scenario in the *Reflect* column. If they were undecided about whether this was independent or conditional probability, the two students wrote out questions they had for their peers or Ms. Shuzhen.

During this task, Ms. Shuzhen moved from group to group, asking specific questions and listening to student conversations. At the same time, she was checking for their understanding by listening to students' descriptions, examples, and analysis of the scenarios. After all, that is what the success criteria were for the day. As she noticed student pairs coming to final decisions about each scenario, she brought the class back together for a whole-group discussion about the learning experience. Her line of questioning for the whole group hinged on the information she gathered about her students' learning during the task. Where did learners struggle in this task? Were there gaps in their learning that needed to be addressed at this point in the learning progression?

OBSERVE–REFLECT–QUESTION GRAPHIC ORGANIZER

Observe	Reflect	Question

Figure 3.8

 This graphic organizer is available for download at resources.corwin.com/vlmathematics-9-12.

Teaching for Clarity at the Close

Ms. Shuzhen decides to provide brief and specific direct/deliberate instruction related to independent and conditional probability. She returns to the learning intention and success criteria before asking them to consider the tossing of a coin and the probability of that coin landing on "tails." Starting with this common scenario, she first activates learners' prior knowledge before reintroducing concepts of independent and conditional probability. After this 10-minute mini-lesson, she provides her learners with two additional examples and asks them to think about which example represents independent probability and which one represents conditional probability. After learners have had a chance to think this over, she asks them to share their reasoning with a neighbor. As she moves around the room, eavesdropping on conversations, this guided practice will allow her to give specific feedback to learners that need additional support.

Finally, she asks her students to return to their symbol partners and adjust their sorting task from the beginning of the lesson, asking them, "What might you change about your sort in light of this mini-lesson?" Ms. Shuzhen provides the answers to the sort so that partners can assess their own thinking and make any edits and revisions before they end the class for today.

For independent practice, learners are asked to complete a Frayer model for either independent or conditional probability (see Figure 3.9). As they do every day, Ms. Shuzhen's learners work right up until the bell, documenting their thinking and learning so that they can start at the right spot in their learning progression tomorrow. Figure 3.10 shows how Ms. Shuzhen made her planning visible so that she could then provide an engaging and rigorous learning experience for her learners.

> **Teaching Takeaway**
>
> Mini-lessons can occur at any point in a lesson. We should use the right approach at the right time.

> EFFECT SIZE FOR SCAFFOLDING = 0.82

> EFFECT SIZE FOR CONCEPT MAPPING = 0.64

FRAYER MODEL GRAPHIC ORGANIZER

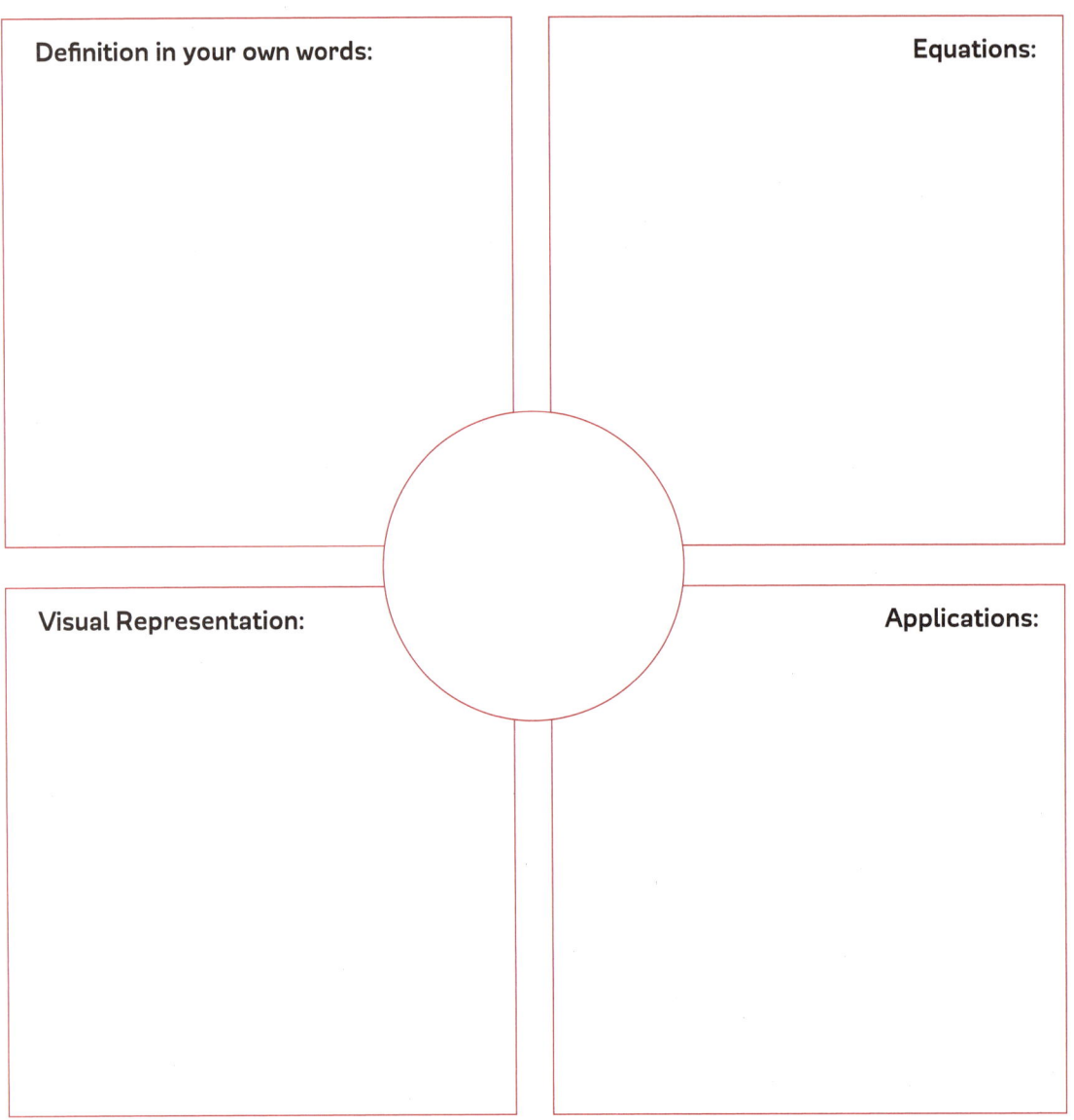

Definition in your own words:

Equations:

Visual Representation:

Applications:

Adapted from "A Schema for Testing the Level of Concept Mastery" by D. A. Frayer, W. C. Frederick, & H. G. Klausmeier, *Technical Report No. 16*. Copyright 1969 by the University of Wisconsin.

Figure 3.9

This graphic organizer is available for download at resources.corwin.com/vlmathematics-9-12.

Ms. Shuzhen's Teaching for Clarity PLANNING GUIDE

ESTABLISHING PURPOSE

1. What are the key content standards I will focus on in this lesson?

Content Standards:

S-CP.A.5 Recognize and explain the concepts of independent and conditional probability in everyday language and everyday situations. For example, compare the chance of having lung cancer if you are a smoker with the chance of being a smoker if you have lung cancer.

Standards for Mathematical Practice:

- Construct viable arguments and critique the reasoning of others.
- Look for and make use of structure.
- Look for and express regularity in repeated reasoning.

2. What are the learning intentions (the goal and *why* of learning, stated in student-friendly language) I will focus on in this lesson?

Content: To understand the specific conditions associated with independent and conditional probability.

Language: To justify my inferences by interpreting and explaining data.

Social: To ask probing questions that help my peers and me advance our thinking about probability.

3 **When will I introduce and reinforce the learning intention(s) so that students understand it, see the relevance, connect it to previous learning, and can clearly communicate it themselves?**

To guide and scaffold learners' thinking, I will open the class with two guiding or probing questions.

How is the probability of an event dependent upon whether the event is independent or conditional?

How are independent and conditional probability different?

SUCCESS CRITERIA

4 **What evidence shows that students have mastered the learning intention(s)? What criteria will I use?**

I can statements:

- *I can describe what is meant by independent and conditional probability.*
- *I can give examples of independent and conditional probability.*
- *I can compare and contrast these two concepts using specific conditions or scenarios.*

5 **How will I check students' understanding (assess learning) during instruction and make accommodations?**

During all aspects of this lesson, student conversation and the discussion of ideas will be used to monitor student learning. In addition, I will use a sorting task and concept map to check for student understanding. I can formatively assess their conversations and responses. This will also give me the chance to note who will need additional guided practice when we transition to collaborative work time. Finally, today's sorting task and exit ticket (Frayer model) comprehensively address and assess each success criterion. I will collect these at the end of the day and use the data to create tomorrow's lesson.

INSTRUCTION

6 What activities and tasks will move students forward in their learning?

As students enter the room, I will distribute grouping cards to each individual. The grouping cards will have a mathematical symbol related to statistics on one side (e.g., union, factorial, different frequency distributions, etc.) and a mathematical formula on the other side of the card (e.g., standard deviation, variance, mean, etc.). Once everyone is in the classroom, I will instruct the learners to find their "symbol partners."

Once learners are seated with their symbol partners, I will share the learning intention and success criteria for the day, then distribute envelopes containing various situations that represent independent or conditional probability.

1. *There is a 75% chance of measurable snow tonight if the cold front crosses the region before the moisture from the Gulf of Mexico arrives.*

2. *Joseph has 12 bow ties in his closet. Only four of the bow ties will match the outfit he has selected for today. What is the probability of him select a bow tie that matches?*

3. *The new F-150 pickup truck comes with several optional features. For example, buyers can select a "back-up" camera, a trailer hitch, or keyless entry. What is the probability of finding an F-150 with all three features?*

4. Suppose you are on a game show and given the choice of three doors. Behind one door is a new car, but behind the others, cans of soup. You pick a door—say, Number 1—and the host, who knows what is behind the doors, opens another door—say, Number 3, which has cans of soup. He says to you, "Do you want to pick door Number 2?"

5. The official tosses the coin to determine who will kick and who will receive the football at the Super Bowl.

6. What is the probability of choosing a "face card" from a deck of cards, replacing the card, and then choosing an even-numbered card?

Following the sorting task, I will return to the guiding questions and guide a whole-group discussion and then close with the Frayer model task. This is an independent task.

7. What resources (materials and sentence frames) are needed?

1. Grouping cards
2. Concept maps and graphic organizers
3. Sorting task cards
4. Frayer model template

8. How will I organize and facilitate the learning? What questions will I ask? How will I initiate closure?

Closure

For independent practice, learners will complete a Frayer model for either independent or conditional probability. The squares of the Frayer model include the labels Definition in Your Own Words, Mathematical Equations Necessary for Calculating Probability, Visual Representations, and Applications.

 This lesson plan is available for download at resources.corwin.com/vlmathematics-9-12.

Figure 3.10   Ms. Shuzhen's Independent Versus Conditional Probability Conceptual Understanding Lesson

Reflection

These three examples from Ms. Rios, Mr. Wittrock, and Ms. Shuzhen exemplify teaching mathematics for conceptual understanding. As in the previous chapter, these three teachers selected a different approach or combination of approaches from the other two classrooms.

Using what you have read in this chapter, reflect on the following questions:

1. In your own words, describe what teaching for conceptual understanding looks like in your mathematics classroom.

2. How does the Teaching for Clarity Planning Guide support your intentions in teaching for conceptual understanding?

3. Compare and contrast the approaches to teaching taken by the classroom teachers featured in this chapter.

4. Consider the following statement: *Conceptual understanding occurs at the surface, deep, and transfer phases of learning.* Do you agree or disagree with the statement? Why or why not? How is this statement reflected in this chapter?

5. How did the classroom teachers featured in this chapter adjust the difficulty and/or complexity of the mathematics tasks to meet the needs of all learners?

TEACHING FOR PROCEDURAL KNOWLEDGE AND FLUENCY 4

CHAPTER 4 SUCCESS CRITERIA:

(1) I can describe what teaching for procedural knowledge in the mathematics classroom looks like.

(2) I can apply the Teaching for Clarity Planning Guide to Teaching Procedural Knowledge.

(3) I can compare and contrast different approaches to teaching for procedural knowledge with those of teaching for conceptual understanding and application.

(4) I can give examples of how to differentiate mathematics tasks designed for procedural knowledge.

In mathematics, you have to be able to solve problems and reason quantitatively. The successful teaching and learning of mathematics may involve the execution of procedures and quantitative reasoning that yield an expression, value, or set of values. Acquiring and consolidating **procedural knowledge**—which is the ability to select, use, and transfer mathematics procedures in problem solving—is a necessary aspect of mathematics if learners are to have the appropriate tools for taking on the next challenge in their learning progression. As we make our final visit to our three featured teachers, we want to take a look at how each teacher created learning experiences that allowed students to learn the necessary procedural skills and progress toward fluency with those skills. Also, you'll notice the adjustments each teacher made to the learning experience so that learners at the surface, deep, and transfer phases of learning could all engage in the mathematics task. And as before, you'll see how Ms. Rios, Mr. Wittrock, and Ms. Shuzhen were able to differentiate the rigor of the mathematics tasks.

> **Procedural knowledge** is the ability to select, use, and transfer mathematics procedures in problem solving. With procedural knowledge, learners know when one procedure is more appropriate than another one for a particular problem.

Ms. Rios and Systems of Linear Equations

The students in Ms. Rios's class were largely successful in developing a conceptual understanding of solutions to systems of equations over the past few days. She feels confident that her students have the foundation required for today's lesson, which is focused on building procedural knowledge, to take root and have meaning. Today, students will be graphing systems of linear equations as a means of approximating their solutions.

> **Spaced practice** is practice that occurs over time rather than in a single setting or practice session.
>
> EFFECT SIZE FOR SPACED VERSUS MASS PRACTICE = 0.60

Most of her students demonstrated some level of mastery in graphing linear equations by the end of their last unit. Graphing did prove more challenging for some students, however. She designed this lesson with all students in mind and decided to revisit these skills explicitly. She is comfortable with this decision because she knows that **spaced practice**—practice that occurs over time rather than in a single setting or practice session—has a relatively high effect size, and that is exactly what this revisiting will be for many of her students. Additionally, this will give her the space that she needs to provide some explicit reteaching for students who struggled more severely with graphing during the last unit.

What Ms. Rios Wants Her Students to Learn

Ms. Rios's lesson today will focus mostly on the first standard listed, though the second standard will be revisited from the last lesson. Students will be using their ability to explain that intersections of functions signify their solutions—developed in the last lesson—in order to know *which* values to approximate.

> ### MATHEMATICS CONTENT AND PRACTICE STANDARDS
>
> A.REI.6.
>
> Solve systems of linear equations exactly and approximately (e.g., with graphs), focusing on pairs of linear equations in two variables.
>
> A.REI.11.
>
> Explain why the *x*-coordinates of the points where the graphs of the equations $y = f(x)$ and $y = g(x)$ intersect are the solutions of the equation $f(x) = g(x)$; find the solutions approximately (e.g., using technology to graph the functions, make tables of values, or find successive approximations).
>
> **Ms. Rios is helping her learners develop the following Standards for Mathematical Practice:**
>
> - Make sense of problems and persevere in solving them.
> - Reason abstractly and quantitatively.
> - Use appropriate tools strategically.

> **Teaching Takeaway**
>
> Although the effect size for the use of calculators is < 0.40, when integral to the learning the effect size increases.

Ms. Rios will largely focus on the first standard today, but she felt the second was worth readdressing, as it will serve as the springboard for new learning.

Learning Intentions and Success Criteria

As usual, Ms. Rios begins her lesson by reading the learning intentions to her students:

> *Content Learning Intention:* To understand that when graphing linear functions, intersections of functions signify their solutions and are a means of solving systems of equations.
>
> *Language Learning Intention:* To communicate the solutions to systems of equations verbally and in writing.
>
> *Social Learning Intention:* To transition smoothly between roles during conversation roundtable.

She elaborates on the language and social learning intentions to explain the flow of the day to her students. She informs them that they will start by taking some notes on the new content, then they will practice the new skills, and finally they will engage in a collaborative task in which they can practice in teams. On days like today when new procedural skills are being taught, Ms. Rios likes to remind her students, "Today is about learning new skills. We are going to get things wrong—we *should* get things wrong! It is OK because today we are practicing. You're supposed to make mistakes when you're practicing." She hopes that her traditional design to today's lesson will help facilitate those mistakes in a positive way that keeps learning moving forward. After all, direct/deliberate instruction of this type has a relatively large effect size due to its deliberate design.

EFFECT SIZE FOR DIRECT/DELIBERATE INSTRUCTION = 0.60

Ms. Rios introduces the success criteria she wrote for today's lesson immediately after introducing the learning intentions. She writes them under the lesson heading in her "master notebook," which she has projected under a document camera. As she talks through them, students copy them down in their own notebooks. They recognize this protocol from their direct/deliberate instruction days and understand they will be redirected to these *I can* statements as part of a daily wrap-up.

EFFECT SIZE FOR NOTE-TAKING = 0.50

> ☐ I can (still) graph linear functions in slope-intercept form.
> ☐ I can (still) graph linear functions in point-slope form.
> ☐ I can approximate solutions to systems of equations by examining graphs.
> ☐ I can explain solutions to systems of equations in writing.

Ms. Rios makes a point of emphasizing the word *still* in the first two success criteria to signify to students that they are revisiting skills that they have previously developed. She writes *I can still* statements like these whenever she is calling on heavy doses of prior knowledge in order to propel a new lesson. She recognizes this type of learning as near transfer within mathematics, whereby students use preexisting mathematical structures in their mind's eye to access new, now-within-reach mathematical constructs. Essentially, students will be using the math they own—which is graphing linear functions in this case—to make sense of the math they don't yet own—which in this case is solving systems of linear functions by graphing. If mathematical prerequisites exist for new learning to occur, then near transfer within mathematics is on the horizon.

Another reason that Ms. Rios chooses to address prior knowledge in specific lessons—and chooses to do so through the use of *I can still* statements—is to continually imprint another one of her mantras—namely, "Mastery requires maintenance." She communicates to her students that learning math is like riding a bike: The basic competency can never be taken away.

> Once you can ride a bike, you can always ride a bike. However, what happens if you don't ride your bike for a long time? What does it feel like when you hop back on? Are you as good as you used to be? Math is the same. If you want to get good, it requires practice and use. If you want to stay good, it requires practice and use. This, students, is because mastery requires maintenance.

She likes to share examples of this from her own learning experiences:

> One of the hardest classes I ever took in college was my second calculus class—it was harder than Calc 3! I worked incredibly hard and passed the final in that class with an *A*. I mastered that math. However, I haven't practiced my Calc 2 in a long time—I've been busy practicing my algebra with all of you! If I took that very same final exam today, I would probably still pass, but I would probably get a *C*. I wouldn't get that same *A*. You know why?

Teaching Takeaway

Using the word *still or continuing* in success criteria signifies to our learners that learning is a process.

EFFECT SIZE FOR PRIOR ABILITY = 0.94

EFFECT SIZE FOR MASTERY LEARNING = 0.57

Her students respond, "Because mastery requires maintenance."

Sharing real stories from her own life doesn't just build positive relationships with her students; it builds credibility. Ms. Rios is respected by her students, and they regard her as a credible academic.

Modeling Strategies and Skills

Now that the purpose of the day is clear to her students and they know that they are required to bring prior knowledge to this new learning, Ms. Rios begins activating that knowledge: "Students, in the last lesson we talked about the concept of a solution to a system of equations. Remind me, what is a solution to a system?"

Ms. Rios takes a number of responses—even after hearing what she was looking for—to engage as many students as possible in this collective think-aloud. She reiterates a few responses that touched on the concept as being "when two equations equal the same thing."

"OK," she continues, "so how were we able to know when two equations equaled the same thing? How could we tell?"

One student raises her hand and responds, "Well, it depended on what kind of function it was."

"Can you tell me more about that?" Ms. Rios uses an open-ended question to elicit further elaboration from her student.

"Well, if the function was a table, then we looked at when the numbers were the same."

"Which numbers?" Ms. Rios asks for clarification. This causes the student to pause briefly as other hands start to shoot up around her. "Hold on," Ms. Rios requests of her other eager students. "She'll ask for help if she needs it."

Ms. Rios knows this thoughtful advocacy will go a long way in developing both this student's agency and the culture of the classroom—thinking is not a race.

The student suddenly perks up and claims, "Both of them! They have to have the same x and y."

> **EFFECT SIZE FOR TEACHER CREDIBILITY = 0.90**

> **Teaching Takeaway**
>
> Activating prior knowledge is important in acquiring and consolidating new learning.

> **EFFECT SIZE FOR QUESTIONING = 0.48**

> **EFFECT SIZE FOR STUDENT FEELINGS OF EFFICACY = 0.92**

"Do we agree?" Ms. Rios looks around as the students display general concurrence. "OK, so what's the other type of function you were going to share?"

"Sometimes they are graphs, and you can just look at where they touch."

"You're absolutely right. What do we call it when graphs touch in math? What's the math language we have for this?" Ms. Rios finds this to be an appropriate space to build her students' attention to precision with mathematical vocabulary.

She hears a lot of *intersect* and *intersection* being called out, so she comfortably moves on. "OK, so we have these two methods of finding solutions based on how our functions are presented. Let's see if these can help with our first example."

With that, Ms. Rios writes down the instructions for Example 1 in her projected notebook: *Approximate the solution to the following system of equations.*

$$y = 2x - 3y \qquad y - 7 = -3(x + 2)$$

"So how could we use what we know to help us with this new kind of problem? Were we given a table of data or a graph?" She pauses for effect. "No. Hmmm. So what can we do? Do either of these look familiar to us?" Students point out to her that the first one "looks like $y = mx + b$" and the second looks like "that other way of graphing lines." Recognizing this as her cue to begin teacher modeling so that she can again help students attend to precision with their mathematical language, Ms. Rios jumps into action.

"I love how you are all looking for familiar structures in these equations—and you're right. This top equation is in slope-intercept form." Ms. Rios explicitly points at the coefficient *2* as she says *slope* and the constant *-3* as she says *intercept*. "And this bottom one is in point-slope form." She uses two fingers to call out the point embedded in the second equation and again gestures at the slope. Her goal in combining gestures with verbal descriptions is to connect the title of each equation with its meaning. She wants to imprint on her students that precise mathematical language is

> **Teaching Takeaway**
>
> Student identity, agency, and self-efficacy in mathematics are important for all learners. This is vital as we support them as they grow in their mathematical proficiency.
>
> **EFFECT SIZE FOR VOCABULARY INSTRUCTION = 0.62**

EXAMPLE OF A SYSTEM OF LINEAR EQUATIONS WITH A SINGLE SOLUTION

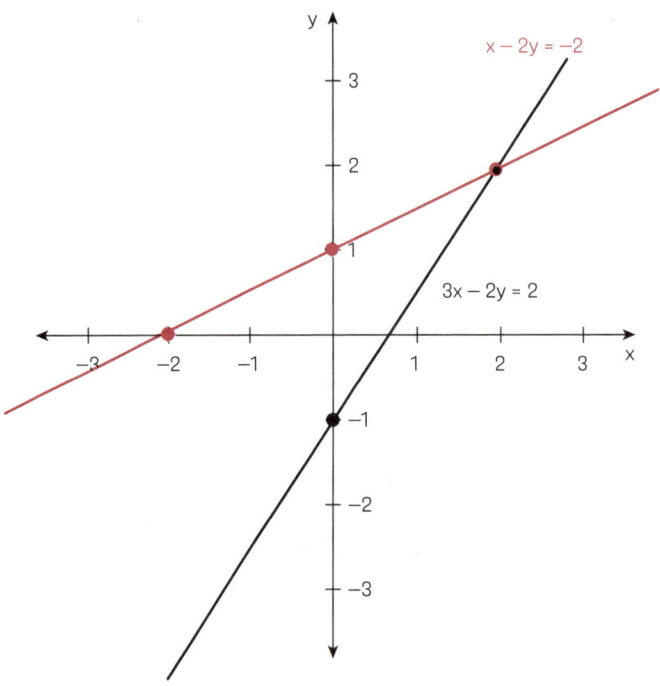

Figure 4.1

actually a tool that alludes to the meaning of mathematical structures—it is not just confusing new jargon.

We have used both of those to graph lines in the past. I am also recognizing that since I know how to graph these equations, I can use their graphs to find their intersection and approximate it to give me the solution. So let's graph! With the first one, what's my slope and how do you know?

Ms. Rios jumps back into questioning as the driver of direct/deliberate instruction since she is now addressing skills that students have previously built. She continues in this way to introduce the rest of the day's content, including graphing lines from point-slope equations,

EFFECT SIZE FOR TEACHER CLARITY = 0.75

approximating solutions to systems by examining their graphs, and explaining those solutions in writing.

This is where teacher clarity comes in. Ms. Rios knows where her students are, she knows which prior knowledge she wishes to access, and she knows where she wants her students to go. This provides her the freedom to open up her classroom—even during the focused instruction described earlier—and allow her students to openly explore their thinking when developing procedural skills. Through this, they discover the need and the utility of procedural skills, not just their mere existence. It is plain to see, then, that clarity is a foundation and a prerequisite to many other influences on learning.

Guiding and Scaffolding Student Thinking

Ms. Rios provides a few examples similar to the one she modeled for students to engage in semi-independently (see Figure 4.1). This means that students try to do what they can but are welcome and encouraged to refer to their notes and to partners to get needed boosts. Ms. Rios uses this time to sit with students she notices having difficulties graphing (some of whom she anticipated from their struggles during the last unit). During this guided practice phase, Ms. Rios uses questioning strategies much like those she uses during the whole-class discussions. The key difference, however, is that these questions are individualized for the student in front of her as she works diligently to understand how they are accessing the content.

EFFECT SIZE FOR REHEARSAL AND MEMORIZATION = 0.73

Additionally, Ms. Rios comfortably diverts from the assigned problem once she is able to formatively assess which key concepts are causing students to struggle. For instance, as she notices one student graphing y-intercepts as x-intercepts instead, she discusses the concept with the student and generates additional mini-examples to build fluency. "Graph the point (0, 0). OK, now do (0, 1). OK, now (0, 14), (0, -3), and (0, 3.7245). What do they all have in common?" she asks.

The student responds with, "They are all on the y-axis."

"Right. Why is that based on the way the points look? What do they all have in common before you graph them?"

"They all have zeros."

> **Teaching Takeaway**
>
> Targeted questioning to find gaps in student learning is essential in facilitating future learning.

EFFECT SIZE FOR DELIBERATE PRACTICE = 0.79

EFFECT SIZE FOR EXPLICIT TEACHING STRATEGIES = 0.57

Video 12
Differentiating Instruction to Support Surface, Deep, and Transfer Learning

https://resources.corwin.com/vlmathematics-9-12

"Great. Zeros where?" The student seems unsure of the question's wording as he looks at Ms. Rios with a "right-in-front-of-you-on-the-paper" sort of look. Ms. Rios recognizes this expression and rephrases her question in the moment. "Where are the zeros? Are they always x-values, always y-values, or both in these examples?"

"Oh! The x is always zero."

"There we go. So why do you think that is? What conclusion can we draw?"

"Y-intercepts happen on the y-axis," the student points to the vertical axis to emphasize his understanding, "and x is always zero."

"Wonderful! Now let's try your graphs again with that approach." Ms. Rios stays with the student and works through graphing the original example.

Guided practice is key for students as they reach for the limits of their "zones of proximal development," as Vygotsky would put it. The zone of proximal development is the current upper bound of new learning that students can reach with the right help. Vygotsky defines the *zone of proximal development* as "the distance between the actual development level as determined by independent problem solving and the level of potential development as determined through problem solving under adult guidance or in collaboration with more capable peers" (Cole, John-Steiner, Scribner, & Souberman, 1978, p. 86). Essentially, the zone of proximal development is what an individual is ready to learn. It is measured as the difference between what an individual can do alone and what he or she can do with support. During guided practice, the teacher is that support.

Instructional Approaches That Promote Procedural Knowledge

Ms. Rios continues the lesson by encouraging students to share their work under the document camera and verbally annotate their thinking as they proceed through each step. Students identify and justify each decision they made along the solution path—much like a think-aloud. What Ms. Rios finds wonderful about this process is that while she catches students emulating some of her strategies and explanations (which warms her heart), she also hears them explain their thinking: "The way *I* see it . . ." or "*I* think about it kind of like . . ." This ownership of the material from peers can help connect students to the content on a different level. Sometimes, Ms. Rios recognizes, they can't necessarily see themselves in the head of the teacher as they can see themselves in the head of their peers, further echoing the need for *collaboration with more capable peers* as previously identified by Vygotsky (Cole et al., 1978).

Armed with conceptual understanding, students have had opportunities to see how their teacher approaches these procedural skills, they have heard how their peers think through problems of this type, and they have had time to practice building their own skillsets. Now, Ms. Rios has planned for them to engage in a collaborative task. She places students into groups of four and provides each student a sheet of graph paper. She prompts them to fold the paper into a diamond-foldable (also referred to as a *conversation roundtable foldable*) (see Figure 4.2).

She then asks students to label each quadrant with the following words, starting on the upper left and working clockwise. She also asks them to draw a coordinate plane along the folds in the middle of the "diamond," as seen in Figure 4.3:

Quadrant 1: Equation: Slope: y-intercept:

Quadrant 2: Equation: Slope: Point:

Quadrant 3: Approximate Solution:

Quadrant 4: Explanation: The solution to this system of equations is approximately _____ because _____.

The idea of a conversation roundtable is that in Quadrant 1, Student 1 identifies the slope and y-intercept from an equation and graphs in the middle; in Quadrant 2, Student 2 identifies the slope and the point from an equation and graphs in the middle; in Quadrant 3, Student 3 analyzes the graph in the middle and approximates a solution to the system; and in Quadrant 4, Student 4 explains the approximate solution in writing.

> EFFECT SIZE FOR RECIPROCAL TEACHING = **0.74**

CONVERSATION ROUNDTABLE FOLDABLE INSTRUCTIONS

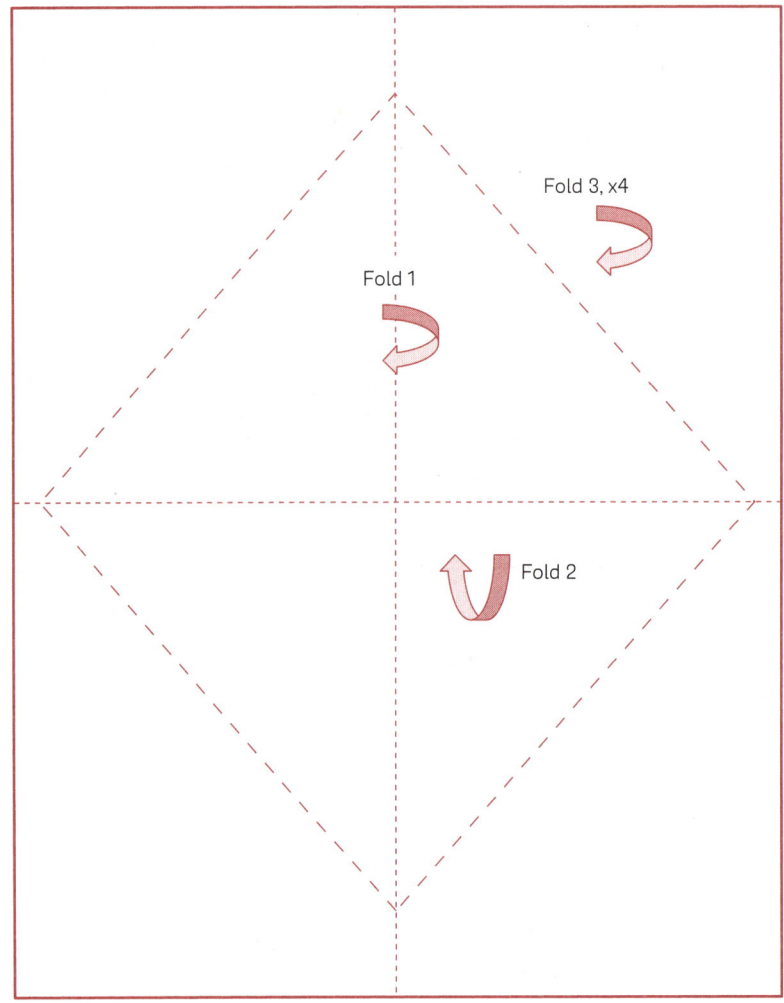

1. Fold in half lengthwise.
2. Fold in half widthwise.
3. Fold each corner toward center.

Source: Adapted from Fisher, 2017.

Figure 4.2

A template for a conversation roundtable foldable is available for download at resources.corwin.com/vlmathematics-9-12.

MS. RIOS'S CONVERSATION ROUNDTABLE FOLDABLE FOR SYSTEMS OF EQUATIONS

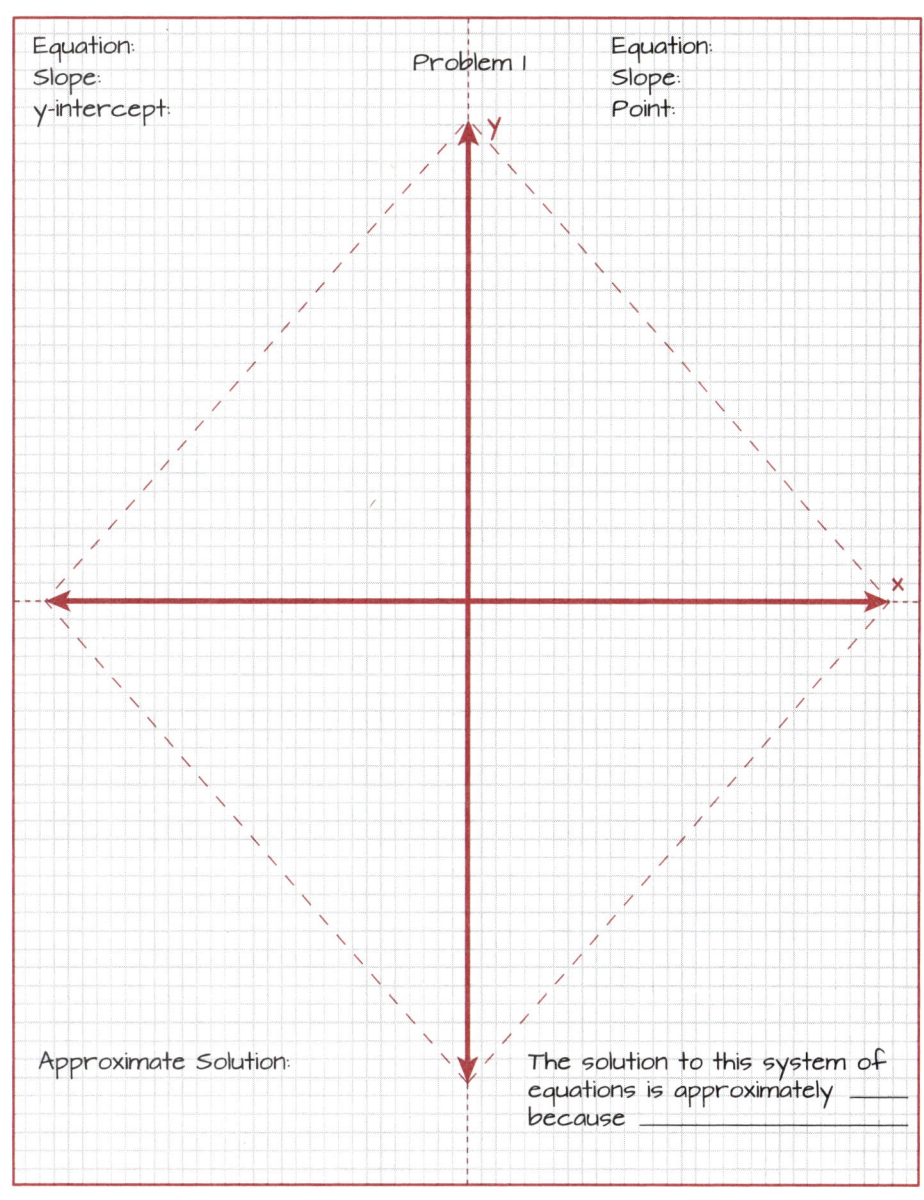

Source: Adapted from Fisher, 2017.

Figure 4.3

She makes sure each student is using a different-colored writing utensil from other members in their groups, as this will help with tracking individual progress and accountability (she provides colored pencils to help with this). She instructs them,

> You will be working on four total problems with your groups. Each of you will work on the same part of a different problem at the same time. For example, during the first round, everyone will be identifying the slope and y-intercept from an equation and using that information to graph the line in the middle of the foldable. Each paper needs to be labeled as either *Problem 1*, *Problem 2*, *Problem 3*, or *Problem 4*. Please decide which is which at your group now.

Ms. Rios uses this pause in instructions to make sure students are getting properly organized and that each group has only one of each labeled problem. She welcomes her students' attention back to her and continues,

> Remember students, it is super important that you pay close attention to instructions today because your social learning intention is to transition smoothly between roles during conversation roundtable. You will need to know what those roles are if you are going to achieve the social learning intention.

Satisfied with the level of attention she has from her students, she continues,

> So after the first round, in which we will all be graphing lines from slope-intercept equations, I will instruct you to pass your paper to the group member to your left. Once we have rotated papers, we will start the second round, and I will project four different equations in point-slope form. After you have all had a chance to graph your own equations, we will pass again (to the left), and I'll project further instructions about approximating solutions. Each step of the task will be individual until the end when we do our error analyses together. Are there any questions about the general flow of this task?

Ms. Rios answers questions and allows students to present a few hypotheticals, just to make sure they truly understand the expectations of the protocol. Once she is confident that they have the gist, she begins by projecting the first four equations. Students work through this protocol as Ms. Rios scans the room and notes how each group is progressing.

> EFFECT SIZE FOR COOPERATIVE LEARNING = **0.40**

Two of the four problems in this task align with student expectations in that they have similar results to the prior in-class examples—a single solution each. The other two, however, are curveballs meant to spur collaborative conversations during the final error analysis phase. One problem has no solutions because the two provided equations result in parallel lines that never intersect. The other curveball problem results in the same graph for each equation and thus infinitely many solutions. Ms. Rios likes introducing special cases in collaborative spaces like this so that students have yet another opportunity to engage in transfer within mathematics. As she sees it, they arguably already possess the tools to make sense of these special cases on their own, so she wants to provide them that opportunity. Sure enough, as the task proceeds she begins hearing the telltale gasps of students being sent into disequilibrium from their results. She even hears a few exacerbated, "What?! They can't do *that*!" types of comments. *It worked*, she thinks to herself. She'll use these perturbations as a bridge toward new conceptual understanding.

> EFFECT SIZE FOR COOPERATIVE LEARNING VERSUS COMPETITIVE LEARNING = **0.53**

> EFFECT SIZE FOR COOPERATIVE LEARNING VERSUS INDIVIDUALISTIC = **0.55**

Teaching for Clarity at the Close

Ms. Rios closes class with a discussion centered on those unexpected curveball cases. She designs her questions to elicit comparing and contrasting of expected and unexpected cases, how to express the solutions (or lack thereof) of these new cases, and what might cause these results. Thus, Ms. Rios demonstrates the often cyclic relationship between procedural knowledge and conceptual understanding. She used conceptual understanding as the driver for teaching procedural knowledge, which in turn became the driver for additional conceptual understanding. Figure 4.4 shows how Ms. Rios made her planning visible so that she could then provide an engaging and rigorous learning experience for her learners.

> EFFECT SIZE FOR TEACHER CREDIBILITY = **0.90**

Ms. Rios's Teaching for Clarity PLANNING GUIDE

ESTABLISHING PURPOSE

1. What are the key content standards I will focus on in this lesson?

Content Standards:

A.REI.6. Solve systems of linear equations exactly and approximately (e.g., with graphs), focusing on pairs of linear equations in two variables.

A.REI.11. Explain why the x-coordinates of the points where the graphs of the equations $y = f(x)$ and $y = g(x)$ intersect are the solutions of the equation $f(x) = g(x)$; find the solutions approximately (e.g., using technology to graph the functions, make tables of values, or find successive approximations).

Standards for Mathematical Practice:

- Make sense of problems and persevere in solving them.
- Reason abstractly and quantitatively.
- Use appropriate tools strategically.

2. What are the learning intentions (the goal and *why* of learning, stated in student-friendly language) I will focus on in this lesson?

Content: To understand that when graphing linear functions, the intersections of functions signify their solutions and are a means of solving systems of equations.

Language: To communicate the solutions to systems of equations verbally and in writing.

Social: To transition smoothly between roles during conversation roundtable.

3 **When will I introduce and reinforce the learning intention(s) so that students understand it, see the relevance, connect it to previous learning, and can clearly communicate it themselves?**

After introducing the learning intentions at the beginning of class, I will rely heavily on the social intention to facilitate the task of the day. I will also explicitly readdress the content and language intentions during direct/deliberate instruction as I model their intent.

SUCCESS CRITERIA

4 **What evidence shows that students have mastered the learning intention(s)? What criteria will I use?**

I can statements:

- I can (still) graph linear functions in slope-intercept form.
- I can (still) graph linear functions in point-slope form.
- I can approximate solutions to systems of equations by examining graphs.
- I can explain solutions to systems of equations in writing.

5 **How will I check students' understanding (assess learning) during instruction and make accommodations?**

I will use whole-group questioning, asking specific questions and using student responses to guide the next steps in today's learning. At the same time, I will be checking for their understanding by observing students, asking questions, and interviewing them about their progress on the diamond task. I will constantly reflect on the learning in the classroom by asking, "Where did learners struggle in the task, and were there gaps in their learning that needed to be addressed at this point in the learning progression?" I will provide feedback to all students as they build their procedural knowledge and fluency.

INSTRUCTION

6 **What activities and tasks will move students forward in their learning?**

Focused Instruction

Students will take notes on graphing systems and approximating their solutions.

Guided Practice

Students will work through an example problem similar to their notes. I will scan the room and sit with students who need more support. Students will explain their methods and solutions at the board.

Collaborative Learning

We will do a collaborative activity involving a conversation roundtable foldable on graph paper. In groups of four, students will work in rounds, completing four separate problems. During the first round, each group member will be graphing a linear function presented in slope-intercept form on the assigned problem. Once time is up, they will pass their foldable to their left and receive a new foldable from their right. During the second round, each group member will now graph an additional linear function presented in point-slope form on their newly received foldables. After passing again and now receiving a third foldable, they will approximate the solution to the system that should be graphed before them. On the fourth and final round, students will use writing to explain the solution provided from Round 3. At the end of this process, the students will have four completed problems. Solutions will be posted for each, and students will conduct an error analysis of their work. Additionally, two of these systems will be unlike the cases discussed in class and will spur a whole-class conversation.

Independent Learning

Students have a short homework assignment aligned to each of the success criteria.

7 **What resources (materials and sentence frames) are needed?**

1. Graph paper for conversation roundtable foldables
2. Colored pencils or pens for foldables (different color for each group member)

8 **How will I organize and facilitate the learning? What questions will I ask? How will I initiate closure?**

This lesson will be an almost-linear path through the gradual release of responsibility. I will begin with focused instruction, then transition to guided practice, and then we will start our collaborative task. After the collaborative task, we will close with a whole-class discussion, and students will be assigned an independent learning homework assignment aligned to today's success criteria.

 This lesson plan is available for download at resources.corwin.com/vlmathematics-9-12.

Figure 4.4   Ms. Rios's Systems of Equations Procedural Lesson

> **Teaching Takeaway**
>
> Visible Learning and Visible Teaching occur when teachers see learning through the eyes of their students and students see themselves as their own teachers.

EFFECT SIZE FOR FEEDBACK = 0.70

Mr. Wittrock and Trigonometric Relationships

Mr. Wittrock loves teaching trigonometry. He sees trigonometry as the perfect geometric vehicle to which students can adhere their algebraic thinking. He also recognizes, however, that trigonometry is often misunderstood as an isolated, disconnected topic and can be generally confusing for students. For these reasons, he likes to space out his course's trigonometry standards over the span of a few units, and he tries to explicitly connect their utility to multiple applications.

Yesterday, the class worked on solving right triangles when given the length of one of its sides and an angle using the sine, cosine, and tangent ratios. Today, Mr. Wittrock will be building on the previous lesson, introducing the concepts of inverse trigonometric functions. His purpose today is to get students to recognize when inverse trigonometric functions are useful and to begin building his students' procedural fluency in using them.

As a practitioner of the peer-assisted reflection (PAR) cycle, Mr. Wittrock begins most class periods with engaging students in part of that cycle. Today is no exception as students trade their draft solutions from the problems assigned the day before and begin providing one another with written feedback. The students are reviewing each other's work on problems aligned to yesterday's two success criteria: *I can use trigonometric functions (sine, cosine, and tangent) to find unknown sides of right triangles*; and *I can solve right triangles, given an angle and a side, and explain my thinking*. Mr. Wittrock has built this routine into his classroom so that the whole process only takes about seven to ten minutes. After students spend a few minutes annotating and adding comments to their peers' work, they finish their written review by ranking their peers' mastery against the given success criteria using the following mini rubric:

0—DO NOT check that box	1—ALMOST check that box	2—CHECK that box
Many mathematical errors and/or incomplete or unclear annotations	Few mathematical errors and/or somewhat incomplete or unclear annotations	No mathematical errors and perfectly complete and clear annotations

Once students finish ranking each other, they begin a brief collaborative discussion, explaining their written comments and fielding each other's questions. This is where most of the new learning on these "old problems" occurs, as students can discuss critical feedback and clarify what they *meant to say* in contrast to what they *actually wrote*—or more often, what they *thought they were supposed to do* in comparison to what they *now know they have to do*. This is, at its core, what is meant by the term *peer-assisted reflection*.

Mr. Wittrock plans on seizing an additional benefit from this process today. Since yesterday's lesson on trigonometric functions is so foundational and a prerequisite to today's lesson on their inverses, Mr. Wittrock will use students' collaborative discussions surrounding their PAR feedback as a means of gathering formative data on their prior knowledge.

He starts this by listening in on a conversation between two students who appear to be agreeing with one another. He hears one student explaining his work as follows:

> So we needed to find the length of this side (he points to a leg of a pictured right triangle), and we were given the information that the other leg was seven inches and the angle next to the one we want is 35 degrees—which is opposite of the seven-inch side. Since I know that we need to use sine to find the missing side, and we don't have the hypotenuse, I set up the sine ratio using the angle and the side we do have to find the hypotenuse.

Mr. Wittrock was very surprised to hear this, as he intended the assigned problem to be an opportunity for students to use the tangent ratio. Though this student's method was mathematically correct, it was akin to taking three left turns in order to go right. Raising additional red flags, the student's partner seemed to be in complete agreement, especially when the student noted that "we need to use sine to find the missing side."

Mr. Wittrock checked in with another pair in which one student was talking the other through the problem-solving process. This pair was

EFFECT SIZE FOR CLASSROOM DISCUSSION = 0.82

Teaching Takeaway

Formative evaluation of learning provides evidence that informs our next instructional decisions.

Video 13
Supporting Surface Learning Needs With a Peer Tutor

https://resources.corwin.com/vlmathematics-9-12

also seeking out the hypotenuse as a necessary problem-solving tool (even though it wasn't). When Mr. Wittrock asked for clarification, he was told, "Yeah, this one is just like our notes," as the student showed him the worked example she was referring to. Mr. Wittrock could now see what was going on. Many students were using their notes as a guide to make sense of this problem—which is great, he thought—but they were using a procedure too rigidly and not demonstrating any flexibility in which trigonometric function to bring to bear. He saw this to be evidence of students emulating a mathematical structure as opposed to genuinely applying new procedural knowledge and decided to take action. He did one final scan and spotted a student who accurately completed the problem in fewer steps using the tangent ratio. Mr. Wittrock briefly conferenced with this student, complimented her work, and asked if she would be willing to explain her process to the class. She agreed, and Mr. Wittrock directed the class to the front of the room.

> EFFECT SIZE FOR FEEDBACK = 0.70

"All right, everybody, if I could have your attention up front, please. I was noticing a few interesting things during your PAR conversations—great job collaborating, by the way—and I wanted to address them together." Mr. Wittrock projected the PAR assignment under the document camera (see Figure 4.5 on page 164). "This first problem is asking us to find the length of the missing leg of this triangle using trigonometry. I noticed many of you chose to begin by setting up a sine ratio. Who can share why you chose to solve the triangle this way?" As he had hoped, Mr. Wittrock elicited the response from one of the students he had interviewed that this was how it was done in the notes, to which he responded,

> **Teaching Takeaway**
>
> If we do not make student thinking visible, we cannot see learning through their eyes.

So I hear what you are saying about the notes. We did have an example where we solved an entire triangle by using the sine function twice. Also, you are absolutely right that we can do that here when we are just looking for this one missing side. It works. But I am wondering, are there any other routes we could have chosen?

With that, he asks the student who solved this problem using the tangent function to come explain her thinking.

The student projects her work under the document camera and begins,

> So what I did was use the tangent to find the missing side. Since we already know this angle is 35 degrees (she pointed to the known angle in the picture of the triangle) and the side that is opposite of it is seven inches (she pointed to the known side), then the side we are looking for is adjacent to the 35 degrees. Since tangent is the one that uses opposite and adjacent—right? SOH CAH TOA? (She voiced her mnemonic as evidence for her claim.) Since tangent uses all the information we have, we can say $tan 35° = \frac{7}{x}$ and solve for x. I used a calculator for the rest.

> **EFFECT SIZE FOR MNEMONICS = 0.76**

Mr. Wittrock thanks the student for her willingness to share and asks the class if they have any clarifying questions for her. Mr. Wittrock was glad to have a student to turn to for this reciprocal teaching review. He was concerned that if he just took the floor and retaught the concept that students might just perceive this information the same way they did the first time. In other words, he wanted to avoid the same miscommunication twice by providing students a different access point through a peer's perspective. Mr. Wittrock then instructs students,

> OK, now that we have seen how others are thinking about this same problem, I am wondering if we consider any routes to be more efficient or less efficient than others. Return to your PAR partners and discuss this idea. For homework tonight, you will be completing your revised solutions and reflecting on how your thinking about this concept changed since the beginning of this PAR process.

> **EFFECT SIZE FOR EXPLICIT TEACHING STRATEGIES = 0.57**

Students return to their discussions and start mapping out their revised solutions.

Through his formative assessment, Mr. Wittrock recognized that students misinterpreted a rigidity in the previous lesson that demanded reteaching. Students needed to be freer thinkers and more purposeful in their strategizing for today's lesson. Now that prior knowledge has been assessed, addressed, and reactivated, Mr. Wittrock is comfortable moving on to his new lesson.

> **EFFECT SIZE FOR PRIOR ACHIEVEMENT = 0.55 AND FOR STRATEGIES TO INTEGRATE WITH PRIOR KNOWLEDGE = 0.93**

TRIANGLE FROM MR. WITTROCK'S DOCUMENT CAMERA

Use trigonometry to find the length of the missing leg of this triangle.

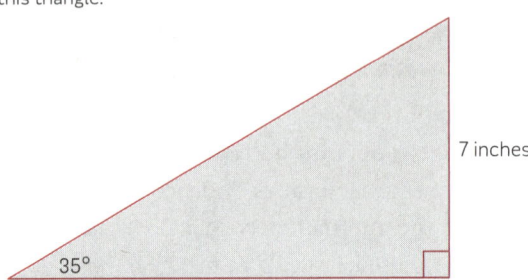

Figure 4.5

What Mr. Wittrock Wants His Students to Learn

By working to develop a surface-level procedural understanding of inverse trigonometric functions in today's lesson, Mr. Wittrock is providing students the connective tissue necessary to begin developing a deep conceptual understanding of trigonometric ratios and right triangles in general. The demand for deep learning is called out in the "use of process skills" language in the following standards addressed in this lesson.

> ### TEXAS ESSENTIAL KNOWLEDGE AND SKILLS (TEKS) GEOMETRY STANDARDS
>
> (9) Similarity, proof, and trigonometry. The student uses the process skills to understand and apply relationships in right triangles. The student is expected to:
>
> (A) determine the lengths of sides and measures of angles in a right triangle by applying the trigonometric ratios sine, cosine, and tangent to solve problems; and
>
> (B) apply the relationships in special right triangles 30°-60°-90° and 45°-45°-90° and the Pythagorean theorem, including Pythagorean triples, to solve problems.

CHAPTER 4. TEACHING FOR PROCEDURAL KNOWLEDGE AND FLUENCY

> **Mr. Wittrock is helping his learners develop the following TEKS Mathematical Process Standards:**
>
> - Create and use representations to organize, record, and communicate mathematical ideas.
>
> - Analyze mathematical relationships to connect and communicate mathematical ideas.
>
> - Display, explain, and justify mathematical ideas and arguments using precise mathematical language in written and oral communication.

Learning Intentions and Success Criteria

After prompting students to put away their PARs and open their math notebooks to a new page, Mr. Wittrock introduces the learning intentions and success criteria for the day:

> *Content Learning Intention:* To understand the relationship between trigonometric functions (sine, cosine, and tangent) and their inverses.
>
> *Language Learning Intention:* To precisely state each inverse trigonometric function as it is being used (i.e., the inverse sine of [this ratio] is [this many degrees]).
>
> *Social Learning Intention*: To hold one another accountable to the language learning intention. #grammarpolice

EFFECT SIZE FOR STUDENT–TEACHER RELATIONSHIP = 0.52

Yes, Mr. Wittrock really uses hashtags in his language and social learning intentions. He argues that this matches the lighthearted humor thematic of his classroom and that it gives him a space to add subtle cues and messages to his students. In this case, he wants students to act like the "grammar police" with each other as they practice their new language regarding inverse trigonometric functions. This expectation, he argues, might "click" a little more than the more general request of holding one another accountable. Are there other ways of accomplishing this? Absolutely. Mr. Wittrock has simply chosen the tone that fits the classroom culture he and his students have built.

Teaching Takeaway

Feedback to learners can come from the teacher, their peers, or their own self-evaluation.

> **Teaching Takeaway**
>
> Having learners record learning intentions and success criteria provides a framework for self-assessing their progress at the end of the lesson.

Today's success criteria have been intentionally structured very similarly to those from yesterday. Mr. Wittrock's goal is for students to recognize analogs between these procedural lessons and apply their algebraic thinking.

☐ I can use inverse trigonometric functions to find unknown angles in right triangles.

☐ I can solve right triangles, given any two of their sides, and explain my thinking.

Instructional Approaches That Promote Procedural Knowledge

As students finish writing their *I can* statements in their math notebooks, Mr. Wittrock begins some focused instruction by posing a problem. "I took the sine of an angle and got *1* as my answer. What was the angle?" Students look around at each other, displaying confused faces. "How about this one: Cosine of what angle equals $\frac{1}{\sqrt{2}}$?"

> **Teaching Takeaway**
>
> When learners document their learning, they can easily monitor their own progress and use this learning in the future.

"Oh!" a student exclaims as he starts to flip backward in his math notebook. "I know this one! We did it yesterday." Mr. Wittrock looks around the room to assess the general state of confused faces as the student finds what he was looking for. "Yesterday, we did sine and cosine of the special right triangles, and cosine of 45 degrees was $\frac{1}{\sqrt{2}}$."

"Do we agree?" Mr. Wittrock looks around at his students, who seem to be generally nodding. "I am sensing that you are convinced of the answer, but not necessarily the method. I mean, let's think about this. Anything that we can do forward in math . . ."

> EFFECT SIZE FOR ENGAGEMENT = 0.56

The students recognize his hanging sentence as their cue to chorally recite, "We can do backward."

"That's right. So if we can take the sine, cosine, or tangent of something, shouldn't we be able to UN-sine, UN-cosine, and UN-tangent things?" He sees students indicating that they are in general agreement and continues, "So how, then, do we do that? Do we just have to memorize a bunch of sines and cosines so that we can recognize the result like we just did with the cosine of 45 degrees?" Mr. Wittrock recognizes that he absolutely has a captive audience at this point. The problem that he posed hooked his students at just the right level—they knew that it was solvable, but didn't know how. They are able to find an answer, but are not satisfied with their method. They are ready and waiting for new procedural knowledge.

> This, folks, is the concept behind inverse trig functions. Today, we are going to delve into the idea and the usefulness of the inverse sine, inverse cosine, and inverse tangent functions. First off, everyone take a look at your graphing calculators and find the sine, cosine, and tangent buttons.

He takes a moment to make sure that everyone has a calculator and is able to locate the buttons.

> Look on top of them, see that little "sine to the -1" on top of the sine button, for example? Well, what that really says is "the inverse sine," and we can use it to find angles if we know the side opposite and the hypotenuse. Let's test it with the example we already did. Press *Second*, then *Inverse Cosine*, then type in $\frac{1}{\sqrt{2}}$. What do we get?

He pauses and makes sure everyone is able to input things correctly. "Look at that—it is exactly the 45 degrees we expected. Why don't we try this out a little bit to make sure we know how to use our calculators?"

With that, Mr. Wittrock assigns a short list of problems for students to practice. The problems are of this form: sine/cosine/tangent of x equals a quantity; find x. He uses this opportunity to scan the room and make sure everyone is able to perform the proper procedures on their calculators.

After troubleshooting some calculator questions, Mr. Wittrock continues his focused instruction. "So now that we have this new tool, how else can we use it? Well, consider this triangle." Mr. Wittrock draws a right triangle with only the right angle and its two legs labeled. "Can we solve this triangle? I think so. In fact, allow me to model my thinking for you as I begin to work through this problem as your 'example zero.'"

EFFECT SIZE FOR DIRECT/DELIBERATE INSTRUCTION = 0.60

Teaching Takeaway

The effect size for the use of calculators increases when calculators reduce the cognitive load on the learner or are necessary for learning the specific content.

EFFECT SIZE FOR THE USE OF CALCULATORS = 0.27

In Mr. Wittrock's class, the students know that this means to put down their pencils and simply observe. Mr. Wittrock will often use an "example zero" problem to eliminate the pressure on students to keep up with their notes while trying to make sense of his think-aloud. Students will instead add the subsequent "example one" to their notes that they complete as guided practice.

> I see that the problem is asking me to "solve this triangle," which means to label all of its sides and all of its angles. I also see that I am given the measurements of its two legs but not its hypotenuse. This means that in order to find one of these missing angles with the given information, I will need to start by setting up a tangent ratio because that is the only trig function that doesn't use the hypotenuse. Then, I can use the inverse tangent function to find the angle. I also recognize that I can do this for either angle, or both.

Mr. Wittrock continues thinking aloud, carefully avoiding expert blind spots, as he solves the triangle in question.

He then provides a similar example for students to add to their notes. This one, however, he treats as a blend between collaborative and guided practice as he primes his students for the "Numbered Heads Together" strategy. In this strategy, students are numbered 1 through 6 and placed into groups of six, each of which is also given a number 1 through 6. An initial die is rolled to signify which group member is going to be responsible for sharing the group's work. This motivates those members (say, the number 3s) from each group to elicit contributions and thinking from all other members. After a question is asked and time is given to construct a response, another die is rolled to signify which group is responsible for answering first. This strategy promotes individual accountability and equitable calling by the teacher, thus ensuring a diversity of student voices. In addition to recording these examples in their notes, students write out and label new notation to assist them in meeting the language learning intention.

Once Mr. Wittrock is satisfied with the apparent development of surface-level procedural skills surrounding inverse trigonometric functions, as students are generally getting correct answers, it is time to

EFFECT SIZE FOR DELIBERATE PRACTICE = 0.79

Teaching Takeaway

To encourage mathematical thinking in our learners, we should model this thinking in our teaching.

spend some energy focusing on deep learning. Mr. Wittrock wants his students to use this new skill to help make connections across all their prior trigonometry and right-triangle knowledge, so he sets up a collaborative task with a focus on strategy. He begins by passing out table-sized whiteboards and dry-erase markers to each group and then poses the following problem:

> Draw and completely label the right triangle with a leg of 15 cm and a hypotenuse of 24 cm.

He preempts their work with, "Take a minute individually and focus on what information we have, what information we need, and which mathematical tools can get us the information we need." He pauses to give students some think time. "OK, now go for it with your groups."

As students start to work through the task, Mr. Wittrock scans the classroom and notices how different groups are already orienting their triangles differently, thus causing some to see value in starting with using inverse sine to find a missing angle, while others start with inverse cosine. One group, he noticed, started by using the Pythagorean theorem to find the missing side. They then found one missing angle using inverse sine and simply subtracted it from 90 degrees to find the final angle. This is exactly what Mr. Wittrock was hoping to see—a diversity of methods all leading to the same accurate solution.

Teaching for Clarity at the Close

As Mr. Wittrock was scanning the classroom, he noted the order in which he wished groups to present on a clipboard based on their method. His list reads:

1. Inverse cosine → sine → inverse cosine
2. Inverse sine → cosine → inverse sine
3. Inverse sine → tangent → 180 degrees
4. Pythagorean → inverse sine → 180 degrees

> **Teaching Takeaway**
>
> Formative evaluation of teaching provides evidence that informs when to move on in teaching and learning.

> EFFECT SIZE FOR COOPERATIVE LEARNING = **0.40**

He has subjectively ordered these methods in order of novelty. He wants to showcase the final group on his list for bringing to bear ideas—such as the Pythagorean theorem and knowledge of degrees in a triangle—that were not directly covered today but are absolutely applicable to this task. With his focus on deep learning and strategic thinking, Mr. Wittrock intends to highlight the value in considering prior knowledge alongside new learning at all times. This, he realizes, is doubly important based on the unintended rigidity many students came away with from yesterday's lesson. Mr. Wittrock hopes to thwart a repeat of that misinterpreted rigidity by celebrating a diversity of methods.

As Mr. Wittrock calls on groups to show their work and illustrate their thinking, he works to emphasize connections between ideas and approaches. He focuses the thinking of the rest of the class with the following questions:

> EFFECT SIZE FOR QUESTIONING = 0.48

- How many different strategies did we see to solve the problem today?
- Which strategy was "the best"?
- Do we see any other strategies now that were not used?
- How are these strategies connected?
- How might you decide which strategy to use, based on the problem itself?

After the final group shares and the discussion comes to a close, Mr. Wittrock hands out a new PAR assignment for independent practice and instructs students that their draft is due for review tomorrow. Thus, the PAR cycle continues. Figure 4.6 shows how Mr. Wittrock made his planning visible so that he could then provide an engaging and rigorous learning experience for his learners.

Mr. Wittrock's Teaching for Clarity PLANNING GUIDE

ESTABLISHING PURPOSE

1

What are the key content standards I will focus on in this lesson?

Content Standards:

TEKS Geometry Standards

(9) Similarity, proof, and trigonometry. The student uses the process skills to understand and apply relationships in right triangles. The student is expected to:

    (A) determine the lengths of sides and measures of angles in a right triangle by applying the trigonometric ratios sine, cosine, and tangent to solve problems; and

    (B) apply the relationships in special right triangles 30°-60°-90° and 45°-45°-90° and the Pythagorean theorem, including Pythagorean triples, to solve problems.

TEKS Mathematical Process Standards:

- Create and use representations to organize, record, and communicate mathematical ideas.
- Analyze mathematical relationships to connect and communicate mathematical ideas.
- Display, explain, and justify mathematical ideas and arguments using precise mathematical language in written and oral communication.

2

What are the learning intentions (the goal and *why* of learning, stated in student-friendly language) I will focus on in this lesson?

Content: To understand the relationship between trigonometric functions (sine, cosine, and tangent) and their inverses.

Language: To precisely state each inverse trigonometric function as it is being used (i.e., the inverse sine of ___ is ___).

Social: To hold one another accountable to the language learning intention. #grammarpolice

SUCCESS CRITERIA

3 **When will I introduce and reinforce the learning intention(s) so that students understand it, see the relevance, connect it to previous learning, and can clearly communicate it themselves?**

After finishing the PAR trade at the beginning of class, the learning intentions will be introduced along with the success criteria. Though today we will be developing a surface-level procedural understanding of inverse trig functions, this is the missing piece for deep learning to occur on the overarching topic of trig functions and their connection to right triangles. I'll know deep learning is occurring when I hear students' audible "Aha!" moments.

---

4 **What evidence shows that students have mastered the learning intention(s)? What criteria will I use?**

I can statements:

- I can use inverse trigonometric functions to find unknown angles in right triangles.
- I can solve right triangles, given any two of their sides, and explain my thinking.

---

5 **How will I check students' understanding (assess learning) during instruction and make accommodations?**

I will assess prior knowledge by listening in on PAR conversations. I will look for areas of common struggle and seek out competent peers for reciprocal teaching.

I will also scan and conduct student interviews during collaborative practice in addition to "numbered heads together" for sharing out.

INSTRUCTION

6 **What activities and tasks will move students forward in their learning?**

Peer-Assisted Reflection (PAR) Trade

Class will begin with students trading their PARs with a partner, providing written feedback, and then discussing the feedback. This will activate the prior knowledge we need to access for today.

Direct/Deliberate Instruction

I'll present a problem that cannot be solved using our current skillset to build the need for new learning. This will generate our discussion of trigonometric functions and their inverses. I'll use a combination of guided questioning and direct teaching to flesh out the concepts. I will model the procedure of using inverse trig functions with a few worked examples.

Collaborative Practice

Students will solve right triangles in collaborative groups using inverse trig functions and other previously learned strategies. I will scan during this time and organize a structured share-out in an intentional order.

Share-Out

In this phase, students from each group will explain how they approached a given problem. The goal is for students to make connections between strategies and start to develop preferences based on efficiency.

Peer-Assisted Reflection (PAR) Homework

Students will receive a new PAR aligned to today's success criteria for independent practice. Their homework tonight is to complete a draft solution.

7 **What resources (materials and sentence frames) are needed?**

1. Table-sized whiteboards and markers for collaborative practice
2. Printed copies of PAR 4.4

8 How will I organize and facilitate the learning? What questions will I ask? How will I initiate closure?

The day will be organized in a linear fashion through the phases listed in Section 7:

1. PAR Trade
   a. Why did you choose to solve this triangle this way?
   b. Are there other routes you could have chosen?
   c. Are any routes more efficient or less efficient than others?

2. Direct/Deliberate Instruction
   a. Can our trigonometry help us find unknown angles?
   b. Sine of what equals 1? $\frac{1}{\sqrt{2}}$? $\frac{\sqrt{3}}{2}$?
   c. How do inverse functions work, and how might they apply to this?

3. Collaborative Practice
   a. What information do we have?
   b. What information do we need?
   c. What mathematical tools can we use to get us the information we need?

4. Share-Out
   a. How many different routes did we see to solve the problem today?
   b. Which one was "the best"?
   c. Do we see any other routes that weren't used?
   d. How might you decide which route to use, based on the problem itself?

 This lesson plan is available for download at resources.corwin.com/vlmathematics-9-12.

Figure 4.6   Mr. Wittrock's Trigonometric Functions Procedural Lesson

Ms. Shuzhen and Probabilities of Compound Events

As the learners in Ms. Shuzhen's class demonstrate their understanding and application of statistics, they must devote time to developing strong procedural knowledge. Ms. Shuzhen knows that this fluency will allow learners to engage in the complex application of statistics and making decisions using statistics. Over the past week, she has noticed that her learners have a strong command of the equations for calculating the number of possible combinations or permutations in a given case. In other words, her students have demonstrated strong surface learning with these procedural skills. However, in many cases, the learners struggled when making decisions about which equation to use in which situation. Her learners did not yet see the deep structures within problems that allowed them to use tools strategically. This lesson will focus on an independent practice task since learners struggled to complete permutations and combinations when the problems were interleaved—they struggled to match the correct procedure with the scenario. Sometimes, Ms. Shuzhen has to engage her learners in several learning experiences around the same content. Learning takes time.

She expects her learners to make connections among these equations and the concepts of permutations and combinations, and eventually, apply their thinking with greater fluency. As learners engage in deep learning, Ms. Shuzhen wants them to make generalizations based on their understanding of permutations and combinations.

What Ms. Shuzhen Wants Her Students to Learn

To match the correct procedure with the scenario, learners must not only be able to use equations to complete a permutation or combination, but also see relations and patterns to these compound events. Thus, the standard addressed requires the application of thinking and concepts.

> **Teaching Takeaway**
>
> Procedural knowledge can be at the deep phase of learning. This occurs when learners make connections between specific procedures or skills in their mathematics learning.

> **MATHEMATICS CONTENT AND PRACTICE STANDARDS**
>
> S-CP.B.9.
>
> Use permutations and combinations to compute probabilities of compound events and solve problems.
>
> **Ms. Shuzhen is helping her learners develop the following Standards for Mathematical Practice:**
>
> - Make sense of problems and persevere in solving them.
> - Reason abstractly and quantitatively.
> - Look for and make use of structure.

However, Ms. Shuzhen recognizes that her learners need additional learning in procedural knowledge—in particular, at the deep level. Together, they will focus on the relationship between the two mathematics procedures and the scenarios to which they are relevant.

Learning Intentions and Success Criteria

Memorizing a formula is one thing. Using the formula at the right time with the right problem is something different. Ms. Shuzhen plans to build on her learners' understanding of the counting principle to connect with the procedural steps in calculating the number of possible combinations or permutations in a given case.

> EFFECT SIZE FOR REHEARSAL AND MEMORIZATION = 0.73

> EFFECT SIZE FOR ASSESSMENT-CAPABLE VISIBLE LEARNERS = 1.33

> EFFECT SIZE FOR TEACHER CLARITY = 0.75

> *Content Learning Intention:* To understand why the rules for permutations and combinations are related to the counting principle.
>
> *Language Learning Intention:* To explain how to compute the probabilities of compound events.
>
> *Social Learning Intention:* To ask probing questions that help my peers and me advance my thinking about probability.

When learners are asked what they are learning and how they know if they are successful, most of Ms. Shuzhen's students can articulate the answers. The main reason for their awareness of what success looks like is the visibility of the criteria for success every day. Today, learners are writing down the success criteria in their mathematics notebooks.

> **SUCCESS CRITERIA FOR TODAY'S LESSON**
>
> ☐ I can explain the difference between a permutation and combination.
> ☐ I can explain how to complete a permutation and combination.
> ☐ I can support my calculations using visual representations of sample spaces.

As learners record these three success criteria in their mathematics notebooks, Ms. Shuzhen points out that they will have to provide evidence that they have met these success criteria. She wants to promote the self-monitoring of their learning.

Modeling Strategies and Skills

Ms. Shuzhen has spent a lot of time thinking about what mastery of these learning intentions and success criteria would look like for her students. If learners are to solve problems involving the probability of compound events with permutations and combinations, she must be intentional about how she checks for understanding and makes learning visible to her students. Her checks for understanding must use strategies that promote quantitative reasoning to use the appropriate tools in solving the problems. Furthermore, learners must make sense of problems, as well as look for and make use of structure in these problems. Only then will her learners be able to construct viable arguments about when to use which algorithm in computing the probability of compound events (© Copyright 2010. National Governors Association Center for Best Practices and Council of Chief State School Officers. All rights reserved.).

With this in mind, the focus questions for today are these:

> *What determines whether something is a permutation or a combination?*
>
> *How does this determine our approach to solving a problem?*

Video 14
Checking for Understanding as Procedural Knowledge Deepens

https://resources.corwin.com/vlmathematics-9-12

EFFECT SIZE FOR DELIBERATE PRACTICE = 0.79

> **EFFECT SIZE FOR ACHIEVING MOTIVATION AND APPROACH = 0.44**

Over the years, Ms. Shuzhen has had great success using guiding questions. She has noticed that her learners are more cognitively and emotionally engaged with the content:

> I am amazed at how the use of guiding or focus questions provides a level of relevancy to their learning. I have students who walked through the door, not caring a single bit about the class, but became driven to find the answer to the focus question each day. As the year has progressed, they talked more about learning statistics, meeting the success criteria, and celebrating that success rather than getting the assignment done and earning a passing grade.

Instructional Approaches That Promote Procedural Knowledge

Given her learners' strong surface learning around permutations and combinations, as well as the capacity to lead their own mathematics discussions, Ms. Shuzhen plans to use the jigsaw strategy to facilitate learning. The **jigsaw**, which allows learners to specialize in one piece of content and then engage in peer instruction to learn the other components of the content, will reinforce students' surface learning, develop fluency with the calculating permutations and combinations, and at the same time foster connections between today's concepts.

> The **jigsaw** is a cooperative learning strategy that allows learners to specialize in one piece of content and then engage in peer instruction to learn the other components of the content.

Ms. Shuzhen divides the day's learning into four parts: permutations, combinations, sample spaces, and compound events. Based on prior checks for understanding, she has strong knowledge about where her students need additional learning and support. The content assigned to each student was determined by the previous checks for understanding and where learners needed the most support. For example, LaShea has a gap in her learning when it comes to visually representing sample spaces. Although she has not mastered the completion of permutations, Ms. Shuzhen wants her to build her procedural fluency with sample spaces and then engage in discussions with her peers about permutations. Therefore, her assigned content will be sample spaces. On the other side of the room, Conner struggles with the calculation of combinations. His content focus in the jigsaw will be combinations.

> **EFFECT SIZE FOR JIGSAW METHOD = 1.20**

> **EFFECT SIZE FOR SCAFFOLDING = 0.82**

In Step 1 of the jigsaw, Ms. Shuzhen assigns one part of the content to each member of a four-person group. In Step 2, once each member has had time to review his or her part independently, he or she will gather with other members of the class who also have been assigned that same part of the jigsaw. For example, in Ms. Shuzhen's second-period class of 32 students, there would be eight students assigned to the component of the jigsaw related to compound events. This expert group develops a teaching strategy for helping their original groups "learn" the content. Now, Ms. Shuzhen recognizes that an expert group of eight is too large. In this case, she asks the expert groups to break up into two groups of four. This is an easy adjustment for large classes.

After some time, Ms. Shuzhen instructs the experts to return to their home groups, and in Step 3, they teach their fellow classmates their specific part of the content. Although the teacher, Ms. Shuzhen, could preset the order of the home group instruction, she leaves this decision to the individual home groups. During each step of the jigsaw, Ms. Shuzhen moves from group to group, listening to student conversations and how they are explaining permutations, combinations, sample spaces, and compound events. At the same time, she monitors their understanding by listening to their descriptions and recording notes on an informal data sheet. Once she notices that each group member has had an opportunity to "teach" her or his content, she brings the class back together for the final step of the Jigsaw.

> In Step 4, you will return to your expert teams and discuss with your peers the new learning from your home group. How did your component fit with the other components from today? For example, the expert group that focused on sample spaces will need to discuss how your topic relates to permutations, combinations, and compound events. This will get you ready for today's exit ticket.

To scaffold the jigsaw process for learners with different levels of readiness, Ms. Shuzhen provided predetermined approaches for teaching content. She also adjusted the content through different modalities—for example, translated into Spanish for some students, provided video clips on permutations and combinations for some learners, and offered graphic organizers to assist with the expert learning process.

Teaching Takeaway

Checks for understanding provide a formative evaluation of student learning. This helps us be more deliberate and intentional about grouping learners.

Video 15
Supporting Learners' Extension Into Transfer

https://resources.corwin.com/vlmathematics-9-12

Teaching for Clarity at the Close

As homework, learners are asked to use today's learning experience and other resources (e.g., textbook and mathematics notebook) to compile evidence of their learning and meeting the success criteria for the day. These miniature portfolios will be shared with her and their peers tomorrow. She tells the class,

> I want you to make a case that you have met the criteria for today. Can you tell the difference between a permutation and combination? Can you complete both of them? The strength of your case will determine the next steps in your learning journey. What will be your evidence?

To wrap up the lesson, Ms. Shuzhen asks each student to respond to the two focus questions for the day. On an exit ticket, learners are to construct a response and turn in that response prior to leaving the classroom. Figure 4.7 shows how Ms. Shuzhen made her planning visible so that she could then provide an engaging and rigorous learning experience for her learners.

Ms. Shuzhen's Teaching for Clarity PLANNING GUIDE

ESTABLISHING PURPOSE

1. What are the key content standards I will focus on in this lesson?

Content Standards:

S-CP.B.9

Use permutations and combinations to compute probabilities of compound events and solve problems.

Standards for Mathematical Practice:

- Make sense of problems and persevere in solving them.
- Reason abstractly and quantitatively.
- Look for and make use of structure.

2. What are the learning intentions (the goal and *why* of learning, stated in student-friendly language) I will focus on in this lesson?

Content: To understand why the rules for permutations and combinations are related to the counting principle.

Language: To explain how to compute the probabilities of compound events.

Social: To ask probing questions that help my peers and me advance my thinking about probability.

3 When will I introduce and reinforce the learning intention(s) so that students understand it, see the relevance, connect it to previous learning, and can clearly communicate it themselves?

After introducing the learning intentions at the beginning of class, I will introduce the guiding questions for today. As we move through today's lesson, we will refer to these questions to monitor our progress, as well as keep our focus on the goals of the lesson.

These guiding questions will serve as the exit ticket and frame the miniportfolios for homework.

The guiding questions are as follows:

What determines whether something is a permutation or a combination?

How does this determine our approach to solving a problem?

SUCCESS CRITERIA

4 What evidence shows that students have mastered the learning intention(s)? What criteria will I use?

I can statements:

- *I can explain the difference between a permutation and combination.*
- *I can explain how to complete a permutation and combination.*
- *I can support my calculations using visual representations of sample spaces.*

5 **How will I check students' understanding (assess learning) during instruction and make accommodations?**

In addition to providing space throughout direct/deliberate instruction for questions, I will monitor the room through the jigsaw activity and engage with learners or groups that need additional support. I will also collect the jigsaw task and exit tickets for formative data.

INSTRUCTION

6 **What activities and tasks will move students forward in their learning?**

Jigsaw

1. *Divide the topic into chunks: permutations, combinations, sample spaces, and compound events.*
2. *Divide the students into expert groups. Inform each group of the chunk they are to become experts in. Embed measures of accountability to ensure that hesitant learners will become actively engaged in complex material.*
3. *Assign students to base groups. The number of students in each base group is equal to the number of expert groups, and each base group member is also a member of a different expert group.*
4. *Have students review the expert material individually.*
5. *Have students meet and collaborate in their expert groups.*
6. *Provide group support for material that may be difficult to master alone, and help students master content in greater depth.*
7. *Provide time for expert groups to complete the activity and prepare their teaching strategy.*
8. *Have experts return to their base group and teach.*
9. *Experts return to their expert groups to debrief and reflect on their teaching.*

7 **What resources (materials and sentence frames) are needed?**

1. Groups (determine who is in what expert group and home group)
2. Instructions for the jigsaw
3. Graphic organizer
4. Directions in Spanish
5. Exit ticket

8 **How will I organize and facilitate the learning? What questions will I ask? How will I initiate closure?**

This lesson will start with a whole-group introduction of the learning intention, success criteria, and guiding questions. Then, learners will transition to their home groups to receive their individual assignments or expert groups. After the jigsaw task is complete, we will close with a whole-class discussion, and students will complete the exit ticket for the day.

 This lesson plan is available for download at resources.corwin.com/vlmathematics-9-12.

Figure 4.7 Ms. Shuzhen's Probabilities of Compound Events Procedural Lesson

Reflection

Our final visit to these three classrooms focused on the development of procedural knowledge and fluency. Using what you have read in this chapter, reflect on the following questions:

1. In your own words, describe what teaching for procedural knowledge looks like in your mathematics classroom.

2. How does the Teaching for Clarity Planning Guide support your intentionality in teaching for procedural knowledge?

3. Compare and contrast the approaches to teaching taken by the classroom teachers featured in this chapter.

4. Consider the following statement: *Procedural knowledge is more than "drill and kill."* Do you agree or disagree with the statement? Why or why not? How is this statement reflected in this chapter?

5. How did the classroom teachers featured in this chapter adjust the difficulty and/or complexity of the mathematics tasks to meet the needs of all learners?

KNOWING YOUR IMPACT: EVALUATING FOR MASTERY

5

CHAPTER 5 SUCCESS CRITERIA:

(1) I can describe what mastery learning is in my classroom.

(2) I can compare and contrast checks for understanding with the evaluation of mastery.

(3) I can explain how to evaluate mastery in my own classroom using tasks and tests.

(4) I can identify characteristics of challenging mathematics tasks.

(5) I can explain the role of feedback in supporting students' journey to mastery.

Let us end right where we began—Ms. Norris's algebra classroom. Ms. Norris established clear learning intentions and success criteria, and she designed a challenging mathematics task that allowed learners to see themselves as their own teachers. Just like Ms. Rios, Mr. Wittrock, and Ms. Shuzhen, Ms. Norris created many opportunities for learners to make their thinking visible through her checks for understanding. Formative evaluation and feedback are critical components to teaching mathematics in the Visible Learning classroom.

> EFFECT SIZE FOR PROVIDING FORMATIVE EVALUATION = 0.48 AND FEEDBACK = 0.70

However, this chapter focuses on determining students' learning over the long haul. In other words, how do teachers assess for mastery? And in doing so, how do teachers and learners make evidence-informed decisions about when to move forward in the learning progression? Knowing our impact on student learning in mathematics involves more than just formative evaluation of learning. Knowing your impact also involves recognizing student mastery in their mathematics learning.

What Is Mastery Learning?

> Mastery learning is the expectation that learners will grasp specific conceptual understanding, procedural knowledge, and the application of specific concepts and thinking skills.

Mastery learning is the expectation that learners will grasp specific conceptual understanding, procedural knowledge, and/or the application of specific concepts and thinking skills. This requires that teachers establish clarity about the learning in mathematics classrooms and then organize a series of logical experiences, noticing which students do and don't learn along the way. When students experience lesson clarity, they progress towards mastery. The claim underlying mastery learning is that all children can learn when provided with clear explanations of what it means to "master" the material being taught. Although mastery learning does not speak to the time learners need to reach mastery, all students continuously receive evaluative feedback on their performance. Learners know where they are at in their learning, where they are going, and what they can do to bridge the gap.

> EFFECT SIZE FOR MASTERY LEARNING = 0.57

> EFFECT SIZE FOR TEACHER CLARITY = 0.75

In true mastery learning, students do not progress to the next unit until they have mastered the previous one. But "moving on" could mean that learners move forward in the learning progression or that they are provided additional learning experiences at the surface, deep, or transfer level to address gaps in their learning if they are not yet able to demonstrate mastery. Ms. Norris notes,

To evaluate student mastery, I develop a rubric that describes each level of proficiency—for example, Levels 1 through 4, with 4 being mastery. My feedback depends on the specific descriptions of each levels. When learners demonstrate, say, a Level 1 or Level 2, I use this information to provide additional scaffolding for these learners. They are not there, yet.

Video 16
Evaluating for Mastery

https://resources.corwin.com/ vlmathematics-9-12

Mastery learning is an essential part of building assessment-capable visible learners in the mathematics classroom. If learners are to know where they are going next in their learning; select the right learning tools to support the next steps (e.g., manipulatives, problem-solving approaches, and/or meta-cognitive strategies); and know what feedback to seek about their own learning, they must have opportunities to assess their own mastery with mathematics content. This, of course, comes after learners have engaged in multiple mathematics tasks replete with checks for understanding that allow teachers and students to adjust learning in the moment. Once that has occurred, it is time to determine students' level of mastery in the mathematics learning. So how do we determine what mastery looks like for specific content in the mathematics classroom?

> **Teaching Takeaway**
>
> Effective feedback is an essential feature of the Visible Learning mathematics classroom.

Using Learning Intentions to Define *Mastery Learning*

Learning intentions provide the framework for defining *mastery* in learning, the development of assessments used to determine student mastery, and the information necessary to plan learning experiences for students. Ms. Norris, Ms. Rios, Mr. Wittrock, and Ms. Shuzhen had to answer the question "What do my students need to learn?" The answer to this question represents mastery for the specific content in each of their classrooms. In the Chapter 1 example from Ms. Norris's classroom, the learning intention stated *I am learning that authentic situations can be modeled or represented with equations*. Therefore, to demonstrate mastery, her learners must model and represent different proportional relationships.

Assessments of mastery require both the teacher and the learners to focus on the essential learning for a particular unit or series of lessons. Teachers must unpack the language of the specific standard

> **Teaching Takeaway**
>
> Features of mastery learning include the following:
>
> 1. Clear learning expectations
>
> 2. Feedback that is specific, constructive, and timely
>
> 3. Sufficient time, attention, and support to ensure learning

to have a clear sense of the conceptual understanding, procedural knowledge, and applications expected in the mastery of the standard (see Figure 5.1). Let us look at another example by first considering another content standard from Ms. Norris's classroom:

> Describe qualitatively the functional relationship between two quantities by analyzing a graph (e.g., where the function is increasing or decreasing, linear or nonlinear). Sketch the graph that exhibits the qualitative features of a function that has been described verbally.

As you can see, this is not very helpful in developing and implementing an assessment of mastery learning. To narrow in on tasks that will allow students to demonstrate mastery, teachers must specifically define what the learner will know, understand, and be able to do. Ms. Norris and her collaborative planning team defined *mastery* as this:

> Given a graph, I can write a mathematics story that explains the qualitative features of increase, decrease, linear, and nonlinear, and describe the intervals over which these characteristics occur.

In addition, Ms. Norris and her colleagues have specifically identified vocabulary that represents key concepts within this standard that learners must use fluently in their work: *discrete, continuous, collinear points, nonlinear, increasing function, constant function, decreasing function, interval of increase, interval of decrease,* and *constant interval.*

Establishing the Expected Level of Mastery

From this preestablished level of mastery, which is based on the standard(s), teachers identify indicators that students are or are not at the level of mastery. These indicators should focus on what students are doing rather than what they are not doing. This helps identify current performance levels and is suggestive of the types of experiences students need to have to progress in their learning. In other words, what does progress toward mastery look like in this specific standard? Learners progress toward mastery at different rates, and teachers should

EXAMPLE OF DEFINED MASTERY FOR SPECIFIC CONTENT STANDARDS

	Mathematics Content Standard	What Mastery Looks Like
Ms. Rios	From Chapter 3: Explain why the x-coordinates of the points where the graphs of the equations $y = f(x)$ and $y = g(x)$ intersect are the solutions of the equation $f(x) = g(x)$; find the solutions approximately (e.g., using technology to graph the functions, make tables of values, or find successive approximations).	Given an authentic scenario (e.g., best recreational vehicle rental plan on a vacation), learners must model the scenario using a system of equations, calculate a solution, and interpret the mathematical results in the context of the scenario.
Mr. Wittrock	From Chapter 4—Similarity, Proof, and Trigonometry: The student uses the process skills to understand and apply relationships in right triangles. The student is expected to (A) determine the lengths of sides and measures of angles in a right triangle by applying the trigonometric ratios sine, cosine, and tangent to solve problems; and (B) apply the relationships in special right triangles 30°–60°–90° and 45°–45°–90° and the Pythagorean theorem, including Pythagorean triples, to solve problems.	Given an authentic scenario (e.g., building design and construction), learners must model the scenario using relationships in right triangles, calculate a solution, and interpret the mathematical results in the context of the scenario.
Ms. Shuzhen	From Chapter 2: Analyze decisions and strategies using probability concepts (e.g., product testing, medical testing, pulling a hockey goalie at the end of a game).	Given a choice of several options, learners must make a decision and justify their choice using probability and statistical reasoning.

Source: Ashley Norris, Mathematics Teacher, Columbia County Public Schools, Georgia

Figure 5.1

map out that progress so that both the teacher and the learners can make an informed decision about where they are in their learning.

Ms. Norris and her colleagues identified the incremental steps along the pathway to achieving mastery for the functional relationship standard using the SOLO Taxonomy (see Figure 1.5 in Chapter 1). If students perceive or actually are far from meeting the highest level of proficiency, making the progression visible allows them to answer the questions "Where am I going, how am I going, and where to go next?" These are essential in developing assessment-capable visible learners. Together, Ms. Norris and her colleagues developed the progression in Figure 5.2.

EXAMPLE OF PROGRESS TOWARD MASTERY FOR SPECIFIC CONTENT STANDARD

Content Standard	Learning Intention:					Vocabulary
Describe qualitatively the functional relationship between two quantities by analyzing a graph (e.g., where the function is increasing or decreasing, linear or nonlinear). Sketch the graph that exhibits the qualitative features of a function that has been described verbally.	I am learning to determine graphical characteristics of a relation, such as whether the relation is increasing or decreasing, and state the intervals of increase and decrease. I am also learning what types of graphs and equations are linear or nonlinear.					discrete
	How will I know when I have it? The following mastery levels will let you know how you are progressing toward this learning goal.					continuous
						collinear points
	Level 4	Level 3	Level 2	Level 1	Level 0	nonlinear
						increasing function
	Given a graph, I can write a story that creatively explains the qualitative features of increase, decrease, linear, and nonlinear, and describe the intervals over which these characteristics occur.	Given a story, I can sketch a graph that accounts for the characteristics given in the story and accurately graph the intervals described in the story.	Given a graph, I can identify qualitative characteristics such as increase, decrease, linear, and nonlinear.	Given a graph, I can identify qualitative characteristics such as increase, decrease, linear, and nonlinear, but I struggle with some of the characteristics.	I struggle to understand the characteristics of a graph.	constant function
						decreasing function
						interval of increase
						interval of decrease
						constant interval

Source: Ashley Norris, Mathematics Teacher, Columbia County Public Schools, Georgia

Figure 5.2

Teaching Takeaway

In addition to knowing what we want our students to learn, we have to know what evidence will demonstrate that they have learned it.

When we revisit the classrooms of Ms. Rios, Mr. Wittrock, and Ms. Shuzhen, we see that they provide similar levels of clarity about what mastery looks like as their learners progress through the big ideas around the content standards (see Figure 5.3). Teachers know their students best and therefore can use evaluation of student learning—within a set of learning intentions—to designate their students' levels of proficiency on the pathway to mastery. That said, there are no prescribed number of these levels.

Collecting Evidence of Progress Toward Mastery

To determine progress and to support the grades given to students, teachers must be able to answer clearly the question "What evidence suggests that the learners have mastered the learning or are moving toward mastery?" The evidence used to determine mastery is typically

EXAMPLES OF LEVELS OF PROFICIENCY TOWARD MASTERY FOR SPECIFIC CONTENT STANDARDS

	Mathematics Content Standard	Levels of Proficiency—Progress Toward Mastery
Ms. Rios	**From Chapter 3:** Explain why the x-coordinates of the points where the graphs of the equations $y = f(x)$ and $y = g(x)$ intersect are the solutions of the equation $f(x) = g(x)$; find the solutions approximately (e.g., using technology to graph the functions, make tables of values, or find successive approximations).	**Level 1:** Shows minimal attempt on the problem (guess and check); has no clear problem-solving approach; provides no reasoning with the answer; or provides no answer. **Level 2:** Shows signs of coherent problem solving; gives minimal evidence to support the answer; fails to address some of the constraints of the problem; occasionally makes sense of quantities in relationships in the problem; has trouble generalizing or using the mathematical results. **Level 3:** Response shows the main elements of solving the problem and an organized approach to solving the problem; there are errors, but of a kind that the student could well fix, with more time for checking and revision and some limited help; makes sense of quantities and their relationships in the specific situation; response uses assumptions, definitions, and previously established results. **Level 4:** Shows understanding and use of stated assumptions, definitions, and previously established results in construction arguments; makes conjectures and builds a logical progression of statements; routinely interprets mathematical results in the context of the situation and reflects on whether the results make sense; communication is precise, using definitions clearly.
Mr. Wittrock	**From Chapter 4:** The student uses the process skills to understand and apply relationships in right triangles. The student is expected to (A) determine the lengths of sides and measures of angles in a right triangle by applying the trigonometric ratios sine, cosine, and tangent to solve problems; and	**Level 1:** Shows minimal attempt on the problem (guess and check); has no clear problem-solving approach; provides no reasoning with the answer; or provides no answer. **Level 2:** Shows signs of coherent problem solving; gives minimal evidence to support the answer; fails to address some of the constraints of the problem; occasionally makes sense of quantities in relationships in the problem; has trouble generalizing or using the mathematical results. **Level 3:** Response shows the main elements of solving the problem and an organized approach to solving the problem; there are errors, but of a kind that the student could well fix, with more time for checking and revision and some limited help; makes sense of quantities and their relationships in the specific situation; response uses assumptions, definitions, and previously established results.

(Continued)

(Continued)

	Mathematics Content Standard	Levels of Proficiency—Progress Toward Mastery
	(B) apply the relationships in special right triangles 30°–60°–90° and 45°–45°–90° and the Pythagorean theorem, including Pythagorean triples, to solve problems.	**Level 4**: Shows understanding and use of stated assumptions, definitions, and previously established results in construction arguments; makes conjectures and builds a logical progression of statements; routinely interprets mathematical results in the context of the situation and reflects on whether the results make sense; communication is precise, using definitions clearly.
Ms. Shuzhen	**From Chapter 2:** Analyze decisions and strategies using probability concepts (e.g., product testing, medical testing, pulling a hockey goalie at the end of a game).	**Level 1**: No solution is provided, or the solution has no relationship to the task; solution addresses none of the mathematical components presented in the task; inappropriate concepts are applied and/or procedures are used. **Level 2**: Solution is not complete, indicating that parts of the problem are not understood; solution addresses some, but not all, of the mathematical components presented in the task. **Level 3**: Solution shows that the student has a broad understanding of the problem and the major concepts necessary for its solution; solution addresses all of the components presented in the task. **Level 4**: Solution shows a deep understanding of the problem, including the ability to identify the appropriate mathematical concepts and the information necessary for its solution; solution completely addresses all mathematical components presented in the task; solution puts to use the underlying mathematical concepts upon which the task is designed.

Figure 5.3

more formal than the evidence used to check for understanding. For example, an exit slip could easily be used to determine which students mastered a given learning intention on a given day. But that probably will not be sufficient evidence for determining mastery of a standard or set of standards. Checks for understanding gather and provide *evidence of learners' progress* toward a learning intention, whereas an evaluation of mastery provides *evidence that a student has demonstrated mastery* of a standard or set of standards.

RELATIONSHIP BETWEEN LEARNING INTENTIONS AND CHECKS FOR UNDERSTANDING

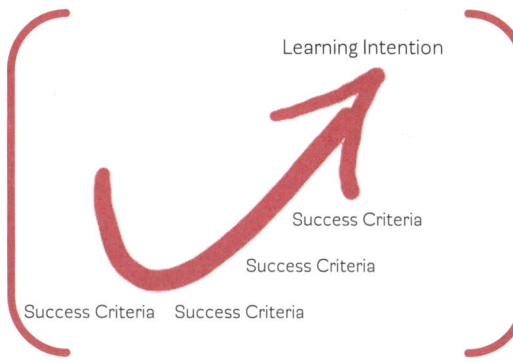

Checks for Understanding gather and provide *evidence of learners' progress* toward a learning intention using the success criteria as guides for this progression.

Figure 5.4

The difference between checks for understanding and evaluating for mastery lies in the focus of the task, as well as the use of the evidence. In a check for understanding, teachers and students are gathering evidence about learning around specific learning intentions and success criteria (see Figure 5.4).

Ms. Rios, Mr. Wittrock, and Ms. Shuzhen had multiple checks for understanding throughout their lessons. In each of their classrooms, learners engaged in checks for understanding that targeted the specific learning intentions and success criteria for the lesson.

Although we can use formative assessments collected over time to evaluate mastery—evidence over time—our classrooms require single tasks that evaluate mastery (e.g., performance-based learning tasks and well-designed standardized tests). These tasks evaluate student mastery by focusing on the standard(s), asking learners to assimilate all of the learning into *a challenging mathematics task* (sometimes called a *rich mathematical task*). Again, evaluating student mastery brings together multiple concepts, procedures, and applications into a single task rather than rich tasks that target specific success criteria within a standard or standards. These tasks can include, but are not limited to, performance-based learning tasks and well-designed standardized tests (see Figure 5.5).

INGREDIENTS FOR PROGRESS TOWARD MASTERY

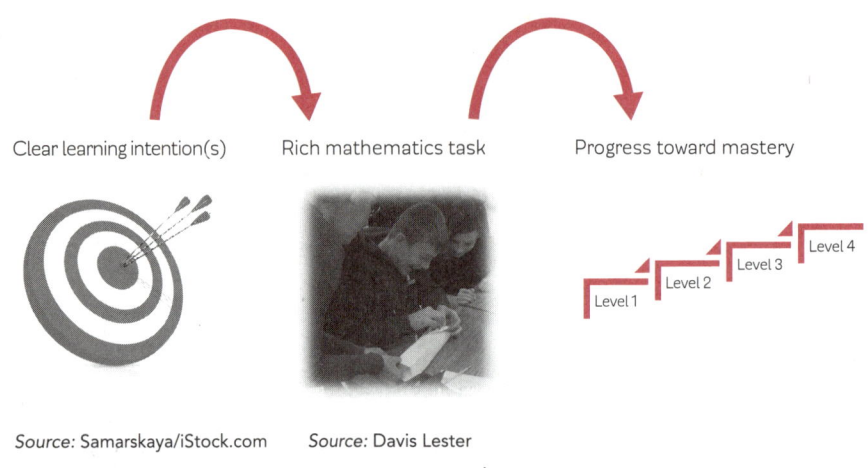

Figure 5.5

Figure 5.6 includes a checklist useful in creating assessment of mastery. As Ms. Norris says,

> After our team develops an assessment for mastery, we use the checklist to make sure that it's the best assessment we can develop. We don't want false positives or false negatives, meaning data that suggest students are mastering content when they are not or students who need more learning but look like they have mastered it based on the assessment.

Poorly designed tasks yield poor evidence and poor decisions about where to go next.

A poorly designed task washes out the benefit of determining learner mastery. For example, a group of teachers was looking to see if learners could compare the properties of two functions represented multiple ways. The teachers developed a sorting and matching task, but that did not provide them with the evidence needed to make a decision about student proficiency. Furthermore, if the task is not engaging and relevant to our students, their level of persistence will likely skew the evidence as well. Whether the evaluation of mastery provides evidence to the teacher and student about the current level of mastery is in the

CHECKLIST FOR CREATING OR SELECTING TASKS THAT ASSESS MASTERY

All Items

- ☐ Is this the most appropriate type of item to use for the intended learning outcomes?
- ☐ Does each item or task require students to demonstrate the performance described in the specific learning outcome it measures (relevance)?
- ☐ Does each item present a clear and definite task to be performed (clarity)?
- ☐ Is each item or task presented in simple, readable language and free from excessive verbiage (conciseness)?
- ☐ Does each item provide an appropriate challenge (ideal difficulty)?
- ☐ Does each item have an answer that would be agreed upon by experts (correctness)?
- ☐ Is there a clear basis for awarding partial credit on items or tasks with multiple points (scoring rubric)?
- ☐ Is each item or task free from technical errors and irrelevant clues (technical soundness)?
- ☐ Is each test item free from cultural bias?
- ☐ Have the items been set aside for a time before reviewing them (or being reviewed by a colleague)?

Performance Items

- ☐ Does the item focus on learning outcomes that require complex cognitive skills and student performances?
- ☐ Does the task represent the content, skills, processes, and practices that are central to learning outcomes?
- ☐ Does the item minimize dependence on skills that are irrelevant to the intended purpose of the assessment task?
- ☐ Does the task provide the necessary scaffolding for students to be able to understand the task and achieve the task?
- ☐ Do the directions clearly describe the task?
- ☐ Are students aware of the basis (expectations) on which their performances will be evaluated in terms of scoring rubrics?

Source: Adapted from Linn and Gronlund (2000).

Figure 5.6

 This checklist is available for download at resources.corwin.com/vlmathematics-9-12.

nature of the task itself. In other words, poorly designed tasks yield poor evidence and poor decisions about where to go next.

In order to develop an effective evaluation that provides opportunities for learners to demonstrate mastery while at the same time provides evidence for feedback or next steps, teachers should consider the ways students can make their mathematics thinking visible.

> What separates a challenging, rich mathematics task from a rote exercise is the nature of the cognitive engagement required to complete the task.

What separates a challenging, rich mathematics task from a rote exercise is the nature of the cognitive engagement required to complete the task. In mathematics exercises, learners repeat terms, concepts, ideas, procedures, or processes and apply those in novel situations.

Let us look back to the set of mastery tasks developed by Ms. Norris and her team. How learners approach these tasks and the thinking these tasks generate provide valuable information to both the teacher and the learners, allowing the learners to gain an understanding of where they are in their learning progression, identify where they need to go next in their learning, and what learning tools are needed to support this next step. What do we mean by *challenging, rich mathematics tasks*? There are many definitions:

- Accessible to all learners ("low floor, high ceiling")
- Real-life task or application
- Multiple approaches and representations
- Collaboration and discussion
- Engagement, curiosity, and creativity
- Making connections within and/or across topics and domains, vertically and horizontally
- Opportunities for extension (adapted from Boaler, 2015, 2016; Wolf, 2015)

These tasks are far different from forced-choice items that may only assess the guesswork of mathematics learners. Bringing the previous definitions to life, Antonetti and Garver (2015) reported on data from classroom walk-throughs that focused on eight features that differentiated mathematics tasks from mere rote exercises. Observers measured consistent and sustained engagement when three or more of the features were present. The eight characteristics of challenging mathematics tasks are as follows:

1. **Personal response**: Do the students have the opportunity to bring their own personal experiences with mathematics to the task? Examples include any task that invites learners to

bring their own background, interests, or expertise to the task. This might be an activity that provides learners with the option to create their own analogies or metaphors, allowing them to select how they will share their responses to a question (e.g., writing, drawing, speaking, etc.) or letting learners select the context in which a concept is explored (e.g., selection of a specific book or creation of their own problem). These examples have one thing in common: They allow learners to personalize their responses to meet their background, interests, or expertise. As we evaluate mastery, insight into how learners are making meaning of the conceptual understanding, procedural knowledge, and the application of concepts and thinking skills is important.

2. **Clear and modeled expectations**: Do the learners have a clear understanding of what they are supposed to do in this mathematics task? This characteristic refers us to clear learning intentions, success criteria, learning progressions, exemplars, models, worked examples, and rubrics (we will take an additional look at the role of rubrics later in this chapter). Do your learners know what success looks like in this task, or are they blindly hoping to hit the end target that you have in mind for them?

3. **Sense of audience**: Do the learners have a sense that this mathematics work matters to someone other than the teacher and the gradebook? Tasks that have a sense of audience are those tasks that mean something to individuals beyond the teacher, which provides authenticity. Sense of audience can be established by cooperative learning or group work in which individual members have specific roles, as in a jigsaw. Other examples include community-based projects or service projects that use mathematics and contribute to the local, school, or classroom community (e.g., analyzing data from a local stream).

4. **Social interaction**: Do the learners have opportunities to socially interact with their peers? Providing learners with opportunities to talk about mathematics and interact with their peers supports their meaning making and development of conceptual

understanding as well as the application of concepts and thinking skills. In addition, teachers and learners get to hear other students' mathematics thinking.

5. **Emotional safety**: Do the learners feel safe in asking questions or making mistakes? Even though this task seeks to evaluate the level of mastery in mathematics content, learners must still believe that they will learn from mistakes and that errors are welcomed even at this stage of their learning. To be blunt, if learners feel threatened in your mathematics classroom, they will not engage in any mathematics task.

6. **Choice**: Do the learners have choices in how they access the mathematics task? As learners engage with procedures, concepts, or their application, we should offer choices of whom they work with, what materials and manipulatives are available, and what mathematics learning strategies they can use to accomplish the task. In addition, we should offer them multiple ways to show us what they know about the mathematics content.

7. **Novelty**: Does the task require the learners to approach the mathematics from a unique perspective? Examples of this characteristic include engaging scenarios, discrepant events, scientific phenomena demonstrations, or games and puzzles.

8. **Authenticity**: Does the task represent an authentic learning experience, or is the experience sterile and unrealistic (e.g., a worksheet, problem-solving scenario)? We can offer them a scenario around population biology and exponential functions, have them address engineering tasks that model stress and strain using mathematical data, or manipulate earthquake data and determine the mathematical properties of the Richter scale (adapted from Schlechty, 2011).

To evaluate the level of mastery in mathematics learning, teachers must design and implement tasks that provide opportunities for learners to truly demonstrate what they know, how they know it, and why they know it.

Ensuring Tasks Evaluate Mastery

Ms. Norris is preparing to evaluate students' mastery in understanding proportional relationships and how to graphically represent those relationships. Throughout the week, she has used checks for understanding to gather and provide evidence of her learners' progress in the following tasks:

- Defining the rate of change
- Calculating slope
- Identifying independent and dependent variables
- Describing the relationship between independent and dependent variables
- Comparing and contrasting graphs depicting different rates of change
- Comparing and contrasting proportional relationships in authentic contexts

She aligned her checks for understanding with the success criteria and specific learning intentions for each lesson. Ms. Norris's checks for understanding allow her to evaluate her students' progress and adjust their learning experiences, but they do not allow her to determine mastery of the content. Mastery assessments are used more summatively, where checks for understanding are used more formatively. But know that assessments are neither formative or summative by nature; it's all in the use of the tool. And as you will see, the mastery assessments are often used to guide future learning experiences for students. Thus, they are tools that include multiple learning intentions, are typically administered at the unit level, can be used as evidence of longer-term learning, and are often used as the basis for grades. Having said that, if we really believe in mastery, grades would be updated throughout the year as students demonstrate competency of previous content. Thus, the grades for a unit taught in October might be updated when students demonstrate deeper understanding in December. For more information on competency-based or standards-based grading, see Guskey (2014). To design or select a task or possibly a cohesive set of tasks for evaluating mastery, teachers should do these things:

1. Return to the learning intentions and success criteria associated with content for which we are evaluating mastery. What is it that students were supposed to learn?

2. Create or select a challenging mathematics task (or a set of tasks) that requires learners to demonstrate their proficiency for each specific learning intention and success criterion. In other words, can students do what each of the learning intentions says they should be able to do?

3. Identify criteria for mastery and levels of progress toward mastery.

For proportional relationships and how to graphically represent those relationships, Ms. Norris asked her learners to engage in the following three-part task. She instructed her learners to complete as much of the task as possible, flagging areas where they need additional learning.

TASK 1

Write a mathematics story that explains the characteristics of the graph. Make sure your story explains intervals of increase, decrease, or neither. You can make up specific distances since the graph does not give them.

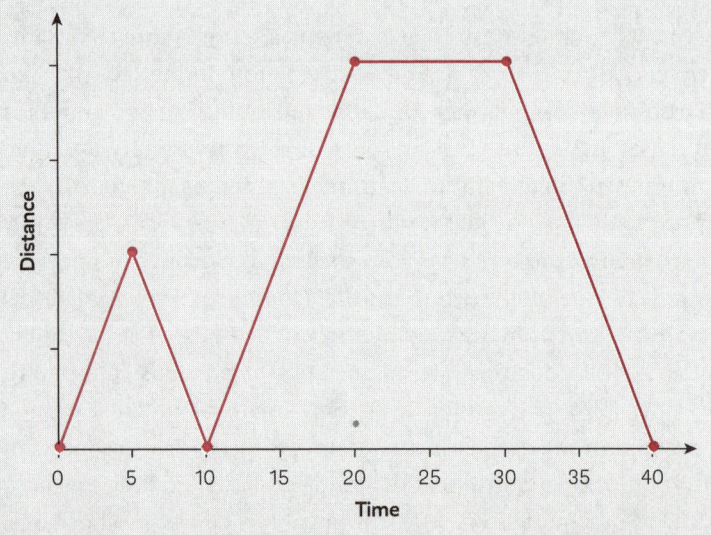

Source: Ashley Norris, Mathematics Teacher, Columbia County Public Schools, Georgia

TASK 2

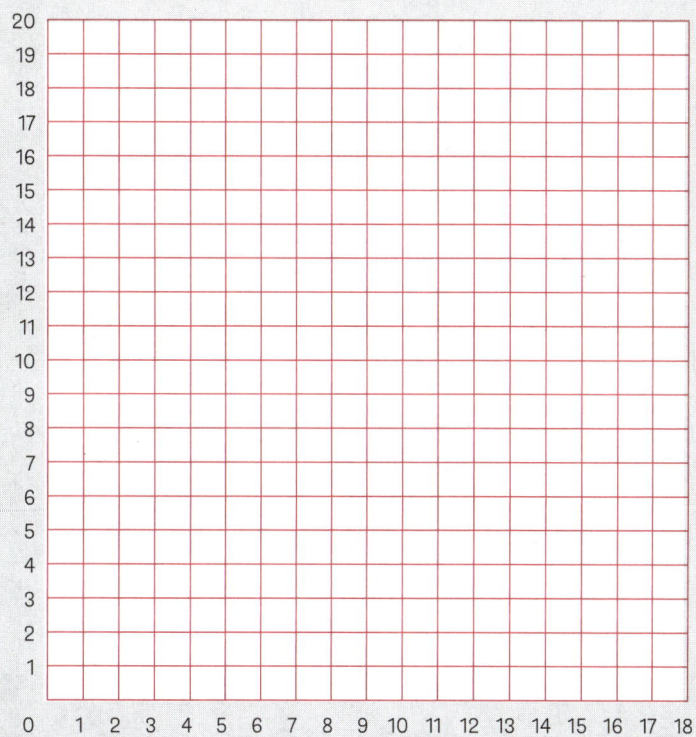

Use the following story to sketch a graph that shows the graphing characteristics given in the story. Be sure to label your axes.

Ben went bushwalking. He started at 8 a.m. and walked seven miles in the first two hours. After resting for 30 minutes, he walked another five miles in one hour. He spent an hour having lunch before beginning the return trip to his starting point. On the return trip, he walked without stopping for three hours.

Source: Ashley Norris, Mathematics Teacher, Columbia County Public Schools, Georgia

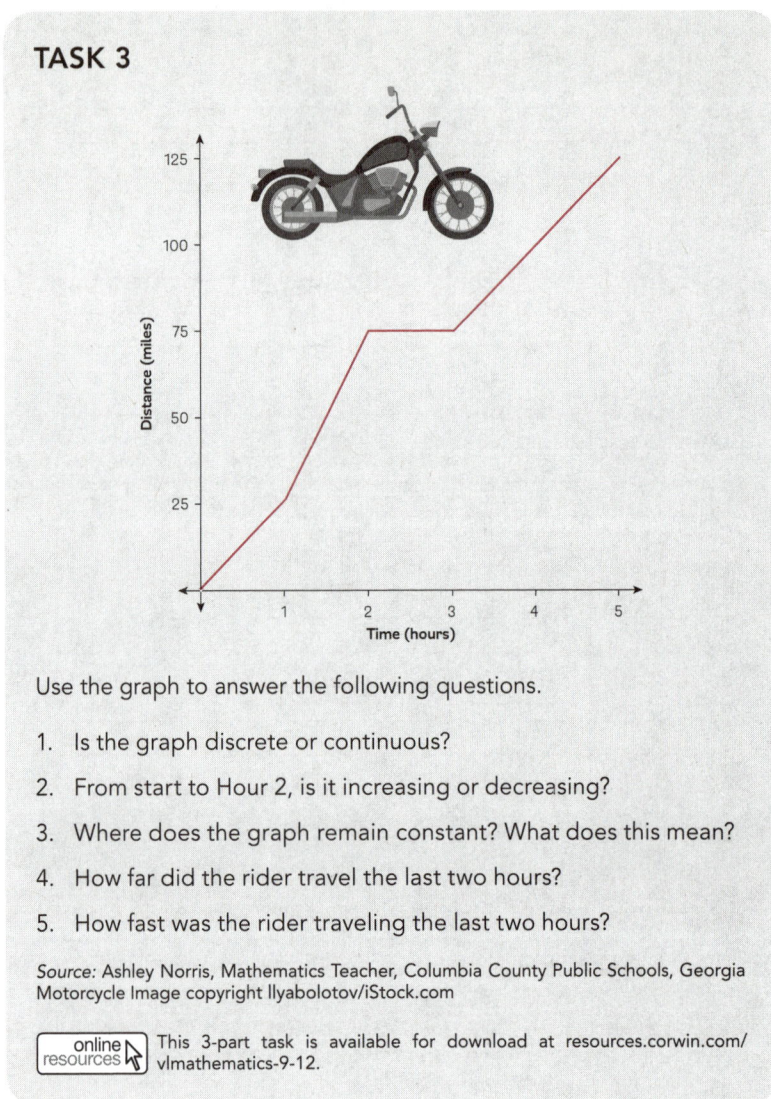

Use the graph to answer the following questions.

1. Is the graph discrete or continuous?
2. From start to Hour 2, is it increasing or decreasing?
3. Where does the graph remain constant? What does this mean?
4. How far did the rider travel the last two hours?
5. How fast was the rider traveling the last two hours?

Source: Ashley Norris, Mathematics Teacher, Columbia County Public Schools, Georgia
Motorcycle Image copyright Ilyabolotov/iStock.com

This 3-part task is available for download at resources.corwin.com/vlmathematics-9-12.

She then developed the tool in Figure 5.7 for evaluating mastery.

Ensuring Tests Evaluate Mastery

Tasks are great, but there will always be mathematics tests. Tests are not only common in the mathematics classroom, but they can be an effective means for determining the mastery of learners. The intention and design of any test determines the usefulness of the evidence generated about learner mastery. Whether multiple-choice or open-ended, tests

EXAMPLE OF PROGRESS TOWARD MASTERY FOR SPECIFIC CONTENT STANDARD

	Learning Intention: I am learning that the unit rate dictates the slope of the line and that different proportional relationships can be represented in different ways.				
	How will I know when I have it? The following mastery levels will let you know how you are progressing toward this learning goal.				
Content Standard	Level 4	Level 3	Level 2	Level 1	Level 0
Graph proportional relationships, interpreting the unit rate as the slope of the graph. Compare two different proportional relationships represented in different ways.	Given a real-world situation, I can identify the rate as the slope, use the rate to write an equation of the form $y = kx$, and graph the relationship. I can also compare two relationships represented differently based on their slope and provide a rationale for my comparison.	Given a real-world situation, I can identify the rate as the slope, use the rate to write an equation of the form $y = kx$, and graph the relationship. I can also compare two relationships based on their slope and provide a rationale for my comparison. I may have made some minor computation errors. I understand the effect rate has on slope, but I struggle with providing a rationale for comparing two functions.	Given the equation $y = kx$, I can identify the slope and graph the function. I can also choose which relationship has the greater rate given different representations.	Given the equation $y = kx$, I can identify the slope and graph the function. I struggle with comparing two functions based on their slope.	I do not understand that unit rate is the slope of a function, and I struggle to graph based on the slope.

Source: Ashley Norris, Mathematics Teacher, Columbia County Public Schools, Georgia

Figure 5.7

 This rubric is available for download at resources.corwin.com/vlmathematics-9-12.

must provide the necessary evidence about student learning so that both the teacher and the learners can make a clear evaluation of their understanding with the specific mathematics content. In designing mathematics tests, we must take into account several aspects of that test if we are to achieve high-quality evaluation of student learning.

Whether in our own classroom or in the classrooms of the teachers featured in this book, a test designed to evaluate learner mastery must

> **The first aspect of a well-designed test is that the test items align with the expectations of the standard and associated learning intentions and success criteria.**

contain questions or items that are consistent with the teaching and learning in that classroom. If the focus in Mr. Wittrock's geometry classroom is on the memorization and execution of formulas (e.g., procedural knowledge in completing the square to find the equation of the circle), then an end-of-unit or standard test cannot contain items that solely focus on conceptual understanding or application to provide a clear evaluation of student mastery (e.g., develop definitions of rotations, reflections, and translation of circles). Likewise, if the focus in Mr. Wittrock's geometry class is on the conceptual understanding of geometric shapes and relationships between the graphical representation of a shape and the associated equation, a test for mastery cannot contain items that only focus on formulas. Therefore, the first aspect of a well-designed test is that the test items align with the expectations of the standard and associated learning intentions and success criteria.

> **Teaching Takeaway**
>
> There should be items on the test that build up to the standard or mastery level.

Test items should provide learners with the opportunity to demonstrate different levels of mastery. In addition to having test items that align with the expectations of the standard, a well-designed test will have questions that fall in the progression toward the standard. For example, in Ms. Rios's algebra class, her students must be able to explain why the x-coordinates of the points where the graphs of the equations $y = f(x)$ and $y = g(x)$ intersect are the solutions of the equation $f(x) = g(x)$. That is the expectation of the standard. The test should include items that ask her learners to find the solution of a system of equations from tables, graphs, and mathematical calculations.

> **Teaching Takeaway**
>
> Students should be familiar with the language of the test.

In addition, the test might ask learners to explain how each approach allows them to locate the solution to a system of equations. Including the components that build up to the standard will allow Ms. Rios to determine how much learners have mastered if they have not fully mastered the standard.

As we reflect on our days as high school mathematics students, we can likely recall instances in which we missed questions on a test because we were not clear on what the questions were asking us to do. When we received feedback on the test, we may have responded to that feedback with, "Oh, that's what you wanted on number 15?" Using consistent language on a test is vital in evaluating the learning of mathematics compared to semantics. As students engage in mathematics learning, we must ensure that the language we expect them to master is the language we use in the learning experiences. For example, if Ms. Shuzhen plans to include questions on her test that use the term *improbability*, then this concept should be introduced during the learning experiences. Likewise, if she is going to use *arrangement* or other terms for a permutation, learners need experiences with that vocabulary or terminology. Using consistent language applies to the cognitive aspects of the questions as well. We must ensure learners know what we mean by *analyze, explain*, or *support your answer*.

Figure 5.8 provides additional guidelines for developing well-designed tests. These checklists help to ensure that our tests provide clear evidence about our learners' mastery in mathematics.

If our ultimate goal is for students to see themselves as their own mathematics teacher, we have to devote time to helping them prepare for tests. Simply telling our learners to "study" is not enough to support them in their journey to becoming assessment-capable visible learners in mathematics. As you can see, we have come full circle in this book. Ensuring that learners have clarity about the learning intentions, success criteria, and their progress toward those items will then help them prepare for this evaluation of mastery. Providing learners with opportunities to connect the learning intentions and success criteria to the type of question they will likely see on a test encourages them to take ownership of their mathematics learning.

Feedback for Mastery

With the learning intention clear, a definition of *success* established, and a challenging mathematics assessment of mastery developed and implemented, the next key item is feedback. The nature of the feedback on learners' performance is an essential and necessary component in the Visible Learning mathematics classroom. Depending on the level of proficiency demonstrated by the learner, specific, constructive, and timely feedback supports learners as they—together with the teacher—evaluate where they are going, how they are going, and where they are going next (see Hattie & Timperley, 2007).

> **Teaching Takeaway**
>
> We must help our learners understand what it means to study for a mathematics test.

> Depending on the level of proficiency demonstrated by the learner, specific, constructive, and timely feedback supports learners as they—together with the teacher—evaluate where they are going, how they are going, and where they are going next.

CHECKLISTS FOR CREATING TESTS THAT ASSESS MASTERY

Short-Answer Items

- ☐ Can the items be answered with a number, symbol, word, or brief phrase?
- ☐ Has textbook language been avoided?
- ☐ Have the items been stated so that only one response is correct?
- ☐ Are the answer blanks equal in length (for fill-in responses)?
- ☐ Are the answer blanks (preferably one per item) at the end of the items, preferably after a question?
- ☐ Are the items free of clues (such as *a* or *an*)?
- ☐ Has the degree of precision been indicated for numerical answers?
- ☐ Have the units been indicated when numerical answers are expressed in units?

Binary (True–False) and Multiple-Binary Items

- ☐ Can each statement be clearly judged true or false with only one concept per statement?
- ☐ Have specific determiners (e.g., *usually*, *always*) been avoided?
- ☐ Have trivial statements been avoided?
- ☐ Have negative statements (especially double negatives) been avoided?
- ☐ Does a superficial analysis suggest a wrong answer?
- ☐ Are opinion statements attributed to some source?
- ☐ Are the true and false items approximately equal in length?
- ☐ Is there approximately an equal number of true and false items?
- ☐ Has a detectable pattern of answers (e.g., *T, F, T, F*) been avoided?

Matching Items

- ☐ Is the material for the two lists homogeneous?
- ☐ Is the list of responses longer or shorter than the list of premises?
- ☐ Are the responses brief and on the right-hand side?
- ☐ Have the responses been placed in alphabetical or numerical order?
- ☐ Do the directions indicate the basis for matching?
- ☐ Do the directions indicate how many times each response may be used?
- ☐ Are all of the matching items on the same page?

Multiple-Choice Items
☐ Does each item stem present a meaningful problem?
☐ Is there too much information in the stem?
☐ Are the item stems free of irrelevant material?
☐ Are the item stems stated in positive terms (if possible)?
☐ If used, has negative wording been given special emphasis (e.g., capitalized)?
☐ Are the distractors brief and free of unnecessary words?
☐ Are the distractors similar in length and form to the answer?
☐ Is there only one correct or clearly best answer?
☐ Are the distractors based on specific misconceptions?
☐ Are the items free of clues that point to the answer?
☐ Are the distractors and answer presented in sensible (e.g., alphabetical, numerical) order?
☐ Has *all of the above* been avoided and *none of the above* used judiciously?
☐ If a stimulus is used, is it necessary for answering the item?
☐ If a stimulus is used, does it require use of skills sought to be assessed?

Source: Adapted from Linn and Gronlund (2000).

Figure 5.8

 These checklists are available for download at resources.corwin.com/vlmathematics-9-12.

Task Feedback

For learners at the earliest level of mastery, task feedback develops student understanding of specific procedures, concepts, and applications. **Task feedback** is corrective, precise, and focused on the accuracy of the learners' responses to the mastery task. For example, Ms. Norris may provide written or verbal feedback that says, "Take a look at your slope calculation for Question 3. The slope of that line is positive, not negative." She may indicate to a learner that a specific question is wrong and needs revisiting before moving on in the learning. On the other hand, she may point out, "You identified correctly the increasing and decreasing intervals for the graph. Now move on to specific distances and speeds."

> **Task feedback** addresses how well the task has been performed—correct or incorrect.

ELEMENTS OF EFFECTIVE FEEDBACK

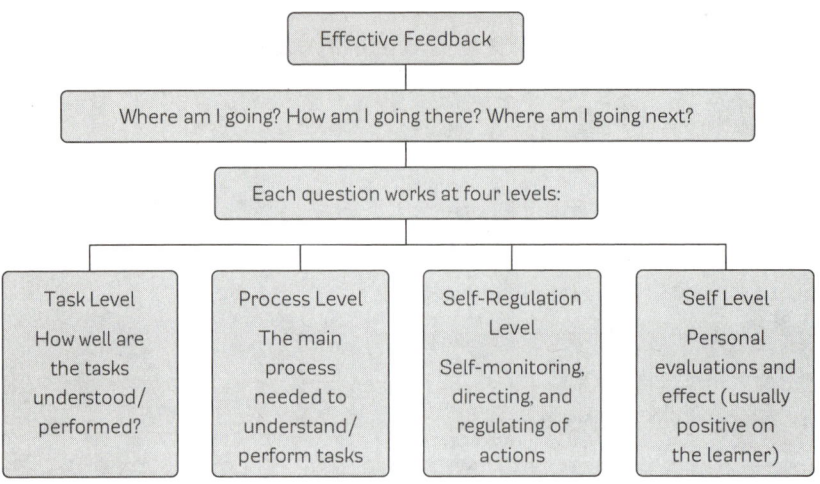

Source: Hattie and Timperley (2007).

Figure 5.9

> **Teaching Takeaway**
>
> Feedback should answer three questions for the learner: Where am I going? How am I going? Where am I going next?

Learners rely on task feedback to add additional structure to their conceptual understanding, procedural knowledge, and application of concepts and thinking skills. This may include examples and non examples, additional learning on procedural steps, and contexts of the task. Ms. Norris may sit down with a learner who has missed a specific question and provide additional examples for finding slope using a graph and using an equation. She may even provide two scenarios and ask the learner to compare and contrast them to clarify understanding. Each learner's successful assimilation of feedback, and thus use of the feedback to decide where to go next, rests solely on whether each learner understands what the feedback means and how he or she can use it to move forward with mathematics learning. Effective feedback (see Figure 5.9) and effective use of that feedback supports this initial learning.

> **Process feedback** focuses on the strategies needed to perform the task.

Process Feedback

As learners begin to develop proficiency with specific content, ideas, and terms, the feedback should increasingly shift to process feedback.

Process feedback is critical as learners explore the *why* and the *how* of specific mathematics content. In their initial assessment of mastery, learners received and assimilated task feedback into their work to develop a deeper understanding of procedures, concepts, and applications. To move learners beyond what is simply right or wrong, example or non example, they must receive and incorporate feedback that focuses on the processes or strategies associated with accomplishing the specific task. Returning to Ms. Norris's classroom, she may not indicate whether a particular response is correct or incorrect, but simply ask, "Why do you believe that this is the interval of increase? What information can you infer from the graph? Do you have any tools that would allow you to verify these assumptions?"

Whether from the teacher or peers, learners should receive feedback on their thinking, not just the accuracy of their response. For example, teachers might engage students in further dialogue about the use of specific strategies to solve a particular problem. Again, this feedback can come from the teacher or their peers. For example, Figure 5.10 shows an example of peer-assisted reflection (PAR). In this scenario, learners complete a draft solution—along with annotations explaining their thought process (not just *what* they did, but *why* they did it)—that is ready to be reviewed by a peer. The peer feedback is offered in two phases. First, peers provide each other written feedback in the form of annotations and a rating toward mastery of each success criterion during a silent review phase. Second, peers discuss the written feedback they provided and ask any clarifying questions they might have about that feedback. The final step for students is to revise their draft solution into a final submission and include a reflection of how their thinking changed throughout this process.

As you may recall from Chapters 3 and 4, Mr. Wittrock uses the PAR system to provide students actionable feedback—often delivered by peers—that they can use to further take control of their own learning and develop into assessment-capable visible learners. The PAR cycle gives students the opportunity to compare and contrast: *This is what I used to be able to do; this is what I can do now. This is how I used to think about this problem; this is how I think about it now. This is what I used to know; this is what I know now.* In addition to these before-and-after snapshots, the feedback and annotation components of PARs can collect much of the connective tissue that bridged students from where they were to where they are. In other words,

> **Teaching Takeaway**
>
> To provide the most amount of feedback to the greatest number of learners as possible, incorporate student-to-student feedback and strategies for student-to-self feedback.

> EFFECT SIZE FOR ASSESSMENT-CAPABLE VISIBLE LEARNERS = **1.33**

PEER-ASSISTED REFLECTION FOR INTRODUCTION TO FUNCTIONS AND INTERVAL NOTATION

Success Criteria

[ ] I can read, understand, and translate between set notation, interval notation, and a number line.

[ ] I can determine whether a relation is also a function.

[ ] I can identify the domain and range of a relation.

[ ] I can categorize a function as one-to-one, onto, both, or neither.

[ ] I can identify whether a function is discrete or continuous.

[ ] I can read, write, and understand function notation: $f(x)$.

[ ] I can evaluate functions for given x-values.

1) The domain of a relation is $\{x | x \geq 0\}$ and the range is $[-4, \infty)$.

   a. Express the domain and range of this relation in set notation, interval notation, and as a number line.

   b. Graph a relation that is **NOT** a function that has this domain and range. Explain why your graph is **NOT** a function.

   c. Graph a relation that is **ALSO** a function that has this domain and range. Explain why your graph **IS** a function.

2) **Claim:** *If a function is onto, then it must be one-to-one as well.* Justify **or** refute this claim using mathematical evidence and logical reasoning.

3) Sara was born exactly two years before Sam.

   a. Write a function that describes Sam's age, given Sara's age.

   b. What do the domain and range represent?

   c. Explain why you think this function is **either** discrete or continuous.

   d. How old was Sam when Sara was ten-and-a-half years old?

Reviewed by: _____

Rate your peer's mastery of the success criterion (this is the *last* thing you do):

[ ] I can read, understand, and translate between set notation, interval notation, and a number line.

0—DO NOT check that box	1—ALMOST check that box	2—CHECK that box
Many mathematical errors and/or incomplete or unclear annotations	Few mathematical errors and/or somewhat incomplete or unclear annotations	No mathematical errors and perfectly complete and clear annotations

[ ] I can determine whether a relation is also a function.

0—DO NOT check that box	1—ALMOST check that box	2—CHECK that box

[ ] I can identify the domain and range of a relation.

0—DO NOT check that box	1—ALMOST check that box	2—CHECK that box

[ ] I can categorize a function as one-to-one, onto, both, or neither.

0—DO NOT check that box	1—ALMOST check that box	2—CHECK that box

[ ] I can identify whether a function is discrete or continuous.

0—DO NOT check that box	1—ALMOST check that box	2—CHECK that box

[ ] I can read, write, and understand function notation: $f(x)$.

0—DO NOT check that box	1—ALMOST check that box	2—CHECK that box

[ ] I can evaluate functions for given x-values.

0—DO NOT check that box	1—ALMOST check that box	2—CHECK that box

DRAFT SOLUTION	ANNOTATIONS (author's and peer's)
FINAL SOLUTION	ANNOTATIONS (author's only)

Figure 5.10

 This peer-assisted reflection task is available for download at resources.corwin.com/vlmathematics-9-12.

not only does growth as an outcome become blatant to students, but students become aware of their own growth process as well.

Process feedback supports making connections, use of multiple strategies, self-explanation, self-monitoring, self-questioning, and critical thinking. For example, Ms. Norris may ask the learner what strategies he or she used in making the decisions about increasing or decreasing intervals and ask if the strategy worked well or if a different strategy may be more efficient. Rather than focusing solely on the correct answer regarding the relationship between an independent and dependent variable, a teacher may ask a student, "What is your explanation for your answer?" The focus of process feedback is on relationships between ideas, students' strategies for evaluating the reasonableness of an answer or solution, explicitly learning from mistakes, and helping the learner identify different strategies for addressing a task.

Like task feedback, process feedback should be specific and constructive and should support learners' pathways toward self-regulation feedback. That is, the feedback should deepen thinking, reasoning, explanations, and connections. Does the teacher prompt learners through strategic questioning related to the learning process? What appears to be wrong, and why? What approach or strategies did the learner use or apply to the task? What is an explanation for the answer, response, or solution? What are the relationships with other parts of the task?

Self-Regulation Feedback

Self-regulation feedback is the learner knowing what to do when she or he approaches a new and different problem, is stuck, or has to apply concepts and thinking in a new way. Learners who have reached a deep level of conceptual understanding and are armed with multiple strategies are equipped to self-regulate as they transfer their learning to more rigorous tasks. Highly proficient learners benefit from self-regulation feedback, although self-regulation feedback is not the only type of feedback that is important to these learners. For example, when teachers detect a misconception that arises or notice a gap in foundational or background learning, learners benefit from both task and process feedback in these situations. However, a majority of the feedback at this part

---

Self-regulation feedback involves the learner self-monitoring his or her own progress toward a specific goal.

EFFECT SIZE FOR SELF-VERBALIZATION AND SELF-QUESTIONING = 0.55 AND EVALUATION AND REFLECTION = 0.75

of the learning process should be self-regulation through metacognition. The teacher's role in the feedback at this level is to ask questions to prompt further metacognition.

Eventually, learners practice metacognition independently through self-verbalization, self-questioning, and self-reflection. Ms. Norris recalls a student working diligently on the first part of the mastery task at the beginning of this chapter. Midway through the task, the learner stopped and began to erase his work, stating, "This answer does not make sense with the picture, and I can't think of a scenario where my answer works. It must be wrong." Learners take personal ownership of their learning, which provides increased motivation and understanding. This has been and continues to be a well-documented finding in education research (e.g., National Research Council, 2000). The ability to think about your own thinking promotes learners' self-awareness, problem solving around the learning task, and understanding of what they need to do to complete the task.

> The ability to think about your own thinking promotes learners' self-awareness, problem solving around the learning task, and understanding of what they need to do to complete the task.

To reiterate, assessment-capable visible learners know what to do when they get stuck, when a new challenge arises, and when their teacher may not be available to help. This is self-regulation feedback.

Conclusion

Over the course of this book, we set out to portray the teaching of mathematics in the Visible Learning classroom. This brought together three elements of mathematics learning (conceptual understanding, procedural knowledge, and the application of concepts and thinking skills) with three phases of learning: surface, deep, and transfer.

Visible mathematics learning is an attainable goal when mathematics teachers *see* learning through the eyes of their students and students *see* themselves as their own mathematics teachers. Together, this type of learning environment develops assessment-capable visible learners. These learners can do the following:

1. Know their current level of mathematics learning
2. Know where they are going next in meeting their current mathematics learning goals and are confident to take on the challenge

3. Select the most appropriate tools, problem-solving approaches, and skills to guide their learning

4. Seek feedback and recognize errors are opportunities to enhance their mathematics learning

5. Monitor their progress and adjust their mathematics learning

6. Recognize their learning and support their peers in their own mathematics learning journey

Teaching mathematics in the Visible Learning classroom demands as much from the teacher as from the learner. We have to create a learning environment that promotes clarity in learning, provides challenging mathematics tasks, checks for understanding, and enables a clear evaluation of mastery. We must know our impact on learning! Yes, there will be days that are better than others. Learning will be stronger with some content than other content. On the most successful days, celebrate the learning that your students do. On days when there is a less-than-desirable impact on student learning, stay focused on the main thing. Keep the main thing *the main thing* by recalibrating our mindframes about teaching and learning in the mathematics classroom. We can do this by asking ourselves these recalibrating questions:

1. What do I want my students to learn?

2. What evidence will convince me that they have learned it?

3. How will I check learners' understanding and progress?

4. What tasks will get my students to mastery?

5. How will I adjust the rigor of the tasks to meet the needs of all learners?

6. What resources do I need?

7. How will I manage the learning?

The classrooms of Ms. Rios, Mr. Wittrock, Ms. Shuzhen, and Ms. Norris do just that daily (see Figures 5.11–5.13 on the opposite page).

MS. RIOS'S VISIBLE LEARNING IN THE MATHEMATICS CLASSROOM

Conceptual Understanding: A system of equations is a set of two or more equations with the same unknowns.

Procedural Knowledge: Graphing linear equations; intersections of equations signify their solutions and are a means of solving systems of equations.

Application: Systems of linear equations to make informed decisions about a real-world problem.

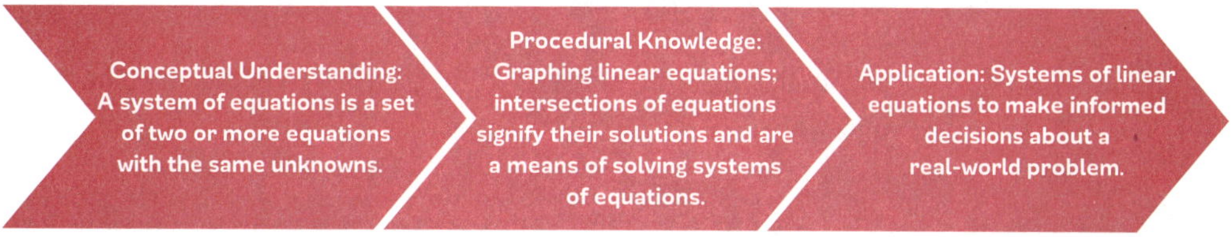

Figure 5.11

MR. WITTROCK'S VISIBLE LEARNING IN THE MATHEMATICS CLASSROOM

Conceptual Understanding: Features of a three-dimensional shape are related to the volume of that shape.

Procedural Knowledge: Relationship between trigonometric functions (sine, cosine, and tangent) and their inverses.

Application: Trigonometric ratios and three-dimensional shapes to measure volumes and surface areas of real-world objects.

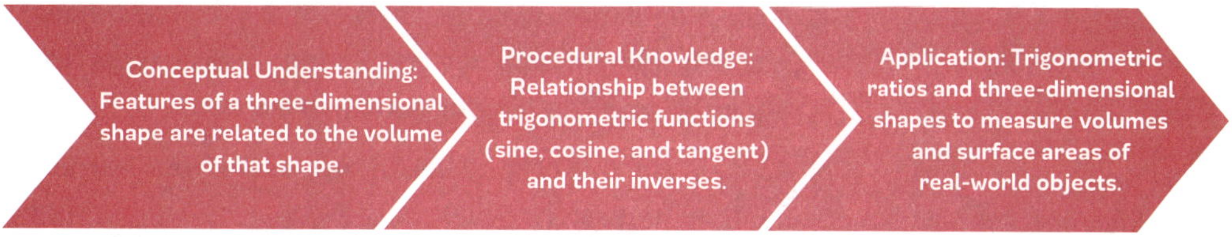

Figure 5.12

MS. SHUZHEN'S VISIBLE LEARNING IN THE MATHEMATICS CLASSROOM

Conceptual Understanding: Specific conditions associated with independent and conditional probability.

Procedural Knowledge: Rules for permutations and combinations are related to the counting principle.

Application: Probability and statistical reasoning to make decisions.

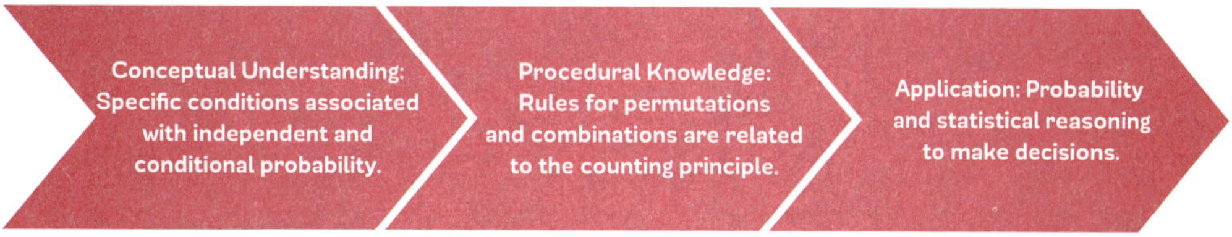

Figure 5.13

Final Reflection

Summarizing the content in this book, reflect on the following questions:

1. Using a specific standard or standards for an upcoming unit, describe what mastery would look like for that content.

2. How will you check for understanding as your learners progress toward mastery? How will these checks be different from your evaluation of their mastery of the standard or standards?

3. How do you plan to evaluate mastery of this particular content—task, test, or both?

4. Reflect on a recent mathematics task in your classroom. Using the definition and characteristics from this chapter, does it "qualify" as a challenging mathematics task?

5. Explain the role of feedback in supporting your learners' journey to mastery.

Appendix A

Effect Sizes

> The Visible Learning research synthesizes findings from **1,800** meta-analyses of **80,000** studies involving **300** million students, into what works best in education.

STUDENT		ES
Prior knowledge and background		
Field independence	●	0.68
Non-standard dialect use	○	−0.29
Piagetian programs	●	1.28
Prior ability	●	0.94
Prior achievement	○	0.55
Relating creativity to achievement	○	0.40
Relations of high school to university achievement	○	0.60
Relations of high school achievement to career performance	●	0.38
Assessment-capable visible learners	●	1.33
Working memory strength	○	0.57
Beliefs, attitudes, and dispositions		
Attitude to content domains	●	0.35
Concentration/persistence/engagement	○	0.56
Grit/incremental vs. entity thinking	●	0.25
Mindfulness	●	0.29
Morning vs. evening		0.12
Perceived task value		0.46
Positive ethnic self-identity		0.12
Positive self-concept	○	0.41
Self-efficacy	●	0.92
Stereotype threat	○	−0.33
Student personality attributes	●	0.26
Motivational approach, orientation		
Achieving motivation and approach	○	0.44
Boredom	○	−0.49
Deep motivation and approach	○	0.69
Depression	○	−0.36
Lack of stress		0.17
Mastery goals		0.06
Motivation	○	0.42
Performance goals	○	−0.01
Reducing anxiety		0.42
Surface motivation and approach	○	−0.11
Physical influences		
ADHD	○	−0.90
ADHD – treatment with drugs	●	0.32
Breastfeeding		0.04
Deafness	○	−0.61
Exercise/relaxation	●	0.26
Gender on achievement		0.08
Lack of illness	●	0.26
Lack of sleep	○	−0.05
Full compared to pre-term/low birth weight	○	0.57
Relative age within a class	○	0.45

CURRICULA		ES
Reading, writing, and the arts		
Comprehensive instructional programs for teachers	●	0.72
Comprehension programs	○	0.47
Drama/arts programs	●	0.38
Exposure to reading	○	0.43
Music programs	●	0.37
Phonics instruction	●	0.70
Repeated reading programs	●	0.75
Second/third chance programs	○	0.53
Sentence combining programs		0.15
Spelling programs	○	0.58
Visual-perception programs	○	0.55
Vocabulary programs	○	0.62
Whole language approach		0.06
Writing programs	○	0.45
Math and sciences		
Manipulative materials on math	●	0.30
Mathematics programs	○	0.59
Science programs	○	0.48
Use of calculators	●	0.27
Other curricula programs		
Bilingual programs	●	0.36
Career interventions	●	0.38
Chess instruction	●	0.34
Conceptual change programs	●	0.99
Creativity programs	○	0.62
Diversity courses		0.09
Extra-curricula programs	●	0.20
Integrated curricula programs	○	0.47
Juvenile delinquent programs		0.12
Motivation/character programs	●	0.34
Outdoor/adventure programs	○	0.43
Perceptual-motor programs		0.08
Play programs	○	0.50
Social skills programs	●	0.39
Tactile stimulation programs	○	0.58

Access the complete and most recent versions of the influence chart at: https://www.visiblelearningplus.com/content/research-john-hattie

APPENDIX A. EFFECT SIZES

HOME	ES
Family structure	
Adopted vs. non-adopted care	● 0.25
Engaged vs. disengaged fathers	● 0.20
Intact (two-parent) families	● 0.23
Other family structure	0.16
Home environment	
Corporal punishment in the home	○ −0.33
Early years' interventions	● 0.44
Home visiting	● 0.29
Moving between schools	○ −0.34
Parental autonomy support	0.15
Parental involvement	● 0.50
Parental military deployment	○ −0.16
Positive family/home dynamics	● 0.52
Television	○ −0.18
Family resources	
Family on welfare/state aid	○ −0.12
Non-immigrant background	0.01
Parental employment	0.03
Socio-economic status	● 0.52

SCHOOL	ES
Leadership	
Collective teacher efficacy	● 1.57
Principals/school leaders	● 0.32
School climate	● 0.32
School resourcing	
External accountability systems	● 0.31
Finances	● 0.21
Types of school	
Charter schools	0.09
Religious schools	● 0.24
Single-sex schools	0.08
Summer school	● 0.23
Summer vacation effect	○ −0.02
School compositional effects	
College halls of residence	0.05
Desegregation	● 0.28
Diverse student body	0.10
Middle schools' interventions	0.08
Out-of-school curricula experiences	● 0.26
School choice programs	0.12
School size (600–900 students at secondary)	● 0.43
Other school factors	
Counseling effects	● 0.35
Generalized school effects	○ 0.48
Modifying school calendars/timetables	0.09
Pre-school programs	● −0.28
Suspension/expelling students	○ −0.20

CLASSROOM	ES
Classroom composition effects	
Detracking	0.09
Mainstreaming/inclusion	● 0.27
Multi-grade/age classes	0.04
Open vs. traditional classrooms	0.01
Reducing class size	● 0.21
Retention (holding students back)	○ −0.32
Small group learning	● 0.47
Tracking/streaming	0.12
Within class grouping	0.18
School curricula for gifted students	
Ability grouping for gifted students	● 0.30
Acceleration programs	● 0.68
Enrichment programs	● 0.53
Classroom influences	
Background music	0.10
Behavioral intervention programs	● 0.62
Classroom management	● 0.35
Cognitive behavioral programs	● 0.29
Decreasing disruptive behavior	● 0.34
Mentoring	0.12
Positive peer influences	● 0.53
Strong classroom cohesion	● 0.44
Students feeling disliked	○ −0.19

TEACHER	ES
Teacher attributes	
Average teacher effects	● 0.32
Teacher clarity	● 0.75
Teacher credibility	● 0.90
Teacher estimates of achievement	● 1.29
Teacher expectations	● 0.43
Teacher personality attributes	● 0.23
Teacher performance pay	0.05
Teacher verbal ability	● 0.22
Teacher-student interactions	
Student rating of quality of teaching	● 0.50
Teachers not labeling students	● 0.61
Teacher-student relationships	● 0.52
Teacher education	
Initial teacher training programs	0.12
Micro-teaching/video review of lessons	● 0.88
Professional development programs	● 0.41
Teacher subject matter knowledge	0.11

Key for rating

● Potential to considerably accelerate student achievement

● Potential to accelerate student achievement

● Likely to have positive impact on student achievement

● Likely to have small positive impact on student achievement

○ Likely to have a negative impact on student achievement

ES Effect size calculated using Cohen's d

corwin.com/visiblelearning

Access the complete and most recent versions of the influence chart at: https://www.visiblelearningplus.com/content/research-john-hattie

The Visible Learning research synthesizes findings from **1,800** meta-analyses of **80,000** studies involving **300** million students, into what works best in education.

TEACHING: Focus on student learning strategies	ES
Strategies emphasizing student meta-cognitive/self-regulated learning	
Elaboration and organization	0.75
Elaborative interrogation	0.42
Evaluation and reflection	0.75
Meta-cognitive strategies	0.60
Help seeking	0.72
Self-regulation strategies	0.52
Self-verbalization and self-questioning	0.55
Strategy monitoring	0.58
Transfer strategies	0.86
Student-focused interventions	
Aptitude/treatment interactions	0.19
Individualized instruction	0.23
Matching style of learning	0.31
Student-centered teaching	0.36
Student control over learning	0.02
Strategies emphasizing student perspectives in learning	
Peer tutoring	0.53
Volunteer tutors	0.26
Learning strategies	
Deliberate practice	0.79
Effort	0.77
Imagery	0.45
Interleaved practice	0.21
Mnemonics	0.76
Note taking	0.50
Outlining and transforming	0.66
Practice testing	0.54
Record keeping	0.52
Rehearsal and memorization	0.73
Spaced vs. mass practice	0.60
Strategy to integrate with prior knowledge	0.93
Study skills	0.46
Summarization	0.79
Teaching test taking and coaching	0.30
Time on task	0.49
Underlining and highlighting	0.50

TEACHING: Focus on teaching/instructional strategies	ES
Strategies emphasizing learning intentions	
Appropriately challenging goals	0.59
Behavioral organizers	0.42
Clear goal intentions	0.48
Cognitive task analysis	1.29
Concept mapping	0.64
Goal commitment	0.40
Learning goals vs. no goals	0.68
Learning hierarchies-based approach	0.19
Planning and prediction	0.76
Setting standards for self-judgement	0.62
Strategies emphasizing success criteria	
Mastery learning	0.57
Worked examples	0.37
Strategies emphasizing feedback	
Classroom discussion	0.82
Different types of testing	0.12
Feedback	0.70
Providing formative evaluation	0.48
Questioning	0.48
Response to intervention	1.29
Teaching/instructional strategies	
Adjunct aids	0.32
Collaborative learning	0.34
Competitive vs. individualistic learning	0.24
Cooperative learning	0.40
Cooperative vs. competitive learning	0.53
Cooperative vs. individualistic learning	0.55
Direct/deliberate instruction	0.60
Discovery-based teaching	0.21
Explicit teaching strategies	0.57
Humor	0.04
Inductive teaching	0.44
Inquiry-based teaching	0.40
Jigsaw method	1.20
Philosophy in schools	0.43
Problem-based learning	0.26
Problem-solving teaching	0.68
Reciprocal teaching	0.74
Scaffolding	0.82
Teaching communication skills and strategies	0.43

Access the complete and most recent versions of the influence chart at: https://www.visiblelearningplus.com/content/research-john-hattie

APPENDIX A. EFFECT SIZES

TEACHING: Focus on implementation method		ES
Implementations using technologies		
Clickers	●	0.22
Gaming/simulations	●	0.35
Information communications technology (ICT)	◐	0.47
Intelligent tutoring systems	◐	0.48
Interactive video methods	◐	0.54
Mobile phones	●	0.37
One-on-one laptops	○	0.16
Online and digital tools	●	0.29
Programmed instruction	●	0.23
Technology in distance education	○	0.01
Technology in mathematics	●	0.33
Technology in other subjects	◐	0.55
Technology in reading/literacy	●	0.29
Technology in science	●	0.23
Technology in small groups	●	0.21
Technology in writing	◐	0.42
Technology with college students	◐	0.42
Technology with elementary students	◐	0.44
Technology with high school students	●	0.30
Technology with learning needs students	◐	0.57
Use of PowerPoint	●	0.26
Visual/audio-visual methods	●	0.22
Web-based learning	○	0.18
Implementations using out-of-school learning		
After-school programs	◐	0.40
Distance education	○	0.13
Home-school programs	○	0.16
Homework	●	0.29
Service learning	◐	0.58
Implementations that emphasize school-wide teaching strategies		
Co- or team teaching	○	0.19
Interventions for students with learning needs	●	0.77
Student support programs – college	●	0.21
Teaching creative thinking	●	0.34
Whole-school improvement programs	●	0.28

Key for rating

● Potential to considerably accelerate student achievement

◐ Potential to accelerate student achievement

● Likely to have positive impact on student achievement

○ Likely to have small positive impact on student achievement

○ Likely to have a negative impact on student achievement

ES Effect size calculated using Cohen's *d*

Access the complete and most recent versions of the influence chart at: https://www.visiblelearningplus.com/content/research-john-hattie

Appendix B

Teaching for Clarity Planning Guide

Teaching for Clarity PLANNING GUIDE

ESTABLISHING PURPOSE

1 **What are the key content standards I will focus on in this lesson?**

2 **What are the learning intentions (the goal and *why* of learning, stated in student-friendly language) I will focus on in this lesson?**

Content:

Language:

Social:

3 **When will I introduce and reinforce the learning intention(s) so that students understand it, see the relevance, connect it to previous learning, and can clearly communicate it themselves?**

SUCCESS CRITERIA

4 **What evidence shows that students have mastered the learning intention(s)? What criteria will I use?**

I can statements:

5 How will I check students' understanding (assess learning) during instruction and make accommodations?

INSTRUCTION

6 What activities and tasks will move students forward in their learning?

7 What resources (materials and sentence frames) are needed?

8 How will I organize and facilitate the learning? What questions will I ask? How will I initiate closure?

 This planning guide is available for download at resources.corwin.com/vlmathematics-9-12.

Appendix C

Learning Intentions and Success Criteria Template

Learning Intentions	Conceptual Understanding	Procedural Knowledge	Application of Concepts and Thinking Skills
Unistructural (one idea)			
Multistructural (many ideas)			
Relational (related ideas)			
Extended abstract (extending ideas)			

Success Criteria	Conceptual Understanding	Procedural Knowledge	Application of Concepts and Thinking Skills
Unistructural (one idea)			
Multistructural (many ideas)			
Relational (related ideas)			
Extended abstract (extending ideas)			

 This template is available for download at resources.corwin.com/vlmathematics-9-12.

Appendix D

A Selection of International Mathematical Practice or Process Standards*

*Note that this is a nonexhaustive list of international mathematical practice/process standards as of June 2016. Because standards are often under review, you can look to your own state or country's individual documents to find the most up-to-date practice/process standards.

USA Common Core State Standards 8 Mathematical Practices[a]	USA Texas Essential Knowledge and Skills TEKS 7 Mathematical Practice Standards[b]	USA Virginia Mathematics 5 Standards of Learning[c]	International Baccalaureate 6 Assessment Objectives[d]	Hong Kong Key Learning Area 7 Generic Skills[e]	Singapore Mathematical Problem-Solving Processes[f]	Australian F-10 Mathematics Curriculum Key Ideas[g]
1. Make sense of problems and persevere in solving them.	A. Apply mathematics to problems arising in everyday life, society, and the workplace.	Mathematical problem solving	Knowledge and understanding	Collaboration skills	Reasoning, communications, and connections	Understanding
2. Reason abstractly and quantitatively.	B. Use a problem-solving model that incorporates analyzing given information, formulating a plan or strategy, determining a solution, justifying the solution, and evaluating the problem-solving process and the reasonableness of the solution.	Mathematical communication	Problem solving	Communication skills	Applications and modeling	Fluency
3. Construct viable arguments and critique the reasoning of others.		Mathematical reasoning	Communication and interpretation	Creativity	Thinking skills and heuristics	Problem solving
		Mathematical connection	Technology	Critical-thinking skills		Reasoning
4. Use appropriate tools strategically.	C. Select tools, including real objects, manipulatives, paper and pencil, and technology as appropriate.	Mathematical representations	Reasoning	Information technology skills		
5. Attend to precision.	D. Communicate mathematical ideas, reasoning, and their implications using multiple representations, including symbols, diagrams, graphs, and language as appropriate.		Inquiry approaches	Numeracy skills		
6. Look for and make use of structure.				Problem-solving skills		

(Continued)

(Continued)

USA Common Core State Standards 8 Mathematical Practices[a]	USA Texas Essential Knowledge and Skills TEKS 7 Mathematical Practice Standards[b]	USA Virginia Mathematics 5 Standards of Learning[c]	International Baccalaureate 6 Assessment Objectives[d]	Hong Kong Key Learning Area 7 Generic Skills[e]	Singapore Mathematical Problem-Solving Processes[f]	Australian F-10 Mathematics Curriculum Key Ideas[g]
7. Look for and express regularity in repeated reasoning.	E. Create and use representations to organize, record, and communicate mathematical ideas.					
8. Model with mathematics.	F. Analyze mathematical relationships to connect and communicate mathematical ideas.					
	G. Display, explain, and justify mathematical ideas and arguments using precise mathematical language in written or oral communication.					

[a] Retrieved June 22, 2016, from http://www.corestandards.org/Math/Practice/.
[b] Retrieved June 22, 2016, from http://ritter.tea.state.tx.us/rules/tac/chapter111/ch111a.html.
[c] Retrieved June 22, 2016, from http://www.doe.virginia.gov/testing/sol/standards_docs/mathematics/2009/stds_math.pdf.
[d] Retrieved June 22, 2016, from http://www.ibo.org/globalassets/publications/recognition/5_mathsl.pdf.
[e] Retrieved June 22, 2016, from http://www.edb.gov.hk/attachment/en/curriculum-development/kla/ma/curr/Math_CAGuide_e_2015.pdf.
[f] Retrieved June 22, 2016, from https://www.moe.gov.sg/docs/default-source/document/education/syllabuses/sciences/files/mathematics-syllabus-(primary-1-to-4).pdf.
[g] Retrieved June 22, 2016, from http://www.australiancurriculum.edu.au/mathematics/curriculum/f-10?layout=1.

Source: Standards for Mathematical Practice, CCSSO.

References

Almarode, J., Fisher, D., Frey, Hattie, J. (2018). *Visible learning for science: What works best to optimize student learning, Grades K–12*. Thousand Oaks, CA: Corwin.Almarode, J. T., & Vandas, K. (in press). *Clarity for learning: Five essential practices for empowering students and teachers*. Thousand Oaks, CA: Corwin.

American Psychological Association, Coalition for Psychology in Schools and Education. (2015). *Top 20 principles from psychology for preK–12 teaching and learning*. Retrieved from http://www.apa.org/ed/schools/cpse/top-twenty-principles.pdf

Antonetti, J., & Garver, J. (2015). *17,000 classroom visits can't be wrong*. Alexandria, VA: Association for Supervision and Curriculum Development.

Biggs, J. B., & Collis, K. F. (1982). *Evaluating the quality of learning: The SOLO taxonomy (structure of the observed learning outcome)*. New York, NY: Academic Press.

Boaler, J. (2015). *What's math got to do with it? How teachers and parents can transform mathematics learning and inspire success* (Rev. ed.). New York, NY: Penguin.

Boaler, J. (2016). *Mathematical mindsets*. New York, NY: Jossey-Bass.

Cole, M., John-Steiner, V., Scribner, S., & Souberman, E. (Eds.). (1978). *Mind in society: The development of higher psychological processes*. L. S. Vygotsky. Oxford, England: Harvard University Press.

Fennell, F. S., Kobett, B. M., & Wray, J. A. (2017). *The formative 5: Everyday assessment techniques for every math classroom*. Thousand Oaks, CA: Corwin.

Fisher, D., & Frey, N. (2008). Homework and the gradual release of responsibility: Making "responsibility" possible. *English Journal, 98*(2), 40–45.

Frayer, D. A., Frederick, W. C., & Klausmeier, H. G. (1969). A schema for testing the level of concept mastery. *Technical Report 16*. Madison: University of Wisconsin.

Frey, N., Hattie, J., & Fisher, D. (2018). *Developing assessment-capable visible learners*. Thousand Oaks, CA: Corwin.

Guskey, T. R. (2014). *On your mark: Challenging the conventions of grading and reporting*. Bloomington, IN: Solution Tree.

Hansen, J., & Thunder, K. (2014). Spanish, mathematics, and English: The languages of success in a grade 8 class. *Voices From the Middle, 21*(3), 18–23.

Hattie, J. (2009). *Visible learning: A synthesis of over 800 meta-analyses relating to achievement*. New York, NY: Routledge.

Hattie, J. (2012). *Visible learning for teachers: Maximizing impact on learning.* New York, NY: Routledge.

Hattie, J., Fisher, D., Frey, N., Gojak, L. M., Moore, S. D., & Mellman, W. (2017). *Visible learning for mathematics: What works best to optimize student learning.* Thousand Oaks, CA: Corwin.

Hattie, J., & Timperley, H. (2007). The power of feedback. *Review of Educational Research, 77*(1), 81–112.

Hattie, J., & Zierer, K. (2018). *Ten mindframes for visible learning: Teaching for success.* New York, NY: Routledge.

Herbel-Eisenmann, B. A., & Breyfogle, M. L. (2005). Questioning our patterns of questioning. *Mathematics Teaching in the Middle School, 10*(9), 484–489.

Hook, P., & Mills, J. (2011). *SOLO taxonomy: A guide for schools. Book 1.* Laughton, United Kingdom: Essential Resources.

Linn, R. L., & Gronlund, N. E. (2000). *Measurement and assessment in teaching* (8th ed.). Upper Saddle River, NJ: Merrill Prentice Hall.

Moss, M. C., & Brookhart, S. M. (2012). *Learning targets: Helping students aim for understanding in today's lesson.* Arlington, VA: ASCD.

National Council of Teachers of Mathematics. (2014). *Principles to actions: Ensuring mathematical success for all.* Reston, VA: Author.

National Governors Association Center for Best Practices, Council of Chief State School Officers. (2010). *Common Core State Standards for Mathematics.* Washington, DC: Author.

National Research Council. (2000). *How people learn: Brain, mind, experience, and school: Expanded edition.* Washington, DC: The National Academies Press. Retrieved from https://doi.org/10.17226/9853

O'Connell, M. J., & Vandas, K. (2015). *Partnering with students: Building ownership of learning.* Thousand Oaks, CA: Corwin.

Reinholz, D. L. (2015). Peer-assisted reflection: A design-based intervention for improving success in calculus. *International Journal of Research in Undergraduate Mathematics Education, 1,* 234–267.

Schlechty, P. C. (2011). *Working on the work: An action plan for teachers, principals, and superintendents.* San Francisco, CA: Jossey-Bass.

Wolf, N. B. (2015). *Modeling with mathematics: Authentic problem solving in middle school.* Portsmouth, NH: Heinemann.

Wood, T. (1998). Alternative patterns of communication in mathematics classes: Funneling or focusing? In H. Steinbring, M. G. Bartolini Bussi, & A. Sierpinska (Eds.), *Language and communication in the mathematics classroom* (pp. 167–178). Reston, VA: NCTM.

Index

Ability grouping
  defined, 5
  effect size for, 5, 111
Ability group with gifted learners, effect size for, 111
Academic diversity, ensuring, 5
Accountability, share-outs and, 168
Agency, developing, 146
Algebraic thinking
  student mastery of, 37
  trigonometry and, 160
Alternate group ranking
  basis of, 112
  example of, 112, 113 (figure)
American Psychological Association, 23
Anchor charts, 132
Antonetti, J., 198
Application tasks
  digital inclinometer, 65–66, 65 (figure), 71, 78, 79
  fruit harvested each year, 101–103, 102 (figure)
  hybrid car prices, 45–46, 51–54, 56–57, 60–62
  incorporating student interest into, 80
  for independent *vs.* conditional probability, 131–132, 137–138
  movie prices, 104 (figure)
  planes leaving the airport, 99–101, 99 (figure)
  rigor adjusted for, 44
  statistical reasoning and probability, 80–81, 85, 90–91
  water tower, 63, 64 (figure), 68–70, 72, 74, 78, 79
  See also Performance-based learning tasks

Assessment
  checks for understanding and, 36
  formative, 84, 195
Assessment-capable visible learners
  achievements of, 11, 13
  application of concepts and thinking skills by, 44
  becoming, 98
  capabilities of, 215–216
  characteristics of, 10–11, 12 (figure)
  clarity in learning and, 19
  developing and supporting, 16
  effect size for, 10, 123, 176, 211
  mastery learning and, 189, 191
  reflection about, 40
  self-regulation feedback and, 215
  well-designed tests and, 207
Australian F-10 Mathematics Curriculum Key Ideas, 231

Balance, in mathematics learning, 2
Barometer of influence
  calculator use, 5–6, 7 (figure)
  classroom discussion, 5, 6 (figure)
  effect sizes and, 4, 5, 5 (figure)
Baseball
  field dimensions and batting statistics in, 80, 85, 90
  streakiness in, 80, 85, 90
Biggs, J. B., 29
Bilingual students, 52
Binary items, on tests assessing mastery, 208 (figure)
Blackjack scenarios, 81, 85, 91

Calculators, effect size for use of, 5–6, 7 (figure), 167, 168
California, math course pathway in, 37

235

Caring, teacher credibility and, 146
"Chalk talk," 4
Checking for Understanding as Procedural Knowledge Deepens (video), 177
Checks for understanding, 8, 14, 35–37
   in evaluating for mastery, 188, 201
   evaluating for mastery differentiated from, 195
   evidence of learners' progress and, 194
   for independent and conditional probability, 132, 136
   in planning for clarity, 8 (figure)
   for probabilities of compound events, 177, 178, 183
   for probability and statistical reasoning, 84, 90
   relationship between learning intentions and, 195 (figure)
   for trigonometric relationships, 167, 172
   for volume of three-dimensional shapes, 116
   See also Learning intentions; Success criteria
Choice boards, for statistical reasoning and probability, 85, 90–91
Chunking, 115
Clarity
   about learning intention, focus and, 7
   on expectations for content standards, 95
   in learning, defined, 19
   in learning, promoting, 216
   mastery learning and, 188
   as prerequisite to learning, 149
   reflection, 40–41
   See also Planning for clarity
Classroom discussion, effect size for, 4–6, 6 (figure), 52, 99, 132, 161
Classrooms. *See* Collaborative classrooms; Visible Learning classrooms
Close reading, structured, 50–51
Cognitive task analysis, effect size for, 98
Cohen's *d*, 3

Collaborative classrooms, co-teaching in, 10, 13–14
Collaborative discussions, 161–163, 173, 174
Collaborative Learning in an Application Task (video), 69
Collaborative planning, 97
Collis, K. F., 29
Combinations. *See* Permutations and combinations
Combinatorial games, 81, 85, 90
Common Core State Standards 8
   Mathematical Practices, 231–232
Communication skills and strategies, effect size for teaching, 48
Competence, teacher credibility and, 146
Competency-based grading, 201
Competitive learning, cooperative learning *vs.*, effect size for, 18, 131
Complexity, difficulty *vs.*, 32
Compound events
   probability of, solving problems with permutations and combinations, 175, 176, 177, 178, 181, 183
   seeing relations and patterns in, 175
Concept mapping, effect size for, 133
Concepts, application of
   deep-phase learning intentions and, 29 (figure)
   deep-phase success criteria for, 30 (figure)
   Learning Intentions and Success Criteria template, 229
   learning tasks and, 34
   mastery learning and, 188, 190
   in mathematics learning, 2, 7, 14, 20, 21
   reflection, 40
   surface-phase learning intentions and, 28 (figure)
   surface-phase success criteria and, 29 (figure)
   teaching for, 43–92
   transfer-phase learning intentions and, 31 (figure)
   transfer-phase success criteria and, 31 (figure)

Conceptual understanding, 44
  deep-phase learning intentions and, 29 (figure)
  deep-phase success criteria for, 30 (figure)
  in dependent and conditional probability, 82
  Learning Intentions and Success Criteria template, 229
  learning tasks and, 34
  mastery learning and, 188, 190
  in mathematics learning, 2, 7, 14, 15, 20
  procedural knowledge and, 155
  reflection, 40
  self-regulation feedback and, 214
  surface learning and, 123
  surface-phase learning intentions and, 28 (figure)
  surface-phase success criteria and, 29 (figure)
  transfer learning and, 118
  transfer-phase learning intentions and, 31 (figure)
  transfer-phase success criteria and, 31 (figure)
Conditional probability
  S-CP.A.5 standard, 128, 129, 135
  tasks for, 131–132, 137–138
Conferences, formative evaluation and, 116, 118
Consolidating Knowledge Through Deliberate Instruction (video), 132
Content learning intentions
  for graphing linear functions, 144, 156
  for hybrid car application task, 49, 58
  for independent vs. conditional probability, 129, 135
  for permutations/combinations related to counting principle, 176, 181
  for probability and statistical reasoning, 82, 88
  question answered by, 48
  for systems of linear equations, 96, 105
  for understanding trigonometric functions, 165, 171
  for volume of three-dimensional shapes, 115, 125
  for water tower task, 68, 69, 76
Content task analysis, effect size for, 47
Conversation roundtable foldable
  creating, 151
  instructions for, 152 (figure), 154
  for systems of equations, 153 (figure)
Cooperative learning
  competitive learning vs., effect size for, 18, 131
  effect size for, 18, 119, 155, 169
Cooperative learning teams, for creating equations and inequalities, 18–19
Cosine, 160, 164, 165, 169, 171
Co-teaching, in collaborative mathematics classrooms, 10, 13–14
Counting principle, 176
Creating Assessment-Capable Visible Learners (video), 11
Critical thinking, building expectation of, 97
Cylinders, prisms and, 117 (figure)

Decibels, 26
Deep learning, 25, 31, 215
  conceptual understanding and, 97
  cyclical nature of learning and, 119
  defined, 22
  for each component of mathematics learning, 30 (figure)
  impact of, on students' learning, 23, 24 (figure)
  mastery learning and, 188
  in mathematics, 22 (figure)
  procedural knowledge and, 142, 175
  in secondary mathematics classroom, 29–30
  SOLO taxonomy and, 26
  statistical reasoning and, 80
  of trigonometric ratios and right triangles, 164
Deliberate instruction
  description of, 33–34
  effect size for, 98, 144
  for independent and conditional probability, 133
  for trigonometric relationships, 163 173, 174

for water tower task, 70
See also Direct instruction
Deliberate practice
  effect size for, 34, 150, 168, 177
  three-dimensional shapes and, 64
Dialogic instruction, effect size for, 98
Dice combinations, in role-playing games, 81, 85, 91
Differentiating Instruction to Support Surface, Deep, and Transfer Learning (video), 150
Difficulty, complexity *vs.*, 32
Digital inclinometer task, 65–66, 65 (figure), 71, 78, 79
Direct instruction
  effect size for, 34, 98, 144
  negative reputation of, 33
  See also Deliberate instruction
Diversity
  academic, 5
  interpersonal skillset and, 111
  of methods, 169
  of student voice, share-outs and, 168, 174
Document camera
  "master notebook" projected under, 144
  PAR assignment projected under, 162
  student work projected under, 162, 163
  triangle from, 164 (figure)

Effect sizes, 2, 13, 219–223
  for ability grouping, 5, 111
  for ability group with gifted learners, 111
  for assessment-capable visible learners, 10, 123, 176, 211
  for calculator use, 5–6, 7 (figure), 167, 168
  for classroom discussion, 4–6, 5, 6 (figure), 52, 99, 132, 161
  for cognitive task analysis, 98
  for concept mapping, 133
  for content task analysis, 47
  for cooperative learning, 18, 119, 155, 169
  for cooperative learning *vs.* competitive learning, 18, 131
  defined, 3
  for deliberate practice, 34, 150, 168, 177
  for dialogic instruction, 98
  for direct/deliberate instruction, 34, 98, 144
  for elaboration and organization, 23, 104
  for engagement, 165
  for evaluation and reflection, 23, 57, 111
  for feedback, 34, 54, 100, 160
  for formative evaluation, 36, 188
  for goals, 82
  for "Goldilocks" challenge, 32
  greater than 0.40, 4
  for homework, 122
  for imagery, 99
  for inductive teaching, 132
  for inquiry-based teaching, 119
  for jigsaw, 178
  for mastery learning, 146, 188
  for metacognition, 23, 50
  for metacognitive strategies, 123
  for motivation, 113
  for note-taking, 144
  for not labeling students, 111
  for prior ability, 22, 64
  for prior achievement, 22, 64, 163
  for problem-based learning, 73
  for questioning, 35, 56, 146
  range of, in Visible Learning research, 4, 5, 5 (figure)
  for reciprocal teaching, 71, 151
  for rehearsal, 149
  for rehearsal and memorization, 176
  for scaffolding, 34, 52, 133, 178
  for self-efficacy, 96, 146
  for self-questioning, 35, 214
  for self-reflection, 214
  for self-verbalization, 35, 214
  for setting standards for self judgement, 83
  for small-group learning, 52, 111
  for spaced practice, 142
  for spaced *vs.* massed practice, 33
  for strategies to integrate with prior knowledge, 163
  for strategy monitoring, 19, 84
  for strategy to integrate with prior knowledge, 54
  for student feelings of efficacy, 66
  for student-teacher relationships, 84, 96, 165
  for summarization, 56, 103

for teacher clarity, 19, 148, 176, 188
for teacher credibility, 96, 146, 155
for teacher expectations, 66
for teaching communication skills and strategies, 48
for teaching strategies, 150, 163
for transfer strategies, 116
for treadmill effect, 3
understanding, 3
for vocabulary instruction, 147
Elaboration and organization, effect size for, 23, 104
Engagement, effect size for, 165
English language learners (ELLs), 52, 60
Equations and inequalities, creating, engaging learners in, 18–19
Equations or formulas, preassessing learners and, 26
Errors, as learning opportunities, 11
Evaluating for Mastery (video), 189
Evaluation
 effect size for, 23
 making mathematics learning visible with, 15
Evaluation and reflection, effect size for, 57, 111
Evidence of learning, generating, importance of, 14
Evidence of progress toward mastery, collecting, 192, 194–200
"Example zero" problem, 167–168
Exit tasks, 83, 84
Exit tickets, 11, 54, 103, 129, 131, 179, 180
Expert groups, 179, 183
Expert modeling via a think-aloud, 101, 103
Explicit teacher modeling, difficulty with, 103
Extending thinking, 29
Extension, 35

Feedback, 39, 70
 adjusting instruction and, 71
 assessment-capable visible mathematics learners and, 11
 checks for understanding and, 36
 effective, 189, 210 (figure)
 effect size for, 34, 54, 100, 160
 instructive and timely, 207
 peer-assisted reflection and, 122, 123
 questions answered by, 210, 210 (figure)
 student-to-self, 211
 student-to-student, 211
 in Visible Learning Classroom, 188
Feedback for mastery, 207, 209–211, 214–215
 process feedback, 210–211, 210 (figure), 214
 self-regulation feedback, 210 (figure), 214–215
 task feedback, 207, 209–210, 210 (figure)
Feedback Through Peer Assisted Reflection (video), 123
Fluency building, 35
Focus/focusing questions, 51, 177, 178
FOIL, 20, 25
Formal assessment, 11
Formative assessment, 84, 195
Formative evaluation
 conferences and, 116, 118
 effective means for, 53
 effect size for, 36, 188
 exit tickets and, 103, 179
 informing instructional decisions and, 161
 student interviews and, 116
 of teaching, 169
 in Visible Learning Classroom, 188
Formulas
 chunking and, 115
 preassessing learners and, 26
Frayer model graphic organizer, 133, 134 (figure), 138
Fruit harvesting application task, 101–103
 graphed system of equations for, 102 (figure)
 modeling strategies and skills, 101–103
Funneling questions, 51

Gallery walks, description of, 54
Garver, J., 198
Gifted learners, effect size for ability group with, 111
Goals, effect size for, 82
"Goldilocks" challenge, effect size for, 32

Grades and grading
  competency-based or standards-based, 201
  evidence used to determine mastery and, 192
Graphic organizers, 132, 133 (figure), 134 (figure), 138
Grouping cards, 131, 137, 138
Guided practice
  "example zero" problem and, 168
  zone of proximal development and, 150
Guiding questions, 84, 130, 178, 182

Hanging sentences, 165
Hashtags, in language and social learning intentions, 165
Hattie, J., 2, 4, 6, 34
Hi-lo strategy, 81, 85, 90
Hinge questions, 84, 86
Homework, effect size of, 122
Hong Kong Key Learning Area 7 Generic Skills, 231
Hybrid car prices application task, 45–46
  collaborative groups and, 52–54, 60
  conclusion questions for, 56–57, 62
  printed scaffolds and, 53, 61
  text-dependent questions in, 51, 61

I can statements
  for graphing linear functions, 144, 157
  for hybrid car pricing task, 46, 50, 59
  for independent vs. conditional probability, 129–130, 136
  for permutations, combinations, and sample spaces, 177, 182
  for probability and statistical reasoning, 83 (figure), 86, 86 (figure), 89
  for solutions to systems of equations, 144, 157
  for systems of linear equations, 97, 100, 104, 106
  for teaching for application of concepts/thinking skills, 43
  for teaching for conceptual understanding, 93
  for teaching procedural knowledge and fluency, 141
  for teaching with clarity in mathematics, 17
  for trigonometric relationships, 166, 172
  for volume of three-dimensional shapes, 115, 120, 125
  for water tower task, 69, 77
I can still statements, 144, 145, 157
Imagery, effect size for, 99
Independent learning, 35
Independent practice, 133
Independent probability
  S-CP.A.5 standard, 128, 129, 135
  tasks for, 131–132, 137–138
Inductive task, 132
Inductive teaching, effect size for, 132
Informal assessment, 11
Inquiry-based teaching
  connections between concepts and ideas and, 122
  effect size for, 119
Instruction. See Direct instruction; Mathematics instruction approaches
Intercepts, 147
International Baccalaureate 6 Assessment Objectives, 231
International Mathematical Practice of Process Standards, selection of, 230–232
Intersection, 147, 148
Interviews, formative assessment and, 84
Inverse cosine, 167, 169
Inverse sine, 167, 169
Inverse tangent, 167
Inverse trigonometric functions, 160, 161, 164, 167, 171, 172, 173, 174

Jigsaw, effect size for, 178
Jigsaw strategy
  defined, 178
  steps in, 179, 183

Labeling students, 111
Language learning intentions
  for communicating solutions to systems of equations, 144, 156
  for computing probabilities of compound events, 176, 181
  for hybrid car application task, 49, 58

for interpreting and explaining
    data, 129, 135
to precisely state each inverse
    trigonometric function,
    165, 171
for probability and statistical
    reasoning, 82, 88
question answered by, 48
for systems of linear equations,
    96, 105
for volume of three-dimensional
    shapes, 115, 125
for water tower task, 68, 69, 76
Language support, 5
Learners
    seeing themselves as their own
        teachers, 2, 10, 19, 80, 98,
        160, 188, 215
    tests and ownership of
        mathematics learning by, 207
    See also Assessment-capable visible
        learners
Learning, 25, 26
    clarity as prerequisite to, 149
    cooperative, effect size for, 119
    cooperative *vs.* competitive, effect
        size for, 131
    cyclical nature of, 119
    documenting, 165
    learners taking personal ownership
        of, 215
    moving learners through phases
        of, 26
    as process, phases in, 21
    right approach at the right time
        for, 7
    self-monitoring of, 177
    small-group, 111
    whole-group, 111
    See also Cooperative learning;
        Deep learning; Formative
        evaluation; Mastery learning;
        Surface learning; Transfer
        learning
Learning events, possible, 53 (figure)
Learning intentions
    checks for understanding related
        to, 195 (figure)
    clear, establishing, 39
    deep-phase, for mathematics
        learning components,
        30 (figure)

defined, 18
example of progress toward
    mastery for specific content
    standard, 192 (figure)
mastery assessments and, 201
planning for clarity, 8 (figure)
recording, 166
surface-phase, for mathematics
    learning components, 28, 28
    (figure)
toward mastery in understanding
    proportional relationships,
    205 (figure)
transfer-phase, for mathematics
    learning components, 31
    (figure)
using to define mastery learning,
    189–190
well-designed tests and, 206, 207
See also Checks for understanding;
    Content learning intentions;
    Language learning intentions;
    Social learning intentions;
    Success criteria
Learning Intentions and Success
    Criteria in an Application Lesson
    (video), 50
Learning Intentions and Success
    Criteria template, 229
Linear functions, 94
    hybrid car prices task and, 45–46, 52
Linked learning experiences, 21
Logarithmic functions
    preassessing learners and, 26
    surface learning level and, 27
Low-floor questions, 116

Making Learning Visible Through
    Learner Notebooks (video), 104
Managing Student-Led Dialogic
    Learning (video), 99
Manipulatives, 46
    cooperative learning teams and, 18
    mastery learning and, 189
Mastery
    checklist for creating/selecting tasks
        for assessment of, 197 (figure)
    checks for understanding *vs.*
        evaluating for, 195
    collecting evidence of progress
        toward, 192, 194–200
    defining, 190

ensuring tasks evaluate, in understanding proportional relationships, 201–204, 202 (figure), 203 (figure), 204 (figure)
establishing expected level of, 190–192
example of defined, for specific content standards, 191 (figure)
example of progress toward, for specific content standard, 192 (figure)
examples of levels of proficiency toward, for specific content standards, 193–194 (figure)
feedback for, 207, 209–211, 210 (figure), 214–215
ingredients for progress toward, 195, 196 (figure)
of standards, demonstrated evidence of, 194
success criteria in evaluating for, 187
tests to ensure evaluation of, 204–207
See also Feedback for mastery
Mastery learning
assessment-capable visible learners and, 189, 191
content standards for, 190, 191 (figure)
defined, 188
effect size for, 146, 188
evaluating, 189
features of, 189
learning intentions used in defining, 189–190
Mastery requires maintenance mantra, 145–146
Matching items, on tests that assess mastery, 208 (figure)
Mathematical Practice of Process Standards, international selection of, 230–232
Mathematical thinking, modeling in teaching, 168
Mathematics
as a process *vs.* as collection of products, 103
surface, deep, and transfer learning in, 22 (figure)

Mathematics instruction approaches, 33–35
deliberate instruction, 33–34
independent, 35
student-led dialogic, 34–35
teacher-led dialogic, 34
Mathematics learning
balance in, 2
effective, components of, 20–21
Mathematics tasks, challenging and rich, 216
authenticity in, 200
characteristics of, 198–200
choice in, 200
clear and modeled expectations in, 199
definitions of, 198
emotional safety and, 200
novelty of, 200
personal response and, 198–199
rote exercise *vs.*, 198
sense of audience in, 199
social interaction and, 199–200
See also Application tasks; Performance-based learning tasks
Mathematics teachers
profiles of, 37–39
seeing learning through the eyes of their students, 2, 19, 160, 215
Mathematics teaching practices, effective, 25 (figure)
Mathematics tests. *See* Tests
Memorization
effect size for rehearsal and, 176
surface learning and, 22
Meta-analysis, defined, 3
Metacognition
building expectation of, 97
effect size for, 23, 50
Metacognitive strategies, effect size for, 123
Mindframes
about teaching, recalibrating, 216
defined, 1
Miniature portfolios, 180
Mini-examples, 149
Mini-lessons, 133
Mistakes, practicing and, 144
Modeling a Close Read (video), 50
Monte Carlo simulations, 81, 85, 90
Monty Hall theory, 81, 85, 90

Motivation, effect size for, 113
Movie prices task, graphed system of equations in context, 104 (figure)
Multiple-choice items, on tests that assess mastery, 209 (figure)
Multiple-choice tests, 205

National Council for Teachers of Mathematics, Effective Teaching Practices outlined by, 23
Near transfer learning, 145. *See also* Transfer learning
Norris, Ashley (fictional teacher), 216
  algebra class, learning intentions and success criteria, 18, 28
  cooperative learning groups, 18–19, 33
  introduction to, 1
  Visible Learning in algebra classroom, 19–20
Norris, Ashley, evaluating for mastery
  on checklist for creating assessment for mastery, 196
  defining mastery, 190
  effective feedback and initial learning, 210
  ensuring tasks evaluate mastery in understanding proportional relationships, 201–204, 202 (figure), 203 (figure), 204 (figure), 205 (figure)
  example of progress toward mastery for specific content standard, 192 (figure)
  formative evaluation, 188
  learning intentions, 18, 189
  mastery tasks developed by, 196, 198
  process feedback, 211, 214
  self-regulation feedback, 215
  success criteria, 18
Notebooks, learner, 104
Note-taking, effect size for, 144
Not labeling students, effect size for, 111
"Numbered Heads Together" strategy, 168

Observation recording tool, 54, 55 (figure), 56
Observations, 54
  formative assessment and, 84
  formative evaluations and, 53

Observe-Reflect-Question graphic organizer, 132, 133 (figure)
Open-ended questions, 146
Open-ended tests, 205

PAR. *See* Peer-assisted reflection (PAR)
PBL. *See* Problem-based learning (PBL)
Peer-assisted learning, 34–35
Peer-assisted reflection (PAR), 119, 120–121 (figure), 123, 126, 127
  actionable feedback and, 123
  benefits of, 122–123
  defined, 122
  draft solution example, 211
  for introduction to functions and interval notation, 212–213 (figure)
  meaning of, 161
  risk-taking and, 122–123
  on trigonometric functions, 160, 170, 173, 174
Peer groups, classroom discussion and, 4
PEMDAS, 20, 25
Performance-based learning tasks
  checklist for creating/selecting, in assessing mastery, 197 (figure)
  ensuring evaluation of mastery with, 201–204, 202 (figure), 203 (figure), 204 (figure)
  poorly designed, 196–197
  in progress toward mastery, 195, 196 (figure)
  See also Application tasks
Permutations and combinations, 175
  I can statements related to, 182
  involving probability of compound events with, problem-solving for, 175, 176, 177, 178, 181, 183
  relation to counting principle, 176
  S-CP.B.9 content standard and, 176
pH scale, 26
Planes leaving the airport task, graphed system of equations in context, 99, 99 (figure)
Planning for clarity
  establishing purpose, 8 (figure)
  instruction, 9 (figure)
  success criteria, 9 (figure)
  See also Teaching for clarity planning guide

Point-slope form, 147
Portfolios, miniature, 180
Preassessing learners, 26
Prezi, blackjack scenarios and, 86
Principles to Actions: Ensuring Mathematical Success for All (National Council for Teachers of Mathematics), 23
Prior ability, effect size for, 22, 64
Prior achievement, effect size for, 22, 64, 163
Prior knowledge of learners
  activating, new learning and, 146
  effect size of strategy to integrate with, 54
  identifying, 26
Prism and Cylinder Lab, 116, 117 (figure), 126, 127
Prisms, cylinders and, 117 (figure)
Probability, choice boards and concepts/skills related to, 80–81
Probing questions, 130
Problem-based learning (PBL)
  effect size for, 73
  water tower task and, 73
Problem solving
  mastery learning and, 189
  procedural knowledge in, 142
  trigonometric functions and, 161–163
Procedural knowledge, 44
  conceptual understanding and, 155
  deep-phase learning intentions and, 29 (figure)
  deep-phase success criteria for, 30 (figure)
  defined, 142
  dependent and conditional probability and, 82
  Learning Intentions and Success Criteria template, 229
  learning tasks and, 34
  mastery learning and, 188, 190
  in mathematics learning, 2, 7, 14, 15, 20, 21
  reflection, 40, 185
  surface-phase learning intentions and, 28 (figure)
  surface-phase success criteria and, 29 (figure)
  transfer-phase learning intentions and, 31 (figure)
  transfer-phase success criteria and, 31 (figure)
Process feedback, 210–211, 210 (figure), 214
Productive failure, 52, 53 (figure)
Productive success, 52, 53 (figure)
Proportional relationships, 189
  ensuring tasks evaluate mastery in, 201–204, 202 (figure), 203 (figure), 204 (figure)
  example of progress toward mastery in understanding of, 205 (figure)
Pyramid Sand Lab, 118–119, 118 (figure), 126, 127
Pythagorean theorem, 164, 169, 170, 171
Pythagorean triples, 164, 171

Questions/questioning
  considering types of, 100
  effect size for, 35, 56, 146
  focus/focusing, 51, 177, 178
  funneling, 51
  guiding, 84, 130, 178, 182
  hinge, 84, 86
  low-floor, 116
  open-ended, 146
  probing, 130
  recalibrating, 216
  targeted, 150
  text-dependent, 51

Radian measure of an angle, success criteria for lesson on, 32–33
Recalibrating questions, 216
Reciprocal teaching
  effect size for, 71, 151
  review, 163
Rectangular prisms, 117 (figure)
Reflection
  on development of procedural knowledge, 185
  effect size for, 23
  final, 218
  on teaching for application of concepts/thinking skills, 91
  on teaching for conceptual understanding, 139

on teaching mathematics in Visible Learning classroom, 40–41
See also Evaluation and reflection; Peer-assisted reflection (PAR)
Rehearsal, effect size for, 149
Rehearsal and memorization, effect size for, 176
Resources
  for algebra class, 18
  for conversation roundtable foldables, 151, 154, 159
  for digital inclinometer task, 65–66, 78
  for hybrid car prices task, 61
  for independent *vs.* conditional probability, 131, 138
  for probabilities of compound events, 179, 184
  for statistical reasoning and probability, 85, 91
  for systems of linear equations, 107
  for trigonometric relationships, 167, 169, 173
  for volume of three-dimensional shapes, 126
Richter Scale, 26
Right triangles, trigonometric relationships and, 160–163, 166–169, 171, 172, 174
Rigor
  adjusting, for application tasks, 44
  defined, 32
  maximizing, 46, 51
Rios, Maria (fictional teacher), 94, 188, 216
  assessments of mastery, 189
  checks for understanding, 195
  introduction to, 1
  profile of, 37
  rigor adjusted for application task, 44
  well-designed tests and, 206
Rios, Maria, teaching for application of concepts/thinking skills, 44–45, 217
  application task: hybrid car prices, 45–46
  conclusion questions, 56
  content standards, 47–48, 58
  focusing and funneling questions, 51

  guiding and scaffolding student thinking, 50–54
  I can statements and success criteria, 46, 59
  instruction, 60
  learning intentions and success criteria, 48–50, 56
  process questions, 56–57
  reflection questions, 57, 92
  Standards for Mathematical Practice, 48, 58
  and systems of linear equations, 44–54, 56–63
  Teaching for Clarity at the Close, 54, 56–57
  teaching for clarity planning guide, 58–63
  what she wants students to learn, 47–48
Rios, Maria, teaching for conceptual understanding, 94–110, 217
  collaborative task, 107
  content standards, 95, 105
  deliberate instruction, 98, 107
  example of defined mastery for specific content standard, 191 (figure)
  expert modeling via a think-aloud strategy, 101–103
  fruit harvested each year task, 101–103, 102 (figure)
  I can statements and success criteria, 96–97, 100, 104, 106
  instruction, 96–97, 107
  learning intentions and success criteria, 95–98
  levels of proficiency toward mastery for specific content standards, examples of, 193 (figure)
  modeling strategies and skills, 101–104
  movie prices task, 104 (figure)
  planes leaving the airport task, 99–101, 99 (figure)
  promoting, instructional approaches for, 98–101
  reflection, 139
  Standards for Mathematical Practice, 95, 105
  and systems of linear equations, 94–110

Teaching for Clarity at the Close, 104
teaching for clarity planning guide, 105–110
think-pair-share deliberate instruction combo, 98, 107
think-pair-share strategy, 98–101, 103, 108
what she wants students to learn, 95
Rios, Maria, teaching for procedural knowledge and fluency, 142–159, 217
   collaboration with more capable peers, 151
   content standards, 143, 156
   conversation roundtable foldable, 151, 158
   conversation roundtable foldable for systems of equations, 153 (figure)
   conversation roundtable foldable instructions, 152 (figure), 154
   guiding and scaffolding student thinking, 149–150, 158
   I can statements and success criteria, 144–145, 157
   instruction, 150–151, 154–155, 158–159
   instructional approaches promoting procedural knowledge, 150–151, 154–155
   learning intentions and success criteria, 143–146, 156
   modeling strategies and skills, 146–149
   sharing real stories, 145–146
   solution to system of linear equations with single solution, 147–148, 148 (figure)
   spaced practice, 142
   Standards for Mathematical Practice, 143, 156
   and systems of linear equations, 142–159
   Teaching for Clarity at the Close, 155
   teaching for clarity planning guide, 156–159
   what she wants students to learn, 143
Rote exercise, challenging, rich mathematics task *vs.*, 198

Sample spaces, 178, 179, 182
Scaffolding
   complexity of inferencing mathematics from a situation, 52
   effect size for, 34, 52, 133, 178
   jigsaw process and, 179
   See also Guiding and scaffolding student thinking under individual teachers
Self-assessment, building expectation of, 97
Self-awareness, promoting, 215
Self-efficacy
   developing, 100
   effect size for, 96, 146
Self-judgement standards, effect size for setting, 83
Self-questioning, effect size for, 35, 214
Self-reflection, effect size for, 214
Self-regulation feedback, 214–215
   assessment-capable visible learners and, 215
   defined, 214
   teacher's role in, 215
Self-verbalization, effect size for, 35, 214
Setting the Stage for Conceptual Learning (video), 97
Share-outs, 168, 174
Short-answer items, on tests that assess mastery, 208 (figure)
"Show-me" moments, formative assessment and, 84
Shuzhen, Li (fictional teacher), 94, 188, 216
   assessments of mastery, 189
   checks for understanding, 195
   introduction to, 1
   profile of, 38–39
   rigor adjusted for application task, 44
   well-designed tests, 207
Shuzhen, Li, and independent *vs.* conditional probability, 128–139, 217
   content standards, 129, 135
   Frayer model graphic organizer, 133, 134 (figure), 138
   guiding and scaffolding learners' thinking, 130, 136
   I can statements and success criteria, 129–130, 136

instruction, 131–132, 137–138
instructional approaches that promote conceptual understanding, 131–132
learning intentions and success criteria, 129, 136
modeling strategies and skills, 130–131
Observe-Reflect-Question graphic organizer, 132, 133 (figure)
reflection on teaching for conceptual understanding, 139
surface learning building, 128
Teaching for Clarity at the Close, 133
teaching for clarity planning guide, 135–138
teaching for conceptual understanding, 128–139
what she wants students to learn, 128
Shuzhen, Li, and probabilities of compound events, 175–184
content standards, 176, 181
I can statements and success criteria, 177, 182
instruction, 178–179, 183
instructional approaches that promote procedural knowledge, 178–179
jigsaw strategy, 178–179, 183
learning intentions and success criteria, 176–177, 181
modeling strategies and skills, 177–178
Standards for Mathematical Practice, 176, 181
Teaching for Clarity at the Close, 180
teaching for clarity planning guide, 181–184
teaching for procedural knowledge and fluency, 175–184
what she wants students to learn, 175–176
Shuzhen, Li, and statistical reasoning, 80–92, 217
checks for understanding, 84, 90
choice boards for problem-solving scenarios, 85
content standards, 81, 88
example of defined mastery for specific content standard, 191 (figure)
guiding questions, 84
hinge questions, 86
I can statements and success criteria, 83 (figure), 86, 89
instruction, 84–85, 90–91
learning intentions and success criteria, 82–83
levels of proficiency toward mastery for specific content standards, examples of, 193–194 (figure)
modeling strategies and skills, 83–87
reflection, 92
remediation needs, 84
Standards for Mathematical Practice, 81, 83, 88
Teaching for Clarity at the Close, 87
teaching for clarity planning guide, 88–92
teaching for the application of concepts/thinking skills, 80–92
what she wants students to learn, 80–82
Sine, 160, 164, 165, 169, 171
Singapore Mathematical Problem-Solving Processes, 231
Small-group learning
  effect size for, 52, 111
  implementation and recording tool for observations, 54, 55 (figure)
Social learning intentions
  to advance thinking about probability, 129, 135
  "grammar police" and language regarding inverse trigonometric functions, 165, 171
  for hybrid car application task, 49, 58
  for probability and statistical reasoning, 82, 88
  probing questions for advancing thinking about probability, 176, 181
  question answered by, 49
  for systems of linear equations, 96, 105

to transition during conversation roundtable, 144, 156
for volume of three-dimensional shapes, 115, 125
for water tower task, 68, 69, 76
SOLO (structure of observed learning outcomes) Taxonomy, 26 (figure)
    deep learning in, 26, 29
    defined, 26
    mastery learning and, 191
    prestructural level of, 26
    surface learning in, 26, 27
    transfer learning in, 26, 30
Sorting task cards, 131, 138
Spaced practice, 123
    defined, 142
    effect size for, 142
Spaced *vs.* massed practice, effect size for, 33
Spiral review, 35
Standardized tests, well-designed, 195
Standards-based grading, 201
Statistical reasoning, choice boards and concepts/skills related to, 80–81
Strategies to integrate with prior knowledge, effect size for, 163
Strategy monitoring, effect size for, 19, 84
Student feelings of efficacy, effect size for, 66
Student interviews, formative evaluations and, 53, 116
Student-led dialogic, 34–35, 130
Student-teacher relationship
    effect size for, 84, 96, 165
    investing in, 98
Student-to-self feedback, 211
Student-to-student feedback, 211
Success criteria
    aligning checks for understanding with, 201
    breaking down method for, 97
    clear, 37, 39
    co-constructing, 82–83, 89
    deep-phase, for mathematics learning components, 30 (figure)
    defined, 18
    effect size for, 165
    for evaluating for mastery, 187
    for learning, planning for clarity, 8 (figure), 9 (figure)
    learning intentions/checks for understanding relationship and, 195 (figure)
    in PAR for introduction to functions and interval notation, 212 (figure)
    for radian measure of an angle, 32–33
    surface-phase, for mathematics learning components, 29 (figure)
    for teaching for application of concepts/thinking skills, 43
    for teaching for conceptual understanding, 93
    for teaching procedural knowledge and fluency, 141
    for teaching with clarity in mathematics, 17
    transfer-phase, for mathematics learning components, 31 (figure)
    well-designed tests and, 206, 207
    See also Checks for understanding; I can statements; Learning intentions; Learning Intentions and Success Criteria template
Summarization, effect size for, 56, 103
Summative assessment, 11
Supporting Learners' Extension Into Transfer (video), 179
Supporting Surface Learning Needs With a Peer Tutor (video), 161
Surface learning, 25, 31, 215
    conceptual understanding and, 123
    cyclical nature of learning and, 119
    defined, 21
    fluency building and, 35
    impact of, on students' learning, 23, 24 (figure)
    for inverse trigonometric functions, 164, 168
    jigsaw strategy and, 178
    learning intentions for each component of mathematics learning, 28, 28 (figure)

mastery learning and, 188
procedural knowledge and, 142
in secondary mathematics
classroom, 27–28
SOLO taxonomy and, 26
statistical reasoning and, 80
success criteria for each
component of mathematics
learning, 29 (figure)
Symbol partners, 131, 133

Tangent, 160, 164, 165, 169, 171
Tangent ratios, 160
Targeted questioning, 150
Task feedback, 207–208,
210 (figure)
Tasks
design of, 32, 39
differentiating, for complexity and
difficulty, 31–33
wide range of, 33
See also Application tasks
Teacher clarity, effect size for, 19,
148, 176, 188. *See also* Teaching
for clarity planning guide
Teacher credibility
constructs of, 146
effect size for, 96, 146, 155
Teacher expectations, effect size
for, 66
Teacher-led dialogic, 34, 130
Teachers. *See* Mathematics teachers
Teaching
formative evaluation of, 169
inductive, 132
inquiry-based, effect size for, 119
modeling mathematical thinking
in, 168
recalibrating our mindframes
about, 216
Teaching for clarity planning guide
how to use, 8–9
template, 224–228
*See also Teaching for clarity planning
guide under each individual
teacher*
Teaching mathematics
what works best in, 2–6
what works best when, 6–7, 10
Teaching strategies, effect size for,
150, 163
Technology, access to, 46

TEKS (Texas Essential Knowledge and
Skills)
Geometry Standards, 66–67, 75,
113–114, 164
Mathematical Process Standards,
67–68, 76, 114, 165
7 Mathematical Practice Standards,
231–232
Tests
checklists for assessing mastery
with, 207, 208–209 (figure)
consistent language of, student
familiarity with, 206–207
ensuring mastery evaluated in,
204–207
helping students prepare for, 207
multiple-choice, 205
open-ended, 205
well-designed, 205–206
Text-dependent questioning, 51
Theoretical solutions, 81, 85, 90
Think-aloud approach, 98, 101, 103
Thinking
extending, 29
grounding, metacognitive process
and, 50
Thinking skills
deep-phase learning and, 29 (figure)
deep-phase success criteria for, 30
(figure)
Learning Intentions and Success
Criteria template, 229
mastery learning and, 188
in mathematics learning, 2, 7, 14, 20
reflection, 40
surface-phase learning intentions
and, 28 (figure)
surface-phase success criteria and,
29 (figure)
teaching for, 43–92
transfer-phase learning intentions
and, 31 (figure)
transfer-phase success criteria and,
31 (figure)
Think-pair-share/deliberate
instruction combo, 98, 107
Think-pair-share protocol, 98, 103,
108, 129
Three-dimensional shapes
digital inclinometer made with
personal device task, 65–66,
65 (figure), 71, 78, 79

water tower as composite of semi-sphere, cylinder, and cone, 64 (figure)
water tower task, 63, 68–70, 72, 74, 78, 79
See also Volume of three-dimensional shapes
Transfer learning, 25, 31, 215
  conceptual understanding and, 118
  cyclical nature of learning and, 119
  defined, 23
  impact of, on students' learning, 23, 24 (figure)
  learning intentions for mathematics learning components, 31 (figure)
  mastery learning and, 188
  in mathematics, 22 (figure)
  procedural knowledge and, 142
  in secondary mathematics classroom, 30–31
  SOLO taxonomy and, 26
  success criteria for mathematics learning components, 31 (figure)
Transfer strategies, effect size for, 116
Treadmill effect, 3
Triangle, area of
  deep learning and, 29
  surface learning and, 27
Triangles
  knowledge of degrees in, 169, 170
  problems involving, examples of, 27–28, 27 (figure)
  See also Right triangles
Triangular prisms, 117 (figure)
Trigonometric functions, inverse, 160, 161, 164, 167, 171, 172, 173, 174
Trigonometric ratios, 63, 64
Trigonometry
  algebraic thinking and, 160
  first exposure to concepts of, 63
  moving beyond surface understanding of, 111
Trustworthiness, teacher credibility and, 146

UN-cosine, 166
Unproductive failure, 52, 53 (figure)
Unproductive success, 52, 53 (figure)
UN-sine, 166
UN-tangent, 166

Variant shell game, 81, 85, 91
Virginia Mathematics 5 Standards of Learning, 231
Visible Learning
  in algebra class, implementing, 19–20
  clarity about learning intention in, 7
  continual evaluation in, 6
  database, composition of, 3
  description of, 1
  resource investment and, 3–4
  students seen as own teachers with, 2, 10, 19, 98, 160, 188, 215
  summary of, in mathematics classroom, 217 (figure)
  sustaining in mathematics classroom, 2
  Visible Teaching compared with, 20 (figure)
  what works best, 2–6
  See also Visible Learning classrooms
Visible Learning (Hattie), 2
Visible Learning classrooms, 215
  culture shock in, 97
  effective feedback in, 189
  formative evaluation and feedback in, 188
  See also Concepts, application of; Conceptual understanding; Procedural knowledge; Thinking skills
Visible Learning for Mathematics (Hattie, et al.), 13, 23, 32
Visible Learning research findings
  key findings, 23
  scope of, 220
  on students' learning, 6
Visible Teaching
  teachers learning through eyes of their students with, 2, 19, 160, 215
  Visible Learning compared with, 20 (figure)
Vocabulary in mathematics
  building, 147
  progress toward mastery for specific content standard, example of, 192 (figure)
  specific, for mastery learning, 190

Vocabulary instruction, effect size for, 147
Volume of three-dimensional shapes
   peer-assisted reflection (PAR), 120–121 (figure), 126
   Prism and Cylinder Lab, 116, 117 (figure), 126
   Pyramid Sand Lab, 118–119, 118 (figure), 126
Vygotsky, L., 150, 151

Water tower task, 63, 64 (figure), 68–70, 72, 74, 78, 79
   deliberate practice and, 64
   problem-based learning and, 73
   reiterative questioning and, 72
   sentence frames for, 73, 74 (figure)
What Does Teacher Clarity Mean in High School Mathematics? (video), 20
What Is Visible Learning for Mathematics? (video), 3
Whole-group discussions, 132
Whole-group learning, importance of, 111
Wittrock, Benjamin (fictional teacher), 94, 188, 216
   assessments of mastery, 189
   checks for understanding, 195
   introduction to, 1
   profile of, 38
   rigor adjusted for application task, 44
   well-designed tests and, 206
Wittrock, Benjamin, and three-dimensional shapes, 63–79, 217
   deliberate practice, 64
   digital inclinometer application task, 65–66, 65 (figure), 71, 78, 79
   guiding and scaffolding student thinking, 70–71
   I can statements and success criteria, 69, 77
   instruction, 77–78
   learning intentions and success criteria, 68–69
   modeling strategies and skills, 71–72
   reflection, 92
   Teaching for Clarity at the Close, 73
   teaching for clarity planning guide, 75–79
   teaching for the application of concepts/thinking skills, 63–79
   TEKS Geometry Standards, 66–67, 75
   TEKS Mathematical Process Standards, 67–68, 76
   water tower task, 63, 68–70, 72, 74, 78, 79
   what he wants students to learn, 66–68
Wittrock, Benjamin, and trigonometric relationships, 160–174, 217
   collaborative discussions, 161–163, 173, 174
   example of defined mastery for specific content standard, 191 (figure)
   I can statements and success criteria, 160, 166, 172
   instruction, 166–169, 173
   instructional approaches that promote procedural knowledge, 166–169
   learning intentions and success criteria, 165–166, 171
   levels of proficiency toward mastery for specific content standards, examples of, 193–194 (figure)
   peer-assisted reflection (PAR) cycle, 160, 170, 173, 174, 211
   peers' mastery mini rubric, 160–161, 160 (figure)
   share-out, 163, 168, 174
   Teaching for Clarity at the Close, 169–170
   teaching for clarity planning guide, 171–174
   teaching for procedural knowledge and fluency, 160–174
   TEKS geometry standards, 164, 171
   TEKS Mathematical Process Standards, 165, 171
   triangle from Mr. Wittrock's document camera, 164 (figure)
   what he wants students to learn, 164

Wittrock, Benjamin, and volume of three-dimensional shapes, 111–127
   alternate group ranking, 112, 113 (figure)
   content standards, 113–114, 124
   I can statements and success criteria, 115, 120 (figure), 125
   instruction, 113, 116, 118–119, 126
   instructional approaches that promote conceptual understanding, 116, 118–119
   learning intentions and success criteria, 114–116, 125
   new learning groups, 111
   peer-assisted reflection (PAR), 119, 120–121 (figure), 122, 123, 126, 127
   Prism and Cylinder Lab, 116, 117 (figure), 127
   pyramids and cones, 116, 118–119
   Pyramid Sand Lab, 118–119, 118 (figure), 127
   reflection on teaching for conceptual understanding, 139
   Teaching for Clarity at the Close, 119, 122–123
   teaching for conceptual understanding, 111–127
   TEKS Geometry Standards, 113–114, 124
   TEKS Mathematical Process Standards, 114, 124
   what he wants his students to learn, 112–114
Worked examples, 46

Zone of proximal development, defined, 150

All students should have the opportunity to be successfu[l]

Visible Learning^{plus} is based on one simple belief: Every student should experience at least one year's growth over the course of one school year. Visible Learning^{plus} translates the groundbreaking Visible Learning research by professor John Hattie into a practical model of inquiry and evaluation. Bring Visible Learning to your daily classroom practice with these additional resources across mathematics, literacy, and science.

John Hattie, Douglas Fisher, Nancy Frey, Linda M. Gojak, Sara Delano Moore, and William Mellman

Discover the right mathematics strategy to use at each learning phase so all students demonstrate more than a year's worth of learning per school year.

Grades K–2 and 3–5 coming in 2019!

John Almarode, Douglas Fisher, Joseph Assof, Sara Delano Moore, John Hattie, and Nancy Frey

Leverage the most effective teaching practices at the most effective time to meet the surface, deep, and transfer learning needs of every mathematics student.

Douglas Fisher, Nancy Frey, and John Hattie

Ensure students demonstrate more than a year's worth of learning during a school year by implementing the right literacy practice at the right moment.

Douglas Fisher, Nancy Frey, John Hattie, and Marisol Thayre

High-impact strategies to use for all you teach—all in one place. Deliver sustained, comprehensive literacy experiences to K–12 learners each day.

Nancy Frey, John Hattie, and Douglas Fisher

Imagine students who understand their educational goals and monitor their progress. This illuminating book focuses on self-assessment as a springboard for markedly higher levels of student achievement.

John Almarode, Douglas Fisher, Nancy Frey, and John Hattie

Inquiry, laboratory, project-based learning, discovery learning? The authors reveal that it's not which strategy, but when, and plot a vital K–12 framework for choosing the right approach at the right time.

corwin.com

Let us know what you think!

Did the information in this book resonate with you? We're hoping you'll continue to support this book's journey to reaching teachers and having the ultimate impact in the classroom. Here are a few ways you can do that:

>>> **JOIN** the conversation! Share your comments, participate in an online book study, or post a picture of yourself with the book on social media using **#VLClassroom**.

>>> **PROVIDE** your expert review of *Teaching Mathematics in the Visible Learning Classroom, High School* on Amazon.

>>> **LEAD** or join a book study in your school or team to share ideas on how to bring the concepts presented in the book to life.

>>> **FOLLOW** our Corwin in the Classroom Facebook page and share your Visible Learning strategies in the mathematics classroom using **#VLClassroom**.

>>> **RECOMMEND** this book for your Professional Learning Community activities.

>>> **SUGGEST** this book to teacher educators.

Be sure to stay up-to-date on all things Corwin by following us on social media:
Facebook: www.facebook.com/corwinclassroom
Instagram: www.instagram.com/corwin_press, @corwin_press
Twitter: twitter.com/CorwinPress, @CorwinPress
Pinterest: www.pinterest.com/corwinpress/pins

www.corwin.com

A SAGE Publishing Company

Helping educators make the greatest impact

CORWIN HAS ONE MISSION: to enhance education through intentional professional learning.

We build long-term relationships with our authors, educators, clients, and associations who partner with us to develop and continuously improve the best evidence-based practices that establish and support lifelong learning.